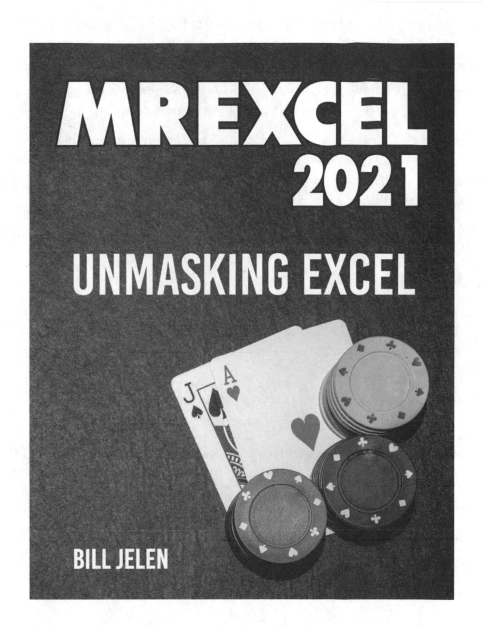

MREXCEL 2021
UNMASKING EXCEL

BILL JELEN

Holy Macro! Books
PO Box 541731, Merritt Island FL 32954

MrExcel 2021 — Unmasking Excel

First Publication: April 2021

Authors: Bill Jelen

Copy Editor: Kitty Wilson

Tech Editors: Roger Govier in 2020, Bob Umlas in 2021

Formula Guru: Richard Simpson.

Indexer: Nellie Jay

Compositor: Jill Cabot

Cover Design: Shannon Travise

Illustrations: Cartoon Bob D'Amico, George Berlin, Walter Moore, Bobby Rosenstock, Chad Thomas

Photography: Sean Carruthers, Mary Ellen Jelen

Published by: Holy Macro! Books, PO Box 541731, Merritt Island FL 32954

Distributed by Independent Publishers Group, Chicago, IL

ISBN 978-1-61547-071-6 (print) 978-1-61547-157-7 (digital)

Library of Congress Control Number: 2021932790

Table of Contents

About the Author

Bill Jelen is the host of MrExcel.com and the author of 61 books about Microsoft Excel including *Excel Gurus Gone Wild and Excel 2019 Inside Out* for Microsoft Press. He has made over 80 guest appearances on TV's *The Lab with Leo / Call for Help with Leo Laporte* and was voted guest of the year on the *Computer America* radio show. He writes the Excel column for *Strategic Finance* magazine. He has produced over 2,300 episodes of his daily video podcast Learn Excel from MrExcel.

About the Illustrators

Cartoonist **Bob D'Amico** creates custom cartoons for business and more. See www.cartoonbob.com for more about his work.

George Berlin is all about delight and wonder! He puts a smile on the world's faces with illustration, animation, and interactive projection art. See more at www.georgeberlin.com.

Walter Moore is famous for his ape cartoons. If you need an illustration of the monkey business at your work, search Bing for Walter Moore Apes.

Bobby Rosenstock is a print maker who specializes in woodcut and letterpress printing. He is owner of the letterpress and design studio in Marietta, Ohio, Just a Jar Design Press - www.justAjar.com.

Chad Thomas is an illustrator who showcases his artwork on his website, www.whiterabbitart.com. His colorful and detailed artwork ranges from pet and people portraits to illustrations for children's books.

Foreword

After 17 years on the road, performing 35 Power Excel seminars a year, I had decided during 2019 to retire from the travel circuit. Little did I know that the pandemic would soon cancel all of the 2020 events. As I write this, we are hopeful that the vaccines work and we can finally unmask for 2021. In the meantime, I have booked a few online-only webinars. Check the MrExcel.com homepage for upcoming events.

The book you are reading was the book that I used in those seminars. I would update the book for a new edition of Excel, print 5000 copies and hit the road. For 2020, this book was produced as an e-book only. For 2021, we are back to print. See what is new in each edition on the last page of the book: "What is New in this 2021 Edition" on page 282.

You will see a number of shortlinks in this book in the format mrx.cl/short. The idea is that it will be easier for you to type mrx.cl than a long URL.

Sample File Downloads

The files used in this book are available for download from mrx.cl/2021bookfiles.

Edge Index

The numbers in the color blocks on the right side of the numbered pages form an edge index in the printed book. The numbers roughly correspond to: 0 is front matter, 1 is favorite techniques, 2 is charting and visualization, 3 is data analysis, 4 is formulas, 5 is tools, and 6 is the index and back matter.

#1 Ask Excel's A.I. a Question About Your Data

A new Natural Language Query feature started rolling out to Microsoft 365 in late 2019. The feature uses artificial intelligence to answer questions about your data.

The feature can be found near the right side of the Home tab. The icon is a blue lightning bolt. The label for the icon has changed between Insights, Ideas, Data Analysis, and Data Ideas.

Note: Microsoft loves to do A|B testing with feature names. As I write this book, they are conducting one such test. One of my computers is calling the feature Data Analysis and the other is calling it Data Ideas. Microsoft might call it Analyze Data or Clippy 2.0. Any name will operate the same. By the time you are reading this, they will have settled on a name. In any case, look for the blue lightning bolt that is second from the right side of the Home tab.

It is the #1 tip in this book because of this problem: (1) The feature has the potential to help millions of people, and (2) it is hidden where no one will find it.

Anyone can perform advanced data analysis by simply asking questions by typing a sentence. Your data set can be up to 250,000 cells. Select one cell in your data. Use the blue lightning bolt icon on the right side of the Home tab.

A box says to Ask A Question About Your Data and it gives you a few sample questions.

Type a question such as "Top 3 Products by 'Sales' where Category is "Bikes"". Excel restates your question and shows you a thumbnail of the report.

If this is the correct analysis, you can use the +Insert Pivot Table icon to insert the results into a new worksheet in your workbook.

Sometimes the feature will give you a chart when you want a table. Try adding "as table" to the end of your sentence.

The "Is this helpful?" link in the lower right is not being used. The original idea was to use Machine Learning to suggest better reports in the future. But the reality is that Microsoft is taking privacy very seriously and they can't learn without retaining your data.

New for 2021 is the "Which Fields Interest You the Most?". This can be used to tell Excel that they should never offer to sum fields such as Year, Part Number, or Cost Center. You can choose to Sum or Average numeric fields. Or you can uncheck the field to make sure it is not in any of the suggestions.

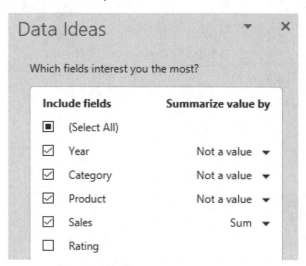

Even before you type a question, Excel will offer you 5-10 suggested reports and a link to load up to 30 more reports. If you aren't sure what you are looking for, it is sometimes interesting to read through these suggested reports.

My one complaint about the feature is shown in the following chart. Ideas was able to find some outliers in this data and offers to create a chart with those points called out in orange. For this chart to work correctly, Excel would have to support conditional formatting in charts and it does not. That means that the pivot chart will always call out these three points, even if the underlying data changes and new outliers emerge. You would have to re-run Ideas and hope that a similar result is offered.

#2 Double-Click the Fill Handle to Copy a Formula

You have thousands of rows of data. You've added a new formula in the top row of your data set, something like =PROPER(A2&" "&B2), as shown here. You need to copy the formula down to all of the rows of your data set.

	A	B	C
C2			=PROPER(A2&" "&B2)
	First Name	Last Name	Name
1	First Name	Last Name	Name
2	PETER	ALBERT	Peter Albert
3	AMY	ANDRAE	
4	FRANK	ARENDT-THEILEN	
5	FR. TONY	AZZARTO	
6	LORNA	BANUILOS	
7	ZACK	BARRESSE	
8	JEREMY	BARTZ	

Many people will grab the Fill Handle and start to drag down. But as you drag down, Excel starts going faster and faster. There is a 200-microsecond pause at the last row of data. 200 microseconds is long enough for you to notice the pause but not long enough for you to react and let go of the mouse button. Before you know it, you've dragged the Fill Handle way too far.

110	RYAN	WILSON
111	PATRICK	WIRZ
112	JOHN C.	WISSE
113		
114	**Excel 2010 does pause here - not long enough for anyone to react, though.**	
115		
116		
117		
118		
119		+
120		

Drag the Fill Handle... You inevitably go too far...

The solution is to double-click the Fill Handle! Go to exactly the same spot where you start to drag the Fill Handle. The mouse pointer changes to a black plus sign. Double-click. Excel looks at the surrounding data, finds the last row with data today, and copies the formula down to the last row of the data set.

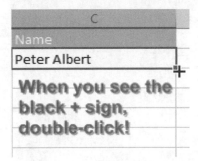

In the past, empty cells in the column to the left would cause the "double-click the Fill Handle" trick to stop working just before the empty cell. But as you can see below, names like Madonna, Cher, or Pele will not cause problems. Provided that there is at least a diagonal path (for example, via B76-A77-B78), Excel will find the true bottom of the data set.

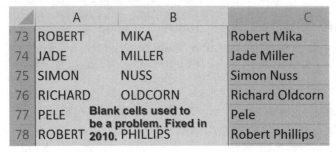

	A	B	C
73	ROBERT	MIKA	Robert Mika
74	JADE	MILLER	Jade Miller
75	SIMON	NUSS	Simon Nuss
76	RICHARD	OLDCORN	Richard Oldcorn
77	PELE	Blank cells used to be a problem. Fixed in	Pele
78	ROBERT	2010. PHILLIPS	Robert Phillips

In my live Power Excel seminars, this trick always elicits a gasp from half the people in the room. It is my number-one time-saving trick.

Alternatives to Double-Clicking the Fill Handle

This trick is an awesome trick if all you've done to this point is drag the Fill Handle to the bottom of the data set. But there are even faster ways to solve this problem:

- Use Tables. If you select one cell in A1:B112 and press Ctrl+T, Excel formats the range as a table. Once you have a table, simply enter the formula in C2. When you press Enter, it is copied to the bottom.

- Use a complex but effective keyboard shortcut. This shortcut requires the adjacent column to have no empty cells. While it seems complicated to explain, the people who tell me about this shortcut can do the entire thing in the blink of an eye.

Here are the steps:

1. From your newly entered formula in C2, press the Left Arrow key to move to cell B2.

2. Press Ctrl+Down Arrow to move to the last row with data—in this case, B112.

3. Press the Right Arrow key to return to the bottom of the mostly empty column C.

4. From cell C112, press Ctrl+Shift+Up Arrow. This selects all of the blank cells next to your data, plus the formula in C2.

5. Press Ctrl+D to fill the formula in C2 to all of the blanks in the selection. Ctrl+D is fill **D**own.

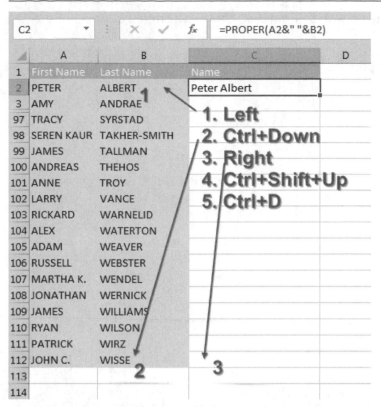

Note: Ctrl+R fills right, which might be useful in other situations.

As an alternative, you can get the same results by pressing Ctrl+C before step 1 and replacing step 5 with pressing Ctrl+V.

Thanks to the following people who suggested this tip: D. Carmichael, Shelley Fishel, Dawn Gilbert, @Knutsford_admi, Francis Logan, Michael Ortenberg, Jon Paterson, Mike Sullivan and Greg Lambert Lane suggested Ctrl+D. Bill Hazlett, author of *Excel for the Math Classroom*, pointed out Ctrl+R.

#3 Break Apart Data

You have just seen how to join data, but people often ask about the opposite problem: how to parse data that is all in a single column. Say you wanted to sort the data in the figure below by zip code:

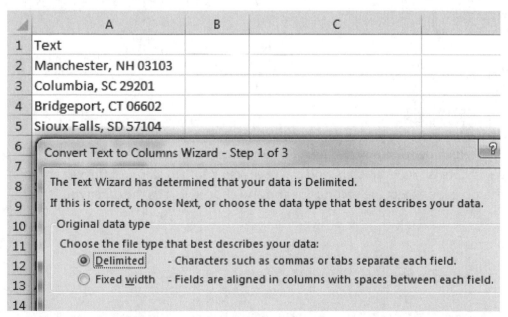

Select the data in A2:A99 and choose Data, Text to Columns. Because some city names, such as Sioux Falls, are two words, you cannot break the data at each occurrence of a space. Instead, you need to use a comma to get the city in column A and the state and zip code in column B, so choose Delimited in step 1 of the wizard and click Next.

In step 2 of the wizard, deselect Tab and select Comma. The preview at the bottom of the dialog shows what your data will look like. Click Next.

Caution: For the rest of the day after you use Text to Columns, Excel will remember the choices you've chosen in step 2 of the Convert Text to Columns Wizard. If you copy data from Notepad and paste to Excel, it will be split at the comma. This is often maddening because most days, the data is not parsed at the comma, but for the rest of today, it will be. To fix it, close and re-open Excel.

Step 3 of the wizard asks you to declare each column as General, Text, or Date. It is fine to leave the columns set as General.

After you've split the state and zip code to column B, select B2:B99 and again choose Data, Text to Columns. This time, since each state is two characters, you can use Fixed Width in step 1 of the wizard. To preserve leading zeros in the zip code, select the second column and choose Text as the data type in step 3 of the wizard.

Tip: A lot of data will work well with Fixed Width, even it doesn't look like it lines up. In the next figure, the first three rows are in Calibri font and don't appear to be lined up. But if you change the font to Courier New, as in rows 4:7, you can see that the columns are perfectly lined up.

	A	B	C	D	E
1	MELANIE	KANE	738 Broadway Highway		
2	KRISTEN	CONRAD	814 Birch Street		Ro:
3	MYRTLE	ZIMMERMAN	567 Fourth Circle		
4	MELANIE	KANE		738 Broadw	
5	KRISTEN	CONRAD		814 Birch	
6	MYRTLE	ZIMMERMAN		567 Fourth	
7	KENNETH	HOLT		962 Centra	

Sometimes, you will find a data set where someone used Alt+Enter to put data on a new line within a cell. You can break out each line to a new column by typing Ctrl+j in the Other box in step 2 of the wizard, as shown below. Why Ctrl+j? Back in the 1980's IBM declared Ctrl+j to be a linefeed. Ctrl+j also can be typed in the Find & Replace dialog box.

There are three special situations that Text to Columns handles easily:

- Dates in YYYYMMDD format can be changed to real dates. In step 3 of the wizard, click the column heading in the dialog, choose Date, then choose YMD from the dropdown.

- If you have negative numbers where the minus sign shows up after the number, go to step 3 of the wizard, click the Advanced Button, and choose Trailing Minus for Negative Numbers.

- Data copied from a Table of Contents will often have dot leaders that extend from the text to the page number as shown below. In step 2 of the wizard, choose Other, type a period, and then select the checkbox for Treat Consecutive Delimiters as One.

◢	A	B	C	D	E
1	Choose				Step 2
2	Date >		Step 3		Consecu
3	YMD		Advanced >		Delimite
4	in Step 3		Trailing Minus		as one
5	20201216		831.25-		A.......1
6	20201017		505 18		Bee 2

#4 Convert Text Numbers to Numbers Quickly

It sometimes happen that you end up with a long column of numbers stored as text and you need to convert those to real numbers.

During 2020, the logic behind Convert to Number was rewritten. In the past, using this feature could take minutes, as Excel would recalculate the worksheet after each cell was converted to a number. Today, however, it is super-fast. Simply select the range of cells where the first cell is a number stored as text. An on-grid drop-down will appear to the left of the top text number. Open the drop-down menu and choose Convert to Number.

Note that this option only appears if you have File, Options, Formula set to these:

Before Convert to Number was rewritten, my favorite method of converting Text Numbers would be to select the column of text numbers and press Alt+D E F. This would run the column through the defaults of Text to Columns.

For completeness, there is a third method. Select a blank cell and enter the number 1. Copy the 1 to the clipboard. Then select the cells with text numbers. From the Paste drop-down menu, choose Paste Special. In the Paste Special dialog, choose both Values and Multipy. When you multiply the 1 times text numbers, they will convert to real numbers. You can also copy any blank cell and then Paste Special Add. This adds a zero to the text numbers.

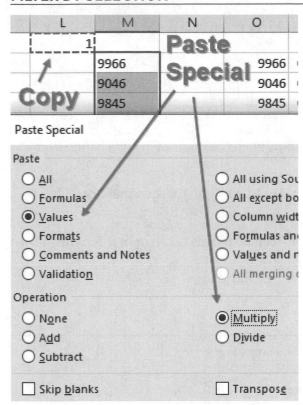

#5 Filter by Selection

The filter dropdowns have been in Excel for decades, but there are two faster ways to filter. Normally, you select a cell in your data, choose Data, Filter, open the dropdown menu on a column heading, uncheck Select All, and scroll through a long list of values, trying to find the desired item.

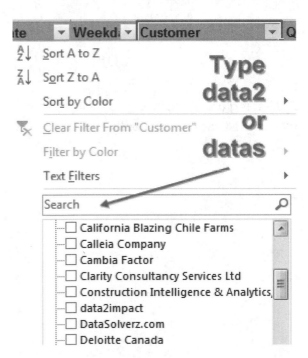

One faster way is to click in the Search box and type enough characters to uniquely identify your selection. Once the only visible items are (Select All Search Results), Add Current Selection to Filter, and the one desired customer, press Enter.

But the fastest way to Filter came from Microsoft Access. Microsoft Access invented a concept called Filter by Selection. It is simple: find a cell that contains the value you want and click Filter by Selection. The filter dropdowns are turned on, and the data is filtered to the selected value. Nothing could be simpler.

Starting in Excel 2007, you can right-click the desired value in the worksheet grid, choose Filter, and then choose By Selected Cells Value.

Guess what? The Filter by Selection trick is also built into Excel, but it is hidden and mislabeled.

Here is how you can add this feature to your Quick Access Toolbar: Right-click anywhere on the Ribbon and choose Customize Quick Access Toolbar.

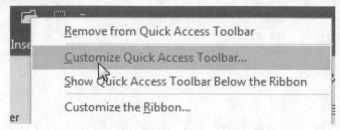

There are two large listboxes in the dialog. Above the left listbox, open the dropdown and change from Popular Commands to Commands Not In The Ribbon.

In the left listbox, scroll to the command AutoFilter and choose it. That's right: The icon that does Filter by Selection is mislabeled AutoFilter.

In the center of the dialog, click the Add>> button. The AutoFilter icon moves to the right listbox, as shown below. Click OK to close the dialog.

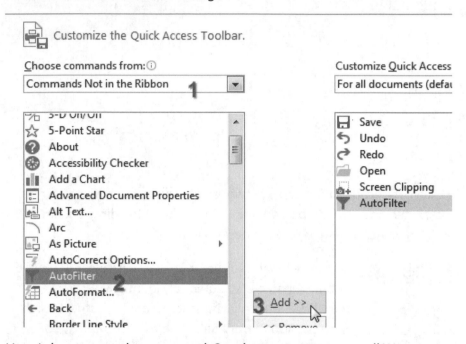

Here is how to use the command: Say that you want to see all West region sales of widgets. First, choose any cell in column B that contains West. Click the AutoFilter icon in the Quick Access Toolbar.

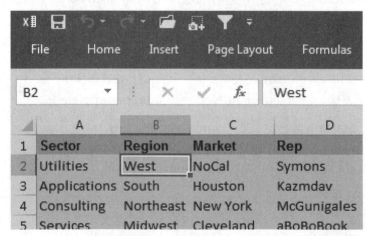

Excel turns on the filter dropdowns and automatically chooses only West from column B.

Next, choose any cell in column E that contains Widget. Click the AutoFilter icon again.

You could continue this process. For example, you could choose a Utilities cell in the Sector column and click AutoFilter.

> **Caution**: It would be great if you could multi-select cells before clicking the AutoFilter icon, but this does not work. If you need to see sales of widgets and gadgets, you could use Filter by Selection to get widgets, but then you have to use the Filter dropdown to add gadgets. Also. Filter by Selection does not work if you are in a Ctrl+T table.

How can it be that this feature has been in Excel since Excel 2003, but Microsoft does not document it? It was never really an official feature. The story is that one of the developers added the feature for internal use. Back in Excel 2003, there was already an AutoFilter icon on the Standard toolbar, so no one would bother to add the apparently redundant AutoFilter icon.

This feature was added to Excel 2007's right-click menu—but three clicks deep: Right-click a value, choose Filter, then choose Filter by Selected Cell's Value.

Bonus Tip: Filter by Selection for Numbers Over/Under

What if you wanted to see all revenue greater than $20,000? Go to the blank row immediately below your revenue column and type >19999. Select that cell and click the AutoFilter icon.

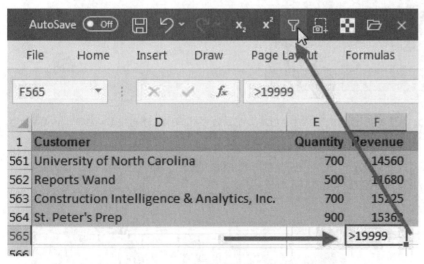

Excel will show only the rows of $20,000 or above.

	D	E	F
1	Customer	Quant ▾	Reven ⊤
2	Vertex42	1000	22810
7	Excelerator BI	1000	21730
9	Berghaus Corporation	900	21438

#6 Total the Visible Rows

After you've applied a filter, say that you want to see the total of the visible cells.

Select the blank cell below each of your numeric columns. Click AutoSum or type Alt+=.

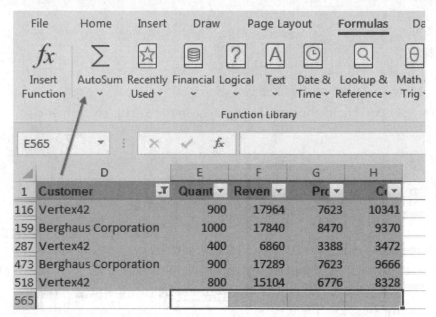

Instead of inserting SUM formulas, Excel inserts =SUBTOTAL(9,…) formulas. The formula below shows the total of only the visible cells.

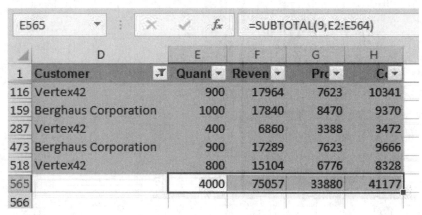

Insert a few blank rows above your data. Cut the formulas from below the data and paste to row 1 with the label Total Visible.

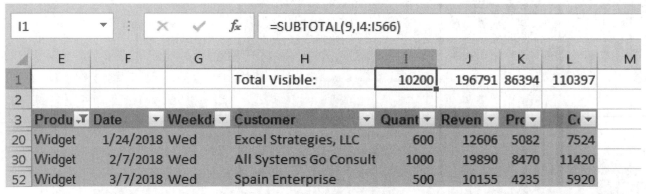

Now, as you change the filters, even if the data fills up more than one full screen, you will see the totals at the top of your worksheet.

Thanks to Sam Radakovitz on the Excel team for Filter by Selection – not for suggesting Filter by Selection, but for formalizing Filter by Selection! Thanks to Taylor & Chris in Albuquerque for the Over/under technique.

#7 Save Filter & Sorting in Sheet View

Do you share a workbook with co-workers? Does you co-worker want to Filter or Sort the workbook differently than you do? Eight years ago, I was ready to strangle my co-worker Scott when he kept filtering our project list to show only his projects.

Amazingly, the Excel team has provided a new solution called "Sheet View". It debuted for Microsoft 365 in March 2020.

Caution: Sheet View only works if you store your workbook in OneDrive or SharePoint online. It is fine for everyone to access the workbook on the PC, but it has to be saved in the cloud.

Below is a small workbook that Andy and Betty share. The Ribbon is showing the new Sheet View settings that are found on the View tab.

Tip: Before you create a view for Andy or Betty, create an unfiltered view called All or Everyone or Default.

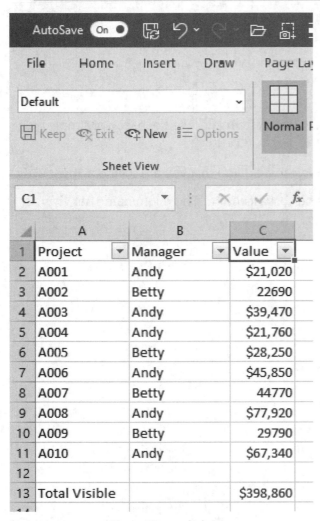

To create a new Sheet View, click New.

The new view is initially called Temporary View. Apply any formatting or sorting. In the image below, Andy has filtered to his records and sorted the projects high-to-low.

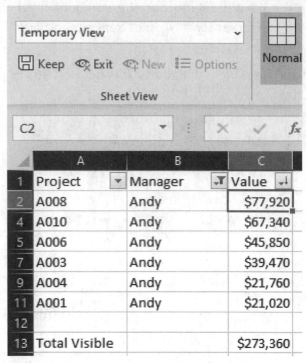

If you want to be able to return to this view in the future, you can either click the Keep icon or simply type a new name such as Andy Descending.

Notice that the Row and Column labels are now black. This is to alert you that you are seeing a Sheet View.

When Betty opens the workbook, she can filter to Betty and sort ascending. She might name her view as BettyAscending.

This next part is absolutely wild. Say that Andy edits cell C2 in his view and changes the value to $100,000.

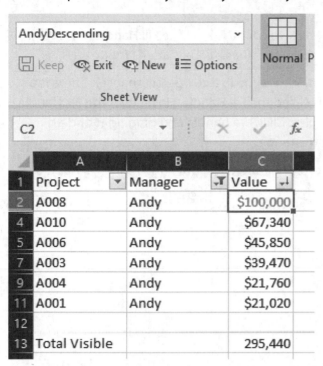

When anyone goes back to the Default view of the workbook, the original sort order is retained. But - the new value for Andy's project A008 is still $100,000!

I've asked the Excel team how they manage to do this behind the scenes, and I still don't know how they manage to keep it all tied together. But it works.

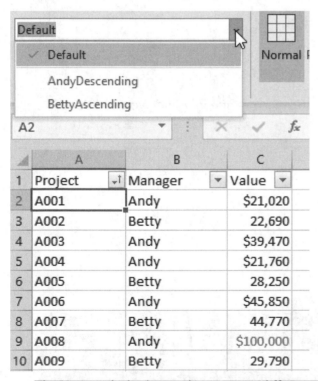

Tip: You might be happy having two different views of the workbook for your own use. But this feature is really designed for when you are collaborating with the whole department. See "#12 Simultaneously Edit a Workbook in Microsoft 365" on page 32.

#8 The Fill Handle Does Know 1, 2, 3...

Why does the Excel Fill Handle pretend it does not know how to count 1, 2, 3? The Fill Handle is great for filling months, weekdays, quarters, and dates. Why doesn't it know that 2 comes after 1?

In case you've never used the Fill Handle, try this: Type a month name in a cell. Select that cell. There is a square dot in the lower right corner of the cell. This dot is called the Fill Handle. Hover over the Fill Handle. The mouse cursor changes from a white cross to a black plus. Click the handle and drag right or drag down. The tooltip increments to show the last month in the range.

Note: If it is not working, select File, Options, Advanced. The third checkbox toggles the Fill Handle.

When you let go of the mouse button, the months will fill in. An icon appears, giving you additional options.

The Fill Handle works great with months or weekdays.

The Fill Handle also works with quarters in many formats.

To do both quarters and years, you have to type a number, then Q, then any punctuation (period, space, apostrophe, dash) before the year.

Q1	Qtr 1	1st Quarter	1Q-2020
Q2	Qtr 2	2nd Quarter	2Q-2020
Q3	Qtr 3	3rd Quarter	3Q-2020
Q4	Qtr 4	4th Quarter	4Q-2020
Q1	Qtr 1	1st Quarter	1Q-2021

When you type 1 and grab the Fill Handle, Excel gives you 1, 1, 1, ... Many people say to enter the 1 and the 2, select them both, then drag the Fill Handle. Here is a faster way.

The secret trick is to hold down Ctrl while dragging. Hold down Ctrl and hover over the fill handle. Instead of the normal icon of a plus sign, you will see a plus sign with a superscript plug sign. When you see the $+^+$, click and drag. Excel fills in 1, 2, 3, ...

Note: Andrew Spain of Spain Enterprise in Huntsville, Alabama taught me a cool variation on this trick. If you start dragging without Ctrl, you can press Ctrl during the drag. A + icon appears at the bottom of the drag rectangle to indicate that you are going to fill instead of copy.

How were we supposed to figure out that Ctrl makes the Fill Handle count instead of copy? I have no idea. I picked up the tip from row 6 at the IMA Meonske seminar in Kent, Ohio. It turns out that Ctrl seems to make the Fill Handle behave in the opposite way: If you Ctrl+drag a date, Excel copies instead of fills.

I've heard another trick: Type 1 in A1. Select A1 and the blank B1. Drag. Excel fills instead of copies.

Right-Click the Fill Handle for More Options

If you right-click and drag the Fill Handle, a menu appears with more options, like Weekdays, Months, and Years. This menu is great for dates.

Normal	Ctrl	Weekday	Months	Years
1/31/2020	1/31/2020	1/31/2020	1/31/2020	1/31/2020
2/1/2020	1/31/2020	2/3/2020	2/29/2020	1/31/2021
2/2/2020	1/31/2020	2/4/2020	3/31/2020	1/31/2022
2/3/2020	1/31/2020	2/5/2020	4/30/2020	1/31/2023

What if your payroll happens on the 15th and on the last day of the month? Put in both dates. Select them both. Right-click and drag the Fill Handle. When you finish dragging, choose Fill Months.

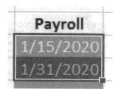

Payroll
1/15/2020
1/31/2020

Teach the Fill Handle a New List

The Fill Handle is a really handy tool. What if you could use it on all sorts of lists? You can teach Excel a new list, provided that you have anywhere from 2 to 240 items. Here is the easy way:

1. Type the list in a column in Excel.

2. Select the list.

3. Select File, Options, Advanced. Scroll almost to the bottom and click Edit Custom Lists.

In the Custom Lists dialog, click Import.

Excel will now understand your list as well as it understands Sunday, Monday, Tuesday. Type any item from the list It does not have to be the first item.

Grab the Fill Handle and drag. Excel fills from your list.

I use this trick for lists that should be in Excel, such as a list of the U.S. states and a list of the letters of the alphabet.

Bonus Tip: Fill Jan, Feb, ..., Dec, Total

A person in one of my seminars wanted to have Jan fill into 13 values: Jan, Feb, Mar, Apr, May, Jun, Jul, Aug, Sep, Oct, Nov, Dec, Total.

While you can edit any custom list that you create, you cannot edit the first four lists in the Custom Lists dialog.

However, if you use the preceding tip to add a new custom list with the 13 values, that list wins. If two custom lists have the value Jan, the lowest one in the dialog box is the one that is used.

If you fiscal year ends March 31, you could set up a list with Apr, May, Jun, ..., Jan, Feb, Mar, Total.

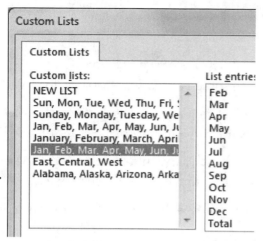

Bonus Tip: Fill 1 to 100,000 in a Flash

What if you have so many items that you can't drag the Fill Handle? Follow these steps:

1. Type the number 1 in a cell.

2. Select that cell.

3. On the Home tab, toward the right, in the Editing group, open the Fill dropdown and choose Series.

4. Select Columns.

5. Enter a Stop Value of 100000.

6. Click OK.

What if you have to fill 100,000 cells of bagel flavors?

1. Type the first bagel flavor in A1.

2. Select A1.

3. Type A100000 in the Name box and press Shift+Enter to select from the current cell to A100000.

4. Home, Fill, Series… and click AutoFill in the Type box. Click OK to fill from the custom list.

Thanks to the person in row 6 at the Meonske Conference in Kent, Ohio, for suggesting this feature.

#9 Fast Worksheet Copy

Yes, you can right-click any sheet tab and choose Move or Copy to make a copy of a worksheet. But that is the very slow way to copy a worksheet. The fast way: Hold down the Ctrl key and drag the worksheet tab to the right.

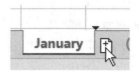

The downside of this trick is that the new sheet is called January (2) instead of February – but that is the case with the Move or Copy method as well. In either case, double-click the sheet name and type a new name.

Ctrl+drag February to the right to create a sheet for March. Rename February (2) to March.

Select January. Shift+select March to select all worksheets. Hold down Ctrl and drag January to the right to create three more worksheets. Rename the three new sheets.

Select January. Shift+select June. Ctrl+drag January to the right, and you've added the final six worksheets for the year. Rename those sheets.

Using this technique, you can quickly come up with 12 copies of the original worksheet.

Illustration: Walter Moore

Bonus Tip: Put the Worksheet Name in a Cell

If you want each report to have the name of the worksheet as a title, use

```
=TRIM(MID(CELL("filename",A1),FIND("]",CELL("filename",A1))+1,20)) &" Report"
```

The CELL() function in this case returns the full path\[File Name]SheetName. By looking for the closing square bracket, you can figure out where the sheet name occurs.

A1		× ✓ *fx*	=TRIM(MID(CELL("filename",A1),FIND("]",CELL("filename", A1))+1,20)) &" Report"						
◢	A	B	C	D	E	F	G	H	I
1	January Report								
2									
3	Flavor	Week 1	Week 2	Week 3	Week 4	Week 5	Total		
4	Asiago	288	132	144	240	264	1068		

January | February | March | April | May | Ju ...

If you plan on using this formula frequently, set up a book.xltx as described in "#10 Use Default Settings for All Future Workbooks" on page 24. In book.xltx, go to Formulas, Define Name. Use a name such as SheetName with a formula of `=TRIM(MID(CELL("filename",book.xltx!$A$1),FIND("]", CELL("filename",book.xltx!$A$1))+1,20))`. Then, in any new workbook `=SheetName&" Report"` will work.

Bonus Tip: Add a Total Row and a Total Column with One AutoSum

Say that you want to add a total row and a total column to a data set. Select all the numbers plus one extra row and one extra column. Click the AutoSum icon or press Alt+=.

	A	B	C	D	E	F
3	Flavor	Q1	Q2	Q3	Q4	Total
4	Asiago	288	132	144	240	
5	Raisin	252	252	252	300	
6	Onion	276	276	132	132	
7	Garlic	72	276	84	240	
8	Total					

Alt+=

Excel adds SUM functions to the total row and the total column as shown in the figure below.

F8		×	✓	fx	=SUM(B8:E8)

	A	B	C	D	E	F
3	Flavor	Q1	Q2	Q3	Q4	Total
4	Asiago	288	132	144	240	804
5	Raisin	252	252	252	300	1056
6	Onion	276	276	132	132	816
7	Garlic	72	276	84	240	672
8	Total	888	936	612	912	3348

Bonus Tip: Power Up the Status Bar Statistics

When you select two or more numeric cells, the total appears in the status bar in the lower right of the Excel window. When you see a total, right-click and choose Average, Count, Numerical Count, Minimum, Maximum, and Sum. You can now see the largest, smallest, and average just by selecting a range of cells:

Asiago	288	132	144	240
Raisin	252	252	252	300
Onion	276	276	132	132
Garlic	72	276	84	240

Average: 209.25   Count: 16   Numerical Count: 16   Min: 72   Max: 300   Sum: 3348

Bonus Tip: Change All Sheets with Group Mode

Any time your manager asks you for something, he or she comes back 15 minutes later and asks for an odd twist that wasn't specified the first time. Now that you can create worksheet copies really quickly, there is more of a chance that you will have to make changes to all 12 sheets instead of just 1 sheet when your manager comes back with a new request.

I will show you an amazingly powerful but incredibly dangerous tool called Group mode.

Say that you have 12 worksheets that are mostly identical. You need to add totals to all 12 worksheets. To enter Group mode, right-click on any worksheet tab and choose Select All Sheets.

The name of the workbook in the title bar now indicates that you are in Group mode.

Anything you do to the January worksheet will now happen to all the sheets in the workbook.

Why is this dangerous? If you get distracted and forget that you are in Group mode, you might start entering January data and overwriting data on the 11 other worksheets!

When you are done adding totals, don't forget to right-click a sheet tab and choose Ungroup Sheets.

Bonus Tip: Create a SUM That Spears Through All Worksheets

So far, you have a workbook with 12 worksheets, 1 for each month. All of the worksheets have the same number of rows and columns. You want a summary worksheet in order to total January through December.

To create it, use the formula =SUM(January:December!B4).

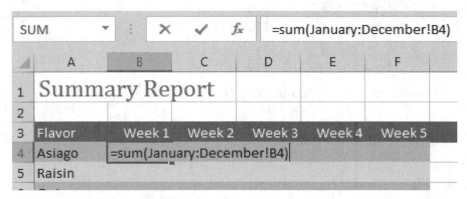

Copy the formula to all cells and you will have a summary of the other 12 worksheets.

Flavor	Week 1	Week 2	Week 3	Week 4	Week 5	Total
Asiago	2400	2040	2004	2388	2688	11520
Raisin	2220	2244	2076	2160	1968	10668

Caution: I make sure to never put spaces in my worksheet names. If you do use spaces, the formula would have to include apostrophes, like this: =SUM('Jan 2018:Mar 2018'!B4).

Tip: If you use 3D spearing formulas frequently, insert two new sheets, one called First and one called Last. Drag the sheet names so they create a sandwich with the desired sheets in the middle. Then, the formula is always =SUM(First:Last!B4).

Here is an easy way to build a 3D spearing formula without having to type the reference: On the summary sheet in cell B4, type =SUM(. Using the mouse, click on the January worksheet tab. Using the mouse, Shift+click on the December worksheet tab. Using the mouse, click on cell B4 on the December worksheet. Type the closing parenthesis and press Enter.

Bonus Tip: Use INDIRECT for a Different Summary Report

Say that you want to build the following report, with months going down column A. In each row, you want to pull the grand total data from each sheet. Each sheet has the same number of rows, so the total is always in row 12.

The first formula would be =January!B12. You could easily copy this formula to columns C:F, but there is not an easy way to copy the formula down to rows 5:15.

B4	▾	⁝	✕ ✓	*fx*	=January!B12	

◢	A	B	C	D	E	F	G
1	Summary Report						
2							
3	Flavor	Week 1	Week 2	Week 3	Week 4	Week 5	Total
4	January	1632					1632
5	February						0
6	March						0

The INDIRECT function evaluates text that looks like a cell reference. INDIRECT returns the value at the address stored in the text. In the next figure, a combination of the ADDRESS and COLUMN functions returns a series of text values that tell Excel where to get the total.

B4	▾	⁝	✕ ✓	*fx*	=$A4&"!"&ADDRESS(12,COLUMN())

◢	A	B	C	D	E
1	Summary Report				
2					
3	Flavor	Week 1	Week 2	Week 3	Week 4
4	January	January!$B$12	January!$C$12	January!$D$12	January!$E$12
5	February	February!$B$12	February!$C$12	February!$D$12	February!$E$12
6	March	March!$B$12	March!$C$12	March!$D$12	March!$E$12

Wrap the previous formula in =INDIRECT() to have Excel pull the totals from each worksheet.

F4	▾	⁝	✕ ✓	*fx*	=INDIRECT($A4&"!"&ADDRESS(12,COLUMN()))

◢	A	B	C	D	E	F	G	H	I	J
1	Summary Report									
2										
3	Month	Week 1	Week 2	Week 3	Week 4	Week 5	Total			
4	January	1632	1836	1368	1716	1608	8160			
5	February	1428	1404	1536	1428	1404	7200			

Caution: INDIRECT will not work for pulling data from other workbooks. Search the Internet for Harlan Grove PULL for a VBA method of doing this.

Thanks to Othneil Denis for the 3D formula tip, Olga Kryuchkova for the Group mode tip, and Al Momrik for status bar.

#10 Use Default Settings for All Future Workbooks

Do you have favorite worksheet settings in Excel? I do. There are things I do to every new workbook I create.

In a few minutes, you can teach Excel your favorite settings. Then, every time you create a new workbook with Ctrl+N or insert a new worksheet, the worksheet will inherit all of your favorite settings.

The key step is to save the workbook as a template into a specific folder with two specific names.

Start with a blank workbook with a single worksheet.

Apply all your favorite settings. There are dozens of possibilities. Here are a few that I use:

On the Page Layout tab, change the Scale to Fit so the Width is 1 page. Leave Height set to Automatic and Width set to 1 Page.

Create a custom header or footer. Use the dialog launcher in the bottom right of the Page Setup group. Go to the Header/Footer tab. Choose Custom Footer. Type whatever is your company standard in the footer.

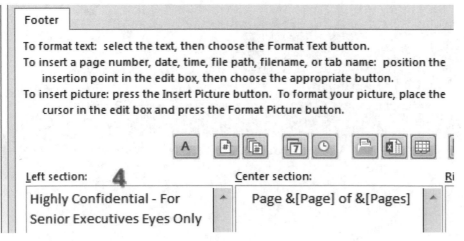

Create custom margins. I like narrow margins – even more narrow than the built-in Narrow margin settings. I've been using 0.25-inch margins since the 1990s, and they're automatically set for me because I've added that to my template.

Choose a theme. I like the colors from Slipstream, but I prefer the Effects from Office 2007–2010.

When you set a pivot table default theme, it only applies to the current workbook. Excel never saves your preference. Create a tiny two-cell data set. Create a pivot table. Change the default formatting. Delete the pivot table and the data set. The template will remember the setting.

Would you use cell styles more often if they weren't so ugly? Do you hate that input cells are orange? Go to Cell Styles, right-click Input, and choose Modify as shown below. Click the Format button and choose a different input color.

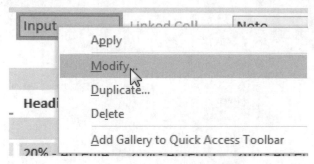

I've just shown you some of my favorite settings. I'm sure you have your own favorites. Maybe you always set up a name to define the tax rate. Add it to your template, and you will never have to set it up again. Turn off gridlines. Do whatever you always do.

Once you've finished customizing your workbook, you need to figure out which file type you use most often. For people who never use macros, this is often XLSX. But I always use macros, so my default file type is XLSM. Maybe you want workbooks to open faster, and you use XLSB. There is a template format related to each of these file types, and you can just change the extension as needed. So, for me, I save the workbook as XLTM. You might save it as XLTX.

As soon as you choose one of these file types, the Save As dialog box moves to a templates folder. You need to save the workbook in a different folder.

C:\Users\Bill\AppData\Roaming\Microsoft\Excel\XLSTART

In the folder bar, type %AppData% and press Enter to get to the AppData\Roaming\ folder on your computer. From there, navigate to Microsoft\Excel\XLSTART.

Save the workbook with the reserved name Book plus the appropriate extension. Use Save As again and save the workbook in the same folder but use Sheet plus the same extension as the name.

Of course, you only have to set this up once. After you do it, any time you use Ctrl+N to create a new workbook, the new workbook will inherit all of the settings from your template named Book.

Why did you have to also save templates named both Book and Sheet? Any time you insert a new worksheet into an existing workbook, Excel uses the Sheet template.

My Rant About New and New...

I've been using Book.xltm for 20 years. In all versions of Excel from Excel 95 up through Excel 2003, the Excel Standard toolbar had an icon called "New". Click that icon, and Excel loaded the Book template. Everything was great.

The File menu offered a New… option, but hardly anyone used it because it was half as many clicks to simply click the New icon on the Standard toolbar. New respects your custom settings in the Book template. New… does not.

If you've set up custom Book and Sheet templates, do not click the Blank Workbook template. Simply dismiss this opening screen by using the Esc key, and your custom Book template loads.

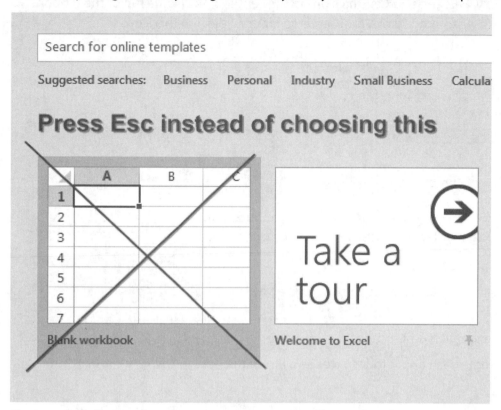

If you get tired of pressing Esc, go to File, Options, General and deselect the checkbox Show the Start Screen When This Application Starts.

Start up options

Choose the extensions you want Excel to open by default

☑ Tell me if Microsoft Excel isn't the default progam for

☐ Show the Start screen when this application starts

Bonus Tip: Changes to Book Template are Cumulative

I've had the opportunity to speak at three consecutive Excelapalooza conferences near Dallas. The conference team arranges two simultaneous tracks about Microsoft Excel. While I am presenting in one ballroom, Lawrence "Mac" McClelland is presenting another track in another ballroom. I picked up this tip from Mac:

Anything you do to Book.xltx is cumulative. Build the workbook with your favorite settings today. If you discover some new settings that you would like to add to Book.xltx in the future, follow these steps:

1. Press Ctrl+N to open a blank version of Book.xltx.

2. Make any changes you would like.

3. Select File, Save As.

4. Change the file type to XLTX or XLTM, depending on whether you regularly use macros.

5. Change Folder to the XLStart folder.

6. Save the file as Book.xltx to replace the existing Book.xltx.

7. Repeat steps 3–5 and save the file as Sheet.xltx.

Bonus Tip: Replace the Comma Style in Book.xltx

The Excel team offers Currency, Percent, and Comma icons in the center of the Home tab of the Ribbon. The tooltip says the Comma Style formats with a thousands separator. I despise this icon.

Why do I despise this icon? Because it turns on Accounting style. Sure, that gives you a thousands separator, but it also adds several things that I hate:

- It turns on two decimal places.

- It uses a right indent of 1 character to move the last digit away from the right edge of the cell.

- It uses parentheses for negative numbers.

- It displays zero with a single dash about four spaces away from the right edge of the cell.

K	L
6,543.21	(4,321.00)
6,543.00	-

There is no way to replace the Comma icon with my own icon or even to change what style it applies. So, I find that I have to click the Dialog Launcher icon at the bottom right of the Number group:

Tip: The Dialog Launcher icon is a diagonal arrow pointing down and to the right. It is found in many groups in the Ribbon and usually offers far more choices than are available in the Ribbon.

Then choose Number from the Category list, choose the checkbox for Use 1000 Separator, and click twice on the down arrow to change 2 decimal places to 0 decimal places. Click OK to close the Format Cells dialog. It takes six clicks to create a simple number format with a comma as the thousands separator. That is why I despise the Comma icon: People who can live with right indents, parentheses, and zeros displayed as dashes can apply that style in one click, but people who just want a comma have to go through six clicks.

The great news: There is a solution. The bad news: Microsoft makes it hard to use the solution. The good news: If you add the solution to the Book.xltx file, the solution will become mostly permanent for all files that you create. Here is what you do:

1. While you are creating Book.xltx, as discussed in "#10 Use Default Settings for All Future Workbooks", type 1234 in a cell. Format the cell using the six clicks discussed above (or your favorite format). Keep that cell selected.

2. Open the Cell Styles gallery. Near the bottom, choose New Cell Style….

3. In the Style box that appears, type a descriptive name for your style, such as CommaGood.

4. If you only want to apply the Number format, unselect the checkboxes for Alignment, Font, Border, Fill, and Protection.

5. Click OK to create the new style.

New styles appear at the top of the Cell Styles gallery, and you now have one-click access to the CommaGood style.

Caution: Any cell style added using this method applies only to the current workbook, making this tip almost useless.

Tip: If you add the CommaGood style to your Book.xltx file, the CommaGood style will be available on all future workbooks that you create with Ctrl+N.

Thanks to Jo Ann Babin for an idea similar to this one.

#11 Recover Unsaved Workbooks

The Auto Recover feature is a lifesaver. It is turned on automatically in Excel 2010 and newer.

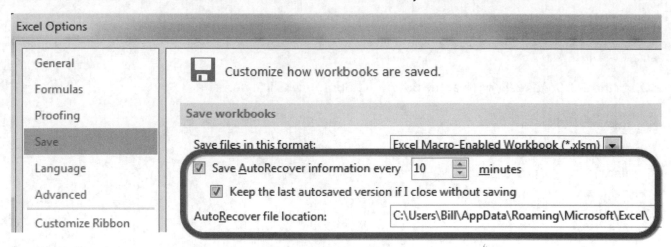

Say it is 4:59 PM on Friday, and you are trying to get the heck out of work. You have a bunch of files open in Excel and issue the Alt+F, X command to exit Excel.

Standing between you and the after-work happy hour are a bunch of dialogs like this one:

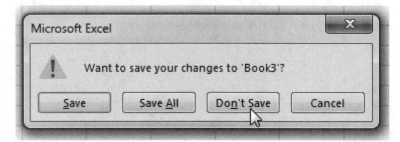

There is no need to save this file, so you click Don't Save. Next file? Don't Save. Next file? Don't Save.

> **Tip**: Hold Shift while clicking Don't Save to perform Don't Save All.

Now you are in a rhythm, clicking Don't Save in perfect synchronization with Excel presenting the message. Then, as you click Don't Save the last time, you realize that *this* workbook had a lot of unsaved changes. And you really needed to save it. You should have clicked Save.

You look at your watch. It will take two hours to re-create all of those changes. Your happy hour plans are sunk. But wait! Excel has your back. If the workbook was open for at least 10 minutes and created an AutoRecover version, Excel kept a copy for you.

Follow these steps to get it back:

1. Open Excel.

2. In the left panel, choose Open Other Workbooks.

3. In the center panel, scroll all the way to the bottom of the recent files. At the very end, click Recover Unsaved Workbooks.

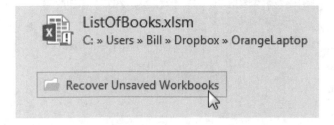

4. Excel shows you all the unsaved workbooks that it has saved for you recently.

Users ▸ Bill ▸ AppData ▸ Local ▸ Microsoft ▸ Office ▸ UnsavedFiles

	Name	Date modified
☐	Book2((Unsaved-3045080039427611400)).xlsb	6/11/2015 6:03 PM
	Book1((Unsaved-3045078414615565691)).xlsb	6/11/2015 4:04 PM

5. Click a workbook and choose Open. If it is the wrong one, go back to File, Open and scroll to the bottom of the list.

6. When you find the right file, click the Save As button to save the workbook. Unsaved workbooks are saved for four days before they are automatically deleted.

RECOVERED UNSAVED FILE   This is a recovered file that is temporarily stored on your computer.   Save As

1

Use AutoRecover Versions to Recover Files Previously Saved

Recover Unsaved Workbooks applies only to files that have never been saved. If your file has been saved, you can use AutoRecover versions to get the file back. If you close a previously saved workbook without saving recent changes, one single AutoRecover version is kept until your next editing session. To access it, reopen the workbook. Use File, Info, Versions to open the last AutoRecover version.

You can also use Windows Explorer to search for the last AutoRecover version. The Excel Options dialog box specifies an AutoRecover File Location. If your file was named Budget2020Data, look for a folder within the AutoRecover File folder that starts with Budget.

While you are editing a workbook, you can access up to the last five AutoRecover versions of a previously saved workbook. You can open them from the Versions section of the Info category. You may make changes to a workbook and want to reference what you previously had. Instead of trying to undo a bunch of revisions or using Save As to save as a new file, you can open an AutoRecover version. AutoRecover versions open in another window so you can reference, copy/paste, save the workbook as a separate file, etc.

Note: An AutoRecover version is created according to the AutoRecover interval AND only if there are changes. So if you leave a workbook open for two hours without making any changes, the last AutoSave version will contain the last revision.

Caution: Both the Save AutoRecover Information option and Keep The Last AutoRecovered Version option must be selected in File, Options, Save for this to work.

Tip: Create a folder called C:\AutoRecover\ and specify it as the AutoRecover File Location. It is much easier than trawling through the Users folder that is the default location.

☑ Save AutoRecover information every 10 ⏶⏷ minutes
   ☑ Keep the last AutoRecovered version if I close without saving
AutoRecover file location: C:\Users\Bill\AppData\Roaming\Microsoft\Excel\

Note: Under the Manage Version options on the Info tab you can select Delete All Unsaved Workbooks. This is an important option to know about if you work on public computers. Note that this option appears only if you're working on a file that has not been saved previously. The easiest way to access it is to create a new workbook.

Thanks to Beth Melton and Paul Seaman and for clarifying the differences between AutoRecover and Recover Unsaved Files.

#12 Simultaneously Edit a Workbook in Microsoft 365

For decades, some people have been wanting a better way to have multiple people in the same workbook at the same time. The old Shared Workbook functionality was awkward. People resorted to only one person having write access at a time", which led to someone opening the file and then forgetting to close it before going for a two-hour lunch and tying up the file that whole time.

After Google's spreadsheet product began offering the ability for multiple people to edit the same worksheet, the Excel team spent many years developing a feature that they call co-authoring. The feature was released to Microsoft 365 customers in the summer of 2017.

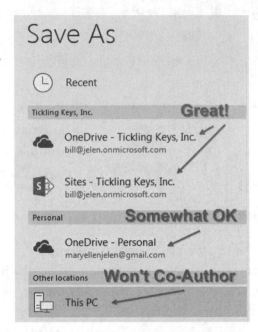

The feature works great if everyone you are sharing with are on the same tenant. For example, if everyone is using a signin ending @YourCo.onmicrosoft.com, then you are on the same tenant.

To start, choose one person to be the owner of the workbook. This person should already have a One Drive For Business or SharePoint Online folder set up. The owner of the document should use File, Save As and choose to save the document in either OneDrive or SharePoint Online.

The owner of the workbook clicks the Share icon in the top right corner of Excel.

The Share panel asks you to invite people by e-mail address. The people you share with will receive an Outlook e-mail with a link to the file. They can also see the workbook in File, Open, Shared With Me.

If you are not in the same tentant, look at the bottom of the panel, you can generate a sharing link.

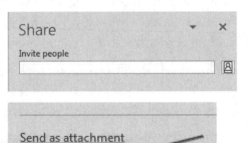

Generate a sharing link where anyone with the link can edit the workbook.

Copy the link and send it to others on your team.

The next step is the annoying part. When they follow the link, they will be taken *as a guest* to Excel Online. The spreadsheet will appear and they can edit in Excel Online. I talked to people from one company who stopped at this point. One person (the workbook owner) would edit in Excel and everyone else was stuck in Excel Online.

> **Caution:** As shown below, the "Edit in Browser" button is very prominent and it is what you are likely to click. In desperation, you might try clicking Download, but this removes the ability to co-author. Not so obvious in the top right corner is the Sign In button.

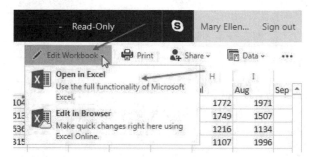

For the other co-authors to use the workbook in the real version of Excel running on a PC, they have to first Sign In to Excel online. Use the credentials that are shown in Excel under File, Account.

Once they have signed in, then the Edit Workbook drop-down menu appears. Open the menu and choose Edit in Excel. This is the only way to have everyone co-author and use the real desktop Excel instead of Excel Online.

While you and others are working in a document, your active cell will be outlined in green. The active cells for others will be other colors. If you want to know who is editing a cell, hover over that cell.

	A	B	C	D	E	F
1	Product	1Q 2020	2Q 2020	3Q 2020	4Q 2020	1Q 2021
2	Apple	1,446	1,540	1,244	3,137	3,296
3	Banana	2,923	1,851	2,311	1,830	2,399
4	Cherry	2,982	2,066	1,330	2,163	1,351
5	Date	1,838	2,547	2,390	1,371	1,622
6	Elderberry	2,549	2,557	2,798	2,591	2,992
7	Fig	1,308	2,854	2,280	2,108	3,318

Co-authoring will work fine provided everyone avoids editing the same cell at the same time.

When someone (probably your manager), dives in to edit a cell that you are already editing, then a confusing set of rules decides who's edit wins. Rather than dealing with these rules, be happy that co-authoring mostly works and have everyone agree not to edit the same cell at the same time.

Co-authoring is a whole new experience. There are good things and bad things that you need to get used to when you are co-authoring.

Bonus Tip: AutoSave is Necessary, But Turn it Off When Not Co-Authoring

The reason that co-authoring is possible is because of AutoSave. Every time that you make a spreadsheet change, that change will be saved to OneDrive so that others can (almost) instantly see what you just typed. AutoSave is necessary if you want ten accountants editing a budget worksheet at the same time.

But let's talk about workbooks that will never be used with co-authoring. These are the run-of-the-mill workbooks that I use 99.9% of the time. I do not want AutoSave to be active for those workbooks. I want to open Excel, know that I can do some "what-if" changes and then close the workbook without saving. If AutoSave is on, those changes are automatically saved. It is terrible.

Or - you likely recognize the scenario: You have a report for January. You need a report for February. You open the January report, change the headings, and then do File, Save As to save for February. This workflow has been fine for decades. But if you allow AutoSave to be on, you will be destroying the January report as soon as you edit A1 and type February over January.

You have four choices. 1. Change your workflow to do the Save a Copy before you make any edits. 2. Always save to a local drive and AutoSave will not automatically be enabled. 3. Toggle AutoSave off for each workbook. Click the "On" icon shown here to turn AutoSave off for the current workbook.

The best choice is 4. Go to File, Options, Save, and unselect the choice for AutoSave OneDrive and SharePoint Online Files By Default.

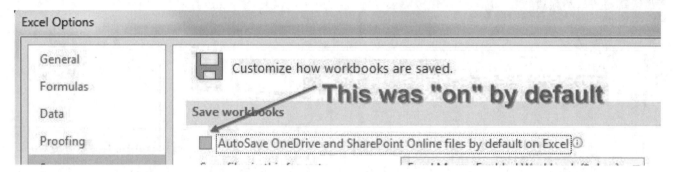

Bonus Tip: Undo an AutoSave

What if you have to undo an AutoSave? Your manager said to merge two regions and then 20 minutes later calls the merger off. AutoSave has been saving after every change in your workbook.

Click the drop-down menu next to the title bar. Click on Version History.

Excel will offer to let you open a previous version of the file. They don't save a version after every change. I (Bill Jelen) made 50 changes to this workbook in the last 20 minutes. The Version History is offering me three versions from those twenty minutes. Note that although all of the changes were made by Bill Jelen, AutoSave is crediting the changes to Mary Ellen Jelen. No one at Microsoft can explain this apparent bug.

#13 New Threaded Comments Allow Conversations

Threaded comments debuted in 2018. When you insert a comment, Excel stores the comment, the author, the date, and time. When a co-worker sees your comment, they can click Reply and add a new comment to the same cell. Each set of comments lists the author, date, and time. Use the ... menu to mark a comment as resolved.

These new threaded comments are indicated by a five-sided purple shape instead of the red triangle used for the old style comments (now known as Notes).

Note: If you are using Excel Online, you have a choice for Comments or Chat. While comments are stored in the workbook, anything typed in Chat will be deleted when you close the workbook.

Bonus Tip: Old Style Comments Are Available as Notes

While the new threaded comments are cool, there are some great tricks that the old legacy comments offered that are lost with the threaded comments. Luckily, if you have a situation requiring one of the special tricks, the old comments are still available as Notes.

Here are some of my favorite Note techniques:

- Individual notes could be set to always show. This is useful for creating helpful instructions for a spreadsheet. Select a cell containing a red-triangle indicator and select Review, Notes, Show/Hide Note.

- Notes can be resized and located in a specific position. Right-click a cell with a note and choose Edit Note. Use the resize handle to change the size or drag an edge to move the comment.

- You can change the shape of a note. To start, Right-click the Ribbon and choose Customize Quick Access Toolbar. In the dialog box, change the top-left drop-down menu to All Commands. Find the

Change Shape icon in the left list and click the Add>> button to add it to the Quick Access Toolbar. Right-click the cell containing the note and choose Show Note. Ctrl+Click on the edge of the note to select the note without entering text edit mode. Use the Change Shape icon in the Quick Access toolbar to choose a new shape. Note that you will often have to resize the note after choosing a shape. You also might try the Center and Align Middle icons to center the text in the shape. After changing the shape, you can return to Hide Note to make the note only visible when you hover over the red triangle indicator.

- You can change the color of a note. This one is tricky because there are two versions of the Format Comment dialog box. While in edit mode, click the border of the comment and then press Ctrl+1 to open the Format Comment dialog box. You should see nine tabs in the dialog. If you only see the Font tab, close the dialog and try clicking the comment border again or Ctrl+Click the comment to leave text edit mode. When you have the dialog with all 9 tabs, use the Colors and Lines tab, Fill Color to change the color of a comment. Use Fill Effects… to add a gradient or a picture.

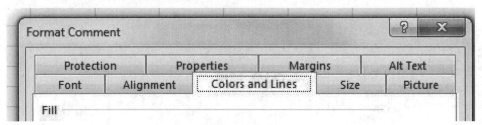

- To create pop-up pictures: edit a note and backspace to remove your name from the note. With a completely blank note, Ctrl+Click the edge and press Ctrl+1. Use Colors and Lines, Fill Color, Fill Effects, Picture and choose a picture from your computer. Hide the note and the picture will pop up when you hover over the triangle.

The following screenshot shows examples of notes with colors, shapes, and a pop-up picture.

Bonus Tip: Add a Tooltip to a Cell with Validation

In the previous Bonus Tip, I suggested using Notes for a help system. The problem with notes: it is possible to arrow in to a cell without ever hovering over the red triangle and the note might be missed. You can use the Data Validation dialog to set up a tooltip for a cell. The tooltip is only visible when the cell is the active cell.

Data Validation is found towards the right side of the Data tab in the Ribbon. I end up using Alt+D L because I always have a difficult time finding the Validation icon. Normally, most people use the Settings tab in Data Validation to control what can be entered in a cell. You will skip the Settings tab and go to the Input Message tab.

On the Input Message tab, type a title and a message. Click OK.

The result: a tooltip that will appear any time the cell is active:

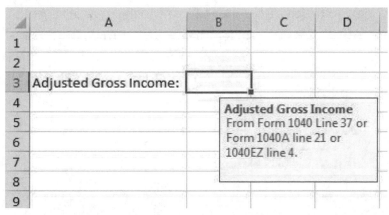

Tip: If you are using Data Validation to create a drop-down list, it is frustrating that you can't search validation using look-ahead typing. Alfred F Vachris Jr. has a great workaround. See: http://mrx.cl/lookahead

#14 Create Perfect One-Click Charts

One-click charts are easy: Select the data and press Alt+F1.

What if you would rather create bar charts instead of the default clustered column chart? To make your life easier, you can change the default chart type. Store your favorite chart settings in a template and then teach Excel to produce your favorite chart in response to Alt+F1.

Say that you want to clean up the chart above. All of those zeros on the left axis take up a lot of space without adding value. Double-click those numbers and change Display Units from None to Millions.

To move the legend to the top, click the + sign next to the chart, choose the arrow to the right of Legend, and choose Top.

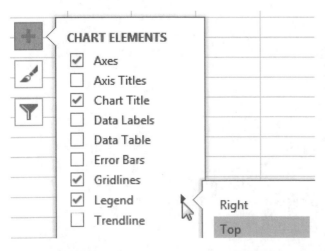

Change the color scheme to something that works with your company colors.

Right-click the chart and choose Save As Template. Then, give the template a name. (I called mine ClusteredColumn.)

Select a chart. In the Design tab of the Ribbon, choose Change Chart Type. Click on the Templates folder to see the template that you just created.

2

Right-click your template and choose Set As Default Chart.

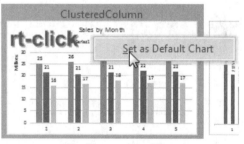

The next time you need to create a chart, select the data and press Alt+F1. All your favorite settings appear in the chart.

Thanks to Areef Ali, Olga Kryuchkova, and Wendy Sprakes for suggesting this feature.

#15 Paste New Data on a Chart

You might be responsible for updating charts every month, week, or day. For example, in my last job, a collection of charts were updated during the month-end close process. The charts would track progress throughout the year.

There is an easy way to add new data to an existing chart. Here, the chart shows data for January through May, and there is new data for June that is not on the chart.

Rather than re-create the chart, you can paste new data on it. Select the new data in the worksheet, including the heading. Press Ctrl+C to copy.

Click on the chart and press Ctrl+V to paste the data on the chart. As shown below, the new data is added to the existing chart.

As you keep adding months to the right side, what if you want to remove data from the left side? Is there any way to Ctrl+X that data off the chart?

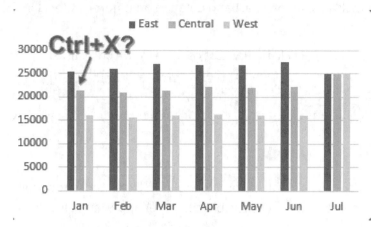

No, but there is another way. Select the chart. Outlines appear around the charted data in the worksheet. A blue box surrounds the data points for the charts, and in each corner of the blue box is a square dot as shown below. The square dot is a resizing handle.

Click on the lower-left resizing handle and drag to the right.

	Jan	Feb	Mar
	25277	26035	27076
	21256	20831	21248
	15915	15597	15909

East　Central　West

The data is removed from the left side of the chart.

You can use resizing handles to resize or drag the blue box to change the data that appears on the chart. Of course, you could have dragged the bottom-right resizing handle to add June to the chart in the first place, but it is good to know this copy-and-paste trick in case the chart and data are on different sheets in the workbook.

> **Tip**: If you want to remove East from the chart, you can click on any East column in the chart and press Delete on your keyboard to remove that series. To temporarily hide a series, you can hide the row or column where the underlying data is stored. In Excel 2013 or newer, you can use the Filter funnel icon located to the right of the chart to hide any series or category from the chart.

#16 Create Interactive Charts

It is easy to create interactive charts without using VBA. By default, if you hide rows in Excel, those rows will be hidden in the chart. The technique is to build a chart with every possible customer and then use a slicer or a filter to hide all except one of the customers.

Say that you have the following list of customers. Make the data into a table by using Ctrl+T.

	Company	Q1	Q2	Q3	Q4
17					
18	Cambia Factor	814	838	897	1032
19	data2impact	860	877	886	877
20	Excel4apps	886	842	775	775
21	excelisfun	632	683	744	789
22	F-Keys Ltd	283	258	243	228
23	SpringBoard	259	220	211	222
24	Surten Excel	493	488	503	513
25	Vertex42	827	769	669	636
26	WSLCB	409	450	513	564
27	Yesenita	835	827	827	819

Select the table and insert a chart. In most cases, Excel will create the wrong chart, with customers along the X-axis.

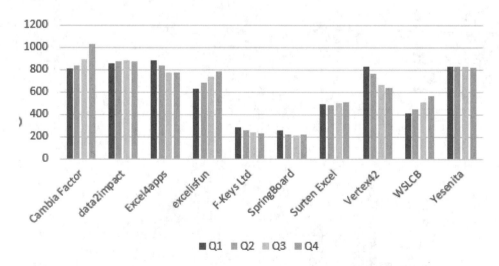

Click the Switch Row/Column icon in the Chart Tools Design tab of the Ribbon.

Select one cell in the table. In Excel 2013 or newer, go to the Insert tab of the Ribbon and choose Slicer. In Excel 2010 or earlier, you have to use the Company dropdown in A17 to choose a single company.

By default, every slicer starts as a single column in the middle of the screen. Plan on dragging the slicer to a new location and size. While the slicer is selected, you can use the Columns spin button near the right side of the Slicer Tools Options tab of the Ribbon to change the number of columns in the slicer.

In the following figure, choose one customer from the slicer and the chart updates to show just that one customer.

Choose a different customer, and the chart updates for that customer.

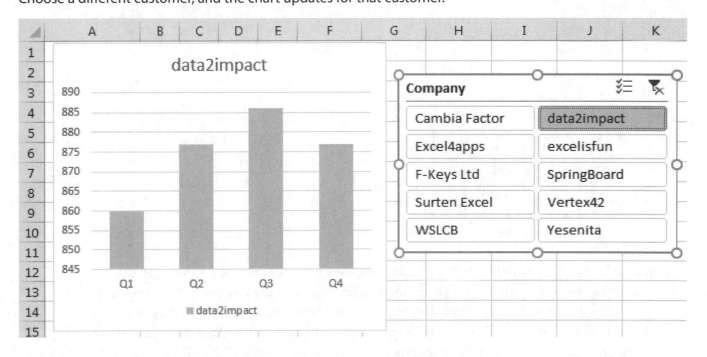

#17 Show Two Different Orders of Magnitude on a Chart

It is nearly impossible to read a chart where one series is dramatically larger than other series. In the following chart, the series for Year to Date Sales is 10 times larger than most of the monthly sales. The blue columns are shortened, and it will be difficult to see subtle changes in monthly sales.

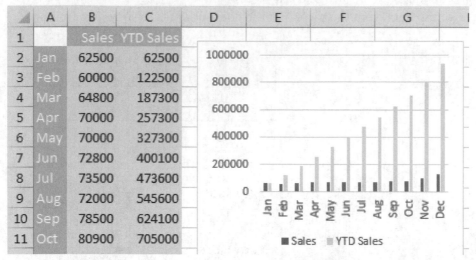

Combo charts were always possible in Excel, but they have a new interface starting in Excel 2013. Choose the chart above and select Change Chart Type. Choose Combo from the category list on the left. You then have the choices shown below. Move the larger number (YTD Sales) to a new scale on the right axis by choosing Secondary Axis. Change the chart style for one series to Line from Clustered Column.

Choose the chart type and axis for your data series:

Series Name	Chart Type	Secondary Axis
Sales	Clustered Column	☐
YTD Sales	Line	☑

The result: Columns for the monthly revenue are taller, so you will be able to make out subtle changes like a decrease from July to August.

To get the additional formatting to the chart above, select the numbers on the left axis. Use the Font Color dropdown on the Home tab to choose a blue to match the blue columns. Select the green line. Select Format, Shape Outline to change to a darker green. Select the numbers on the right axis and change the font color to the same green. Double-click each axis and change Display Units to Thousands. Double-click a blue column and drag the Gap Width setting to be narrower. Double-click the legend and choose to show the legend at the top.

#18 Create Waterfall Charts

For 12 years, I worked at a company doing data analysis. One of my regular tasks was to analyze the profit on sales proposals before they went out the door. I did this with a waterfall chart. For me, the waterfall chart never would have to dip below the zero axis. I used a few tricks to make the columns float and drew the connector lines in by hand, using a ruler and a black pen.

Excel 2016 introduced a built-in Waterfall chart type. Select your range of data and create the chart. In the chart below, three columns are marked as total: Net Price, Gross Profit, and Net Profit. Excel won't automatically know which columns should be totals. Click any column to select all columns in the chart. Then single-click one total column. Right-click and select as Total. Repeat for the other columns that should touch the X-axis.

List Price	$1,400K	
Discount	-$560K	
Net Price	$840K	(mark as total)
Material	-$184K	
Labor	-$15K	
Overhead	-$87K	
Gross Profit	$554K	(mark as total)
Commissions	-$28K	
Net Profit	$526K	(mark as total)

The waterfall charts even work for cash flow charts that might go below zero.

Open	$145K	(mark as total)
Jan	$26K	
Feb	-$68K	
Mar	$20K	
Apr	-$85K	
May	-$76K	
Jun	$59K	
Jul	-$35K	
Aug	$65K	
Sep	$43K	
Oct	-$37K	
Nov	$79K	
Dec	$99K	
Close	$234K	(mark as total)

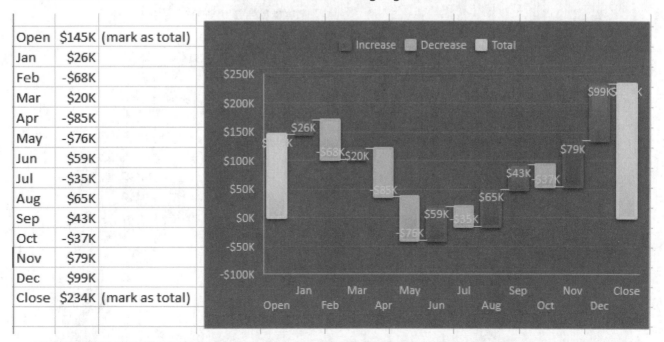

Tip: To change the color for Increase/Decrease or Total: Click on the legend and then click on one item in the legend. Press Ctrl+1 to open the Format panel for that series and choose a new Fill Color.

#19 Create Funnel Charts

In 2016, Microsoft 365 introduced Funnel charts, as well as Treemap, Sunburst, Box & Whisker, Pareto, and Histogram charts. A Funnel chart is great for showing a sales funnel.

#20 Create Filled Map Charts in Microsoft 365

Early in 2017, Map Charts appeared on the Insert tab in Microsoft 365. A Map chart shades closed regions on a map such as countries, states, counties, even zip code boundaries.

When you format a series in a Map, you can choose if it should show all 50 states or only the regions with data. Choose what makes the most sense for your data. In the chart on the left, the series color is a two-color gradient. You can choose three-color gradients or a category map, as shown on the right.

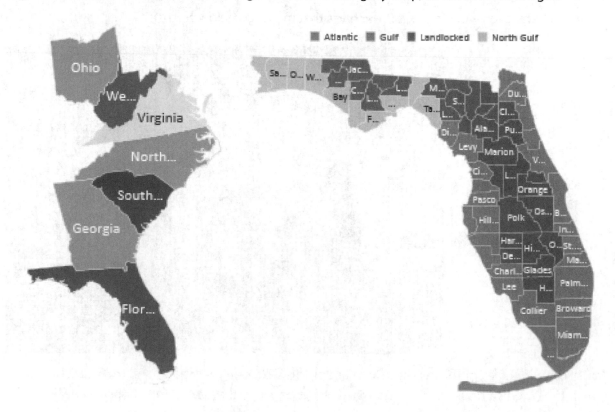

#21 Create a Bell Curve

I have 2200 Excel videos on YouTube. I can never predict which ones will be popular. Many videos hover around 2,000 views. But for some reason, the Bell Curve video collected half a million views. I am not sure why people need to create bell curves, but here are the steps.

A bell curve is defined by an average and a standard deviation. In statistics, 68% of the population will fall within one standard deviation of the mean. 95% falls within two standard deviations of the mean. 99.73% will fall within three standard deviations of the mean.

Say that you want to plot a bell curve that goes from 100 to 200 with the peak at 150. Use 150 as the mean. Since most of the results will fall within 3 standard deviations of the mean, you would use a standard deviation of 50/3 or 16.667.

1. Type 150 in cell B1.

2. Type =50/3 in cell B2.

3. Type headings of Point, X, Y in cells A4:C4.

4. Fill the numbers 1 to 61 in A5:A65. This is enough points to create a smooth curve.

B2			f_x	=50/3	
	A	B	C	D	E
1	Mean	150			
2	Standard Deviation	16.66667	=50/3		
3					
4	Point	X	Y		
5		1			
6		2			
7		3			

5. Go to the midpoint of the data, point 31 in B35. Type a formula there of =B1 to have the mean there.

6. The formula for B36 is =B35+($B$2/10). Copy that formula from row 36 down to row 65.

7. The formula for B34 is =B34-($B$2/10). Copy that formula up to row 5. Note that the notes in columns C:E of this figure do not get entered in your workbook - they are here to add meaning to the figure.

	A	B	C	D	E
1	Mean	150			
2	Standard Deviation	16.66667	=50/3		
3					
4	Point	X	Y		
32		28			
33		29			
34		30	148.3333	=B35-($B$2/10)	Copy up
35		31	150	=B1	
36		32	151.6667	=B35+($B$2/10)	Copy Down
37		33			
38		34			
39		35			

The magic function is called NORM.DIST which stands for Normal Distribution. When statisticians talk about a bell curve, they are talking about a normal distribution. To continue the current example, you want a bell curve from 100 to 200. The numbers 100 to 200 go along the X-axis (the horizontal axis) of the chart. For each point, you need to calculate the height of the curve along the y-axis. NORM.DIST will do this for you. There are four required arguments: =NORM.DIST(This x point, Mean, Standard Deviation, False). The last False says that you want a bell curve and not a S-curve. (The S-Curve shows accumulated probability instead of point probability.)

8. Type =NORM.DIST(B5,$B$1,$B$2,False) in C5 and copy down to row 65.

	A	B	C	D	E	F	G
1	Mean	150					
2	Standard Deviation	16.66667	=50/3				
3							
4	Point	X	Y				
5	1	100	0.000266	=NORM.DIST(B5,$B$1,$B$2,FALSE)			
6	2	101.6667	0.000357				
7	3	103.3333	0.000475	**Several rows**			
33	29	146.6667	0.023463	**hidden (just to**			
34	30	148.3333	0.023817	**make image fit**			
35	31	150	0.023937	**in this book)**			
36	32	151.6667	0.023817				
37	33	153.3333	0.023463				
64	60	198.3333	0.000357				
65	61	200	0.000266				
66							

9. Select B4:C65. On the Insert tab, open the XY-Scatter drop-down menu and choose the thumbnail with a smooth line. Alternatively, choose Recommened Charts and the first option for a bell curve.

The result: a bell curve, as shown here.

#22 Plotting Employees on a Bell Curve

Rather than creating a generic bell curve, how about plotting a list of employees or customers on a bell curve?

Start with a list of people and scores. Use the AVERAGE and STDEV.P functions to find the mean and standard deviation.

	A	B	C	D	E	F	G
1	Name	Score					
2	Andy	62		Mean	78.231	=AVERAGE(B2:B14)	
3	Barb	64		St Dev	14.418	=STDEV.P(B2:B14)	
4	Chris	83					
5	Diane	68					
6	Ed	98					
7	Flo	85					
8	Gary	98					
9	Hank	49					
10	Ike	90					
11	Jared	81					
12	Kelly	93					
13	Lou	71					
14	Mike	75					
15							

Once you know the mean and standard deviation, add a Y column with the formula shown below.

	A	B	C	D	E	F	G
1	Name	Score	Y				
2	Andy	62	=NORM.DIST(B2,$F$7,$F$8,false				
3	Barb	64	NORM.DIST(x, mean, standard_dev, **cumulative**)				
4	Chris	83				TRUE - cumulative d	
5	Diane	68				FALSE - probability	
6	Ed	98					
7	Flo	85			Mean	78.231	
8	Gary	98			St Dev	14.418	
9	Hank	49					

After adding the Y column, sort the data by Score ascending.

	A	B	C
1	Name	Score	Y
2	Hank	49	0.003544
3	Andy	62	0.014683
4	Barb	64	0.017
5	Diane	68	0.021512

Select Score & Y columns and add a Scatter with Smooth Lines as shown in the previous technique. Labelling the chart with names is tricky. Use the + icon to the right of the chart to add data labels. From the Data Labels flyout, choose More Options. In the panel shown below, click the icon with a column chart and then choose Value from Cells and specify the names in column A.

The result:

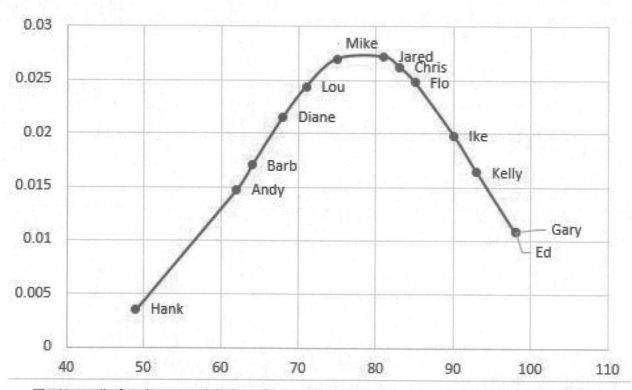

Tip: You will often have two labels in the chart that appear on top of each other. You can rearrange single labels so they appear with a small leader line as shown for Gary and Ed at the right side of the chart. Click on any label and all chart labels are selected. Next, click on either of the labels that appear together. After the second click, you are in "single label selection mode". You can drag that label so it is not on top of the other label.

#23 Add Meaning to Reports Using Data Visualizations

Three easy visualization tools were added to the Conditional Formatting dropdown in Excel 2007: Color Scales, Data Bars, and Icon Sets.

Consider this report, which has way too many decimal places to be useful.

	A	B	C	D	E	F
1	**Reject Rates by Hour and Line**					
3		Line 1	Line 2	Line 3	Line 4	Line 5
4	7AM	0.0000750	0.0106965	0.0066195	0.0012000	0.0010500
5	8AM	0.0004500	0.0066195	0.0036750	0.0006750	0.0016500
6	9AM	0.0002250	0.0021750	0.0088845	0.0015000	0.0012750
7	10AM	0.0005250	0.0070725	0.0104700	0.0018000	0.0007500
8	11AM	0.0006000	0.0061665	0.0104700	0.0014250	0.0015750
9	12PM	0.0006000	0.0014250	0.0054870	0.0017250	0.0008250
10	1PM	0.0006750	0.0031500	0.0086580	0.0016500	0.0015000
11	2PM	0.0013500	0.0031500	0.0113760	0.0023250	0.0033000

Select the numbers in the report and choose Home, Conditional Formatting, Color Scales. Then click on the second icon, which has red at the top and green at the bottom.

With just four clicks, you can now spot trends in the data. Line 2 started out the day with high reject rates but improved. Line 3 was bad the whole day. Line 1 was the best, but even those reject rates began to rise toward the end of the shift.

	Line 1	Line 2	Line 3	Line 4	Line 5
7AM	0.0000750	0.0106965	0.0066195	0.0012000	0.0010500
8AM	0.0004500	0.0066195	0.0036750	0.0006750	0.0016500
9AM	0.0002250	0.0021750	0.0088845	0.0015000	0.0012750
10AM	0.0005250	0.0070725	0.0104700	0.0018000	0.0007500
11AM	0.0006000	0.0061665	0.0104700	0.0014250	0.0015750
12PM	0.0006000	0.0014250	0.0054870	0.0017250	0.0008250
1PM	0.0006750	0.0031500	0.0086580	0.0016500	0.0015000
2PM	0.0013500	0.0031500	0.0113760	0.0023250	0.0033000

The next tool, Data Bar, is like a tiny bar chart that fills a cell. In the following figure, select all of the Revenue cells except for the grand total.

Choose Conditional Formatting, Data Bar, Green. Each number now gets a swath of color, as shown below. Large numbers get more color, and small numbers get hardly any color.

◢	A	B		B
1	Customer	Revenue		Revenue
2	Amazing Yardstick Partners	22810		22810
3	Inventive Opener Corporation	2257		2257
4	Magnificent Tackle Inc.	11240		11240
5	Leading Yogurt Company	9204		9204
6	Excellent Doorbell Company	18552		18552
7	Paramount Doghouse Inc.	9152		9152
8	Flexible Instrument Partners	8456		8456
9	Honest Chopstick Company	21730		21730
10	Wonderful Faucet Corporation	13806		13806
11	Special Doghouse Inc.	16416		16416
12	Ideal Vise Corporation	21015		21015
13	Guaranteed Bicycle Company	21465		21465
14	Astonishing Thermostat Corpora	21438		21438
15	Trustworthy Yogurt Inc.	9144		9144
16	Bright Toothpick Inc.	6267		6267
17	Remarkable Banister Supply	1740		1740
18	Safe Shoe Company	2401		2401
19	Vibrant Vise Company	9345		9345
20	Forceful Furnace Company	11628		11628
21	Guarded Zipper Corporation	5961		5961
22		244027		244027

Caution: Be careful not to include the grand total before selecting Data Bars. In the following example, you can see that the Grand Total gets all of the color, and the other cells get hardly any color.

2401
9345
11628
5961
244027

With the third tool, Icon Sets, you can choose from sets that have three, four, or five different icons.

Most people keep their numbers aligned with the right edge of the cell. Icons always appear on the left edge of the cell. To move the number closer to the icon, use the Increase Indent icon, shown below.

All three of these data visualization tools work by looking at the largest and smallest numbers in the range. Excel breaks that range into three equal-sized parts if you are using an icon set with three icons. That works fine in the example below.

	Q1	Q2	Q3	Q4
Andy	☆ 88	☆ 87	★ 94	☆ 85
Bob	☆ 87	★ 94	☆ 89	★ 94
Charlie	☆ 93	★ 99	★ 100	☆ 91
Dale	☆ 83	☆ 82	☆ 89	☆ 85
Eddy	☆ 80	☆ 83	☆ 82	☆ 91

But in the following figure, Eddy scored horribly in Q1, getting a 30. Because Eddy did poorly, everyone else is awarded a gold star. That doesn't seem fair because their scores did not improve.

	Q1	Q2	Q3	Q4
Andy	⭐ 88	⭐ 87	⭐ 94	⭐ 85
Bob	⭐ 87	⭐ 94	⭐ 89	⭐ 94
Charlie	⭐ 93	⭐ 99	⭐ 100	⭐ 91
Dale	⭐ 83	⭐ 82	⭐ 89	⭐ 85
Eddy	☆ 30	⭐ 83	⭐ 82	⭐ 91

You can take control of where the range for an icon begins and ends. Go to Home, Conditional Formatting, Manage Rules and choose Edit Rule. In the following figure, the Type dropdown offers Percent, Percentile, Formula, and Number. To set the gold star so it requires 90 or above, use the settings shown below. Note that the two other icons have been replaced with No Cell Icon.

#24 Use Cutout People to Add Interest to Your Worksheet

Microsoft 365 subscribers now have access to nearly 2,500 Cutout People in Excel. In a study conducted by YouTube, 90% of the most-watched videos have an emotive human face prominently on the title card. Photos of people attract attention. Try adding a cutout person to your next report to get someone to look at the report.

	A	B	C	D	E	F	G
1	Q3 Results are up 14% over last year!						
2							
3							
4		Jul	Aug	Sep	Q3		
5	Andy	413	547	178	1,138		
6	Barb	142	532	437	1,111		
7	Chris	317	716	905	1,938		
8	Diane	933	299	448	1,680		
9	Ed	533	457	817	1,807		
10	Flo	311	979	354	1,644		
11	Gary	340	292	845	1,477		
12	Hank	501	231	450	1,182		
13	Ike	865	196	222	1,283		
14	Jared	384	400	617	1,401		
15	Total	4,739	4,649	5,273	14,661		
16							

To insert a person, go to Insert, Icons. Across the top of the dialog, you can choose from Images, Icons, People, Stickers, and Illustrations. Click on People.

There are 925 poses of 41 people. Each person has from 15 to 30 multiple poses, exhibiting different emotions. There are people holding their thumb up, or down. Seven of the people offer a series with 1, 2, 3, 4, or 5 fingers extended up.

To find all poses of one person, you might have to know their name to search. Small tiles identify 32 of the 41 people (chosen at random). If you want someone without a name tile, you can type their name in the search box.

The names of people in the photo below are: (Row 1) Addison, Alexander, Alfredo, Angela, Anthony, Babs, Basia, Carrie, Chantel, Charles, Christania, Deepika, Dennis, Elena, Fu, Herlinda, Jian, Jonathan, Kairy, Karun, and Kesha. Row 2: Kevin, Klein, Lance, Mara, Marci, Melanie, Melissa, Nicole, Noah, Pavan, Rachel, Randy, Shao, Sherri, Shreya, Soham, Stanley, Tanvi, Tiyna, and Ursula.

While you can search for people by name, you can also search by emotion or action. You can find people who are happy, excited, frustrated, pointing, or holding a sign. They're also grouped by angle. Searching for "Profile" will find people facing to the side, for example, while searching for "Back" will find people facing away from you.

Below, a series of photos of Karun could be used to illustrate five sequential steps.

Bonus Tip: Add Text to the Sign Held by a Person

There are also poses where the person is holding a blank sign. You can add text to the sign, like in this image of Angela:

Here are the steps for adding text to a sign and making it look natural:

1. Use Insert, Icons, People, and search for "Sign."

2. Select a person and click Insert.

3. Resize the person as needed to fit the situation.

4. Click any cell outside of the picture to unselect the picture.

5. Use Insert, Shapes, Textbox. Draw a text box that aligns closely with the sign.

6. The color of the sign and the default color of the white text box in Excel don't match exactly. With the text box selected, go to Shape Format, Shape Fill, and choose No Fill. This will make the background of the text box transparent and match the color of the sign. On the same tab in the ribbon, choose Shape Outline and choose No Outline.

7. Type your text to appear on the sign. On the Home tab, use Increase Font, Center, Middle Align, Font Color, and Font to make the text on the sign stand out.

> **Note**: I keep picturing the photo shoot where these people were put through the paces of being photographed with up to 270 different emotions. It had to be a tiring day. At the point where they asked people to hold a large blank sign, I doubt that anyone bothered to have a carpenter's level handy to make sure the sign was completely level. In most cases, the sign is tilted by a few degrees.

8. Align the top of the text box with the top of the sign. Make sure the text box is selected. Go to the Shape Format tab in the ribbon and look for the Arrange group toward the right side. The last drop-down in that group is called Rotate. Open the drop-down menu and choose More Rotation Options. This opens the Format Shape task pane. The Rotation spin button allows you to rotate in 1-degree increments. Rotate using the spin button until the text box lines up with the sign.

Bonus Tip: Use a Formula to Toggle Pictures

With the new cutout people, it would be cool if you could toggle in a happy or sad version of a person depending on a formula. Here are the steps:

1. Arrange the various images so they are in a single row or column. Make the cell height and width large enough so each cell completely holds the picture.

2. Copy the cell containing the first photo. Make sure you are copying the cell and not the photo itself. This is often harder than it sounds since the image takes up most of the cell. In the image below, I had to click into B2 and then use the right arrow to select C2.

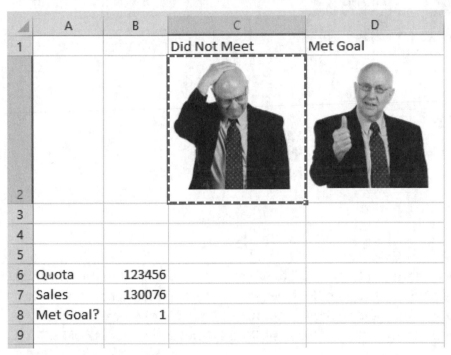

3. Select the spot where you want the photo to appear. Open the Paste drop-down on the Home tab and select the final icon: Paste Linked Picture.

The linked picture appears. When the linked picture is selected, look in the Formula Bar. You will see that the linked picture has a source, currently =$C$2.

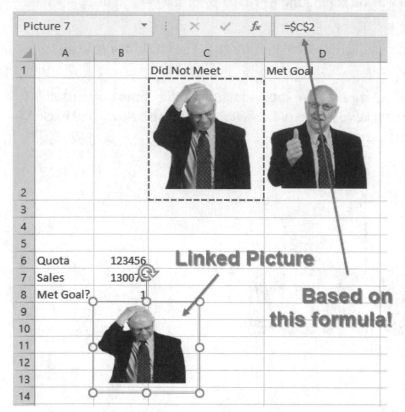

The trick is to change the linked picture formula from =$C$2 to something using OFFSET or INDEX. Notice that B8 is a formula that is currently returning 0 for Did Not Meet or 1 for Met Goal. This lends itself to the OFFSET function: =OFFSET($C$2,0,$B$8). If the formula was returning 1 for Did Not Meet and 2 for Met Goal, then you could use =INDEX($C$2:$C$3,1,$B$8). In this case, INDEX is preferable because OFFSET is volatile.

> **Caution:** You can not type this formula in the Formula Bar. Instead, you have to create a Defined Name. The formula in the Defined Name needs to have the sheet name for each range. If your worksheet name is Dashboard, then the formulas above would become: =OFFSET(Dashboard!$C$2,0,Dashboard!$B$8) or =INDEX(Dashboard!$C$2:$C$3,1,Dashboard!$B$8).

> **Caution:** If you use spaces in your worksheet name, then wrap the sheet name in apostrophes. For example, with a sheet name of My Dashboard, you would need =INDEX('My Dashboard'!$C$2:$C$3,1,'My Dashboard'!$B$8).

4. Go to Formulas, Define Name. Type a name such as WhichRandy. Use a formula like the ones listed above. Click OK.

5. Click on the image in your dashboard that you want to have change. With that linked picture selected, click in the formula bar and change the formula to =WhichRandy.

6. If desired, hide the "1" in B8 by putting it behind Randy's head. Now, as the formula in B8 changes, the image of Randy would change.

#25 Make an Image Semi-Transparent

Semi-transparent images became easier in Microsoft 365 starting in the fall of 2019. If you use Insert, Image, the image always covers the data in the cells. Starting in 2019, you can use the Transparency drop-down on the Picture Format tab of the Ribbon to change the picture transparency.

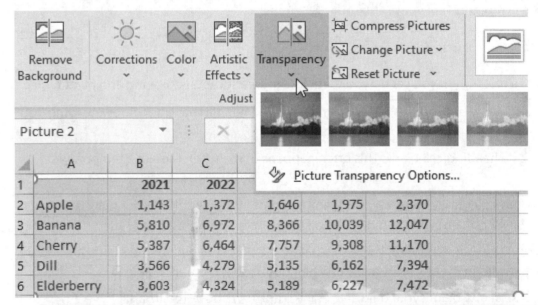

Tip: Picture Transparency is better than the old Page Layout, Background. When you choose a background image, it displays behind the numbers, but it will not print. With Picture transparency, you can control the size and shape of the image.

Caution: In the screenshot above, you will see the Remove Background tool. There is also a Set Transparent Color option under the Color drop-down menu. Both tools are finicky. The Set Transparent Color might work for a sign being held by a Cutout Person, but it won't work for a sky with many shades of blue. The Remove Background tool asks you to mark areas to keep and areas to remove. It seems that when you click a new area, the logic recalculates the old areas. As you remove a new section, the old sections come back. To painlessly remove backgrounds, try PhotoShop or Topaz Mask AI.

#26 Save Any Object as an Image

Starting in 2020 for Microsoft 365, you can right-click any object in Excel and choose Save As Picture. If you want to save a Chart plus a Cutout Person, you can select them both and then choose Group from the Format Picture tab of the Ribbon.

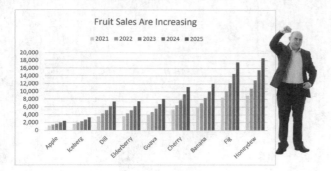

	2021	2022	2023	2024	2025
Apple	1,143	1,372	1,646	1,975	2,370
Iceberg	1,576	1,891	2,269	2,723	3,268
Dill	3,566	4,279	5,135	6,162	7,394
Elderberry	3,603	4,324	5,189	6,227	7,472

Tip: What if you want to save a picture of values in cells? You could use Paste Linked Picture, or simply use the Office Snipping Tool with Win+Shift+S.

#27 Set Up Your Data for Data Analysis

Make sure to follow these rules when you set up your data for sorting, subtotals, filtering and pivot tables.

- Rule 1: Use only a single row of headings above your data. If you need to have a two-row heading, set it up as a single cell with two lines in the row.

- Rule 2: Never leave one heading cell blank. This often happens to me when I set up a temporary column.

- Rule 3: There should be no entirely blank rows or blank columns in the middle of your data. It is okay to have an occasional blank cell, but you should have no entirely blank columns.

- Rule 4: If your heading row is not in row 1, be sure to have a blank row between the report title and the headings. It is fine to make this blank row have a row height of 1 so it is barely visible.

- Rule 5: If you have a total row below your data, leave one blank row above the totals.

- Rule 6: Formatting the heading cells in bold will help the Excel's IntelliSense module understand that these are headings.

Caution: Following these rules may not help if your data is only two columns wide.

Tip: To test, select one cell in your data and press Ctrl+* to select the current region. It should include your data and your headings, but not any Title rows or total row or footnotes.

Bonus Tip: Use Accounting Underline to Avoid Tiny Blank Columns

I once worked for a manager who was very particular about the heading underlines in a report.

The manager hated the regular underlines shown in row 1 below. In cell E1, the underline is only as wide as the characters in the cell. If I tried using a bottom border instead of the underline, you would get a single, long, "uniborder" as shown in row 6.

	A	B	C	D	E	F
1		Apple	Banana	Cherry	Dill	Total
2	Jan	495	824	298	973	2590
3	Feb	994	574	138	705	2411
4	Mar	306	851	719	598	2474
5						
6		Apple	Banana	Cherry	Dill	Total
7	Jan	495	824	298	973	2590

This manager would format his worksheets with tiny little columns between each column. That way, when he used a bottom border, it would go all the way across the cell, but they were still individual borders. This is a data disaster waiting to happen. Someone is going to sort part of the data but not all of the data.

	A	B	C	D	E	F	G	H	I	J
1		Apple		Banana		Cherry		Dill		Total
2	Jan	495		824		298		973		2590
3	Feb	994		574		138		705		2411

There Is an awesome solution, but it is hidden. If you open the Underline drop-down menu on the Home tab of the Ribbon, your only choices are Single or Double. But if you click the dialog launcher in the Font group, the Format Cells dialog offers a drop-down with extra choices for Accounting Underlines. Choose one of those and your underlines will stretch almost all the way across the cell but they will be individual lines instead of a single long line.

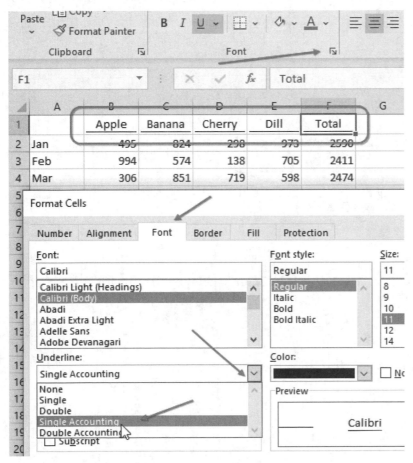

Bonus Tip: Use Alt+Enter to Control Word Wrap

The Gross Profit heading in C1 and C2 violates the rule that each heading should be in a single cell.

◢	A	B	C
1			Gross
2	Revenue	Cost	Profit

In cell C2, type Gross. Then press Alt+Enter. Type Profit. Press Enter. Delete the word Gross from row 1.

◢	A	B	C	
1				
2	Revenue	Cost	Gross Profit	
3				

Excel will see C2 as a single cell. All of the intellisense will continue to work.

Why use Alt+Enter instead of simply turning on Word Wrap? When you have long text that you want to wrap to several lines, the Word Wrap icon frequently wraps at the wrong place.

Alt+Enter prevents this nightmare: in the image below, you type the long heading in D1 and turn on Word Wrap. The results are shown in D3. You don't like where the words are wrapping, so you start typing many spaces at the end of each line as shown in F5. With just the right number of spaces, it will look like D7.

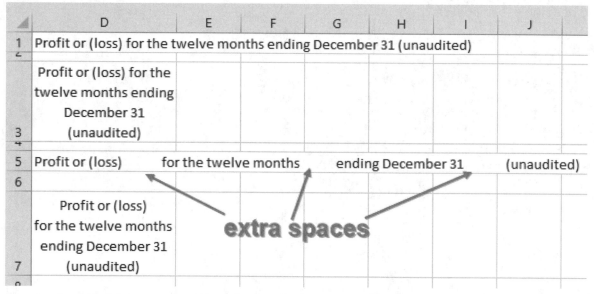

Stop typing all of those spaces. Type the text for line 1, then Alt+Enter. Then type the text for line 2, then Alt+Enter, and so on.

Bonus Tip: Someone went crazy and used Alt+Enter Too Much

Alt-Enter is a great trick until someone uses it in hundreds of cells. I've seen people treat a single cell as if it were Microsoft Word. Pressing Alt+Enter inserts a Character Code 10 in the cell. You might be tempted to fix this by using =SUBSTITUTE(A1,CHAR(10),"").

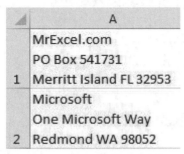

However, the simple solution is to use Data, Text to Columns. In Step 1, choose Delimited. In Step 2, choose Other. Click into the Other box and press Ctrl+J. You won't see anything in the box, but typing Ctrl+J in this dialog or in the Find & Replace dialog will insert a character 10.

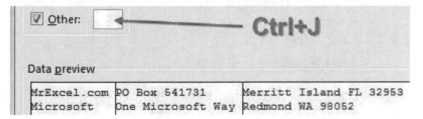

#28 Sort East, Central, and West Using a Custom List

At my last day job, we had three sales regions: East, Central, and West. The company headquarters was in the East, and so the rule was that all reports were sorted with the East region first, then Central, then West. Well, there is no way to do this with a normal sort.

Sort AZ, and you will have Central at the top.

Region	Customer	Revenue
Central	Excel Design Solutions Ltd	810475
Central	Excelerator BI	243675
Central	WSLCB	1116175
East	Budget Wand	692375
East	Deloitte Canada	805775
East	New Hope Laundry	507200
East	SkyWire, Inc.	616200
West	Access Analytic	956425
West	DataSolverz.com	332375
West	Harvest Consulting	437600

Sort the data ZA, and you will have West at the top.

Region	Customer	Revenue
West	Access Analytic	956425
West	DataSolverz.com	332375
West	Harvest Consulting	437600
West	MySpreadsheetLab	651825
West	The Lab with Leo Crew	243925
East	Budget Wand	692375
East	Deloitte Canada	805775
East	New Hope Laundry	507200
East	SkyWire, Inc.	616200
Central	Excel Design Solutions Ltd	810475

I actually went to my manager to ask if he would rename the Central region. "To what?" he asked incredulously. I replied that I didn't care, as long as it started with F through V. Perhaps "Middle"? John shook his head no and went on with his day.

So, over and over, I would sort the report, then Ctrl+X to cut the East region records and paste them before the Central region. If only I had known this trick.

The first thing to do is to set up a custom list with the regions in the correct order: East, Central, West. (See "Teach the Fill Handle a New List" on page 17 for instructions on setting up a custom list.)

Once the custom list is defined, open the Sort dialog by using the Sort icon on the Data tab. Choose to sort by Region. Open the Order dropdown. You don't want A to Z. You don't want Z to A. You want Custom List....

Choose the East, Central, West custom list.

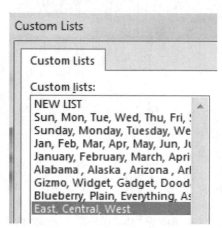

One you've chosen that custom list, you can either sort it East, Central, West or West, Central, East.

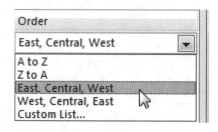

The result: an easy way to sort a list into a nonstandard sequence.

Region	Customer	Revenue
East	Deloitte Canada	805775
East	Budget Wand	692375
East	SkyWire, Inc.	616200
East	New Hope Laundry	507200
Central	WSLCB	1116175
Central	Excel Design Solutions Ltd	810475
Central	Excelerator BI	243675
West	Access Analytic	956425
West	MySpreadsheetLab	651825
West	Harvest Consulting	437600
West	DataSolverz.com	332375
West	The Lab with Leo Crew	243925

Product lines often won't sort correctly: PTC-610, PTC-710, PTC-860, PTC-960, PTC-1100 is the desired order. But PTC-1100 always sorts first in a text sort. A custom list would solve this problem as well.

Thanks to @NeedForExcel for suggesting this tip.

#29 Sort Left to Right

Every day, your IT department sends you a file with the columns in the wrong sequence. It would take them two minutes to change the query, but they have a six-month backlog, so you are stuck rearranging the columns every day.

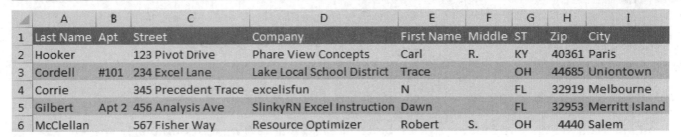

You can reorder the columns with a left-to-right sort.

Add a new row above the data. Type numbers to represent the correct sequence for the columns.

Select Data, Sort. In the Sort dialog, click the Options… button and choose Sort Left to Right. Click OK.

Specify Row 1 in the Sort By dropdown. Click OK.

The problem: The column widths do not travel with the columns.

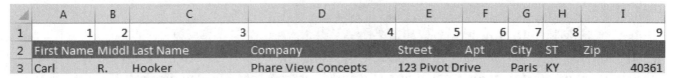

But it is easy to select the data and Press Alt+O, C, A or select Home, Format, Column, AutoFit.

#30 Sort Subtotals

This tip is from my friend Derek Fraley in Springfield, Missouri. I was doing a seminar in Springfield, and I was showing my favorite subtotal tricks.

For those of you who have never used subtotals, here is how to set them up.

Start by making sure your data is sorted. The data below is sorted by customers in column C.

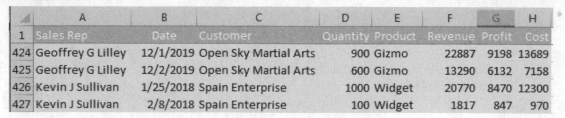

	A	B	C	D	E	F	G	H
1	Sales Rep	Date	Customer	Quantity	Product	Revenue	Profit	Cost
424	Geoffrey G Lilley	12/1/2019	Open Sky Martial Arts	900	Gizmo	22887	9198	13689
425	Geoffrey G Lilley	12/2/2019	Open Sky Martial Arts	600	Gizmo	13290	6132	7158
426	Kevin J Sullivan	1/25/2018	Spain Enterprise	1000	Widget	20770	8470	12300
427	Kevin J Sullivan	2/8/2018	Spain Enterprise	100	Widget	1817	847	970

From the Data tab, choose Subtotals. The Subtotal dialog box always wants to subtotal by the leftmost column. Open the At Each Change In dropdown and choose Customer. Make sure the Use Function box is set to Sum. Choose all of the numeric fields, as shown here.

When you click OK, Excel inserts a subtotal below each group of customers. But, more importantly, it adds Group and Outline buttons to the left of column A.

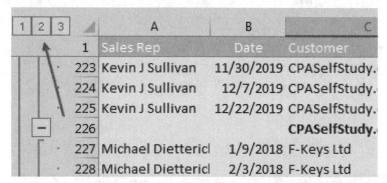

When you click the #2 Group and Outline button, the detail rows are hidden, and you are left with only the subtotal rows and the grand total. This is a beautiful summary of a detailed data set. Of course, at this point, the customers appear in alphabetic sequence. Derek from Springfield showed me that when the data is collapsed in the #2 view, you can sort by any column. In the figure below, a Revenue column cell is selected, and you are about to click the ZA sort button.

`=SUBTOTAL(9,F2:F37)`

Customer	Quantity	Product	Revenue	Profit	Cost
Association for Computers & Taxation Total	20200		430540	190598	239942
Blockhead Data Consultants Total	21500		460086	206861	253225
BradEdgar.com Total	24700		546662	243117	303545
Clarity Consultancy Services Ltd Total	17400		369567	164599	204968
Construction Intelligence & Analytics, Inc. Total	17800		374497	169684	204813

The top customer, Wag More Dog Store, comes to the top of the data set. But it does not come to row 2. Behind the hidden rows, Excel actually sorted a chunk of records. All of the Wag More detail rows moved along with the subtotal row.

	Customer	Quantity	Product	Revenue	Profit	Cost
49	Wag More Dog Store, San Antonio Total	28900		606128	273935	332193
91	BradEdgar.com Total	24700		546662	243117	303545
133	CPASelfStudy.com Total	23400		505279	221591	283688
172	F-Keys Ltd Total	23100		490827	210470	272357
222	Hybrid Software Total	23100		486697	215678	271019
259	Blockhead Data Consultants Total	21500		460086	206861	253225
295	Open Sky Martial Arts Total	20800		448241	196403	251838
332	Association for Computers & Taxation Total	20200		430540	190598	239942
371	Hartville Marketplace & Flea Market Total	19000		410118	181689	228429
408	SurtenExcel.com Total	17600		375472	164413	211059
439	Construction Intelligence & Analytics, Inc. Total	17800		374497	169684	204813
469	Spain Enterprise Total	17600		373852	163926	209926
505	Clarity Consultancy Services Ltd Total	17400		369567	164599	204968
533	The Salem Historical Society, Salem, Ohio Total	15000		329597	145571	184026
559	Juliet Babcock-Hyde CPA, PLLC Total	13900		295018	131416	163602
580	IMA Houston Chapter Total	9900		205231	90443	114788
581	Grand Total	313900		6707812	2978394	3729418

If you go back to the #3 view, you will see the detail records that came along with the subtotal row. Excel did not rearrange the detail records; they remain in their original sequence.

	Customer	Quantity	Product	Revenue
44	Wag More Dog Store, San Antonio	900	Widget	17289
45	Wag More Dog Store, San Antonio	500	Gizmo	10940
46	Wag More Dog Store, San Antonio	1000	Widget	21010
47	Wag More Dog Store, San Antonio	600	Gizmo	13680
48	Wag More Dog Store, San Antonio	800	Gadget	17136
49	Wag More Dog Store, San Antonio Total	28900		606128

To me, this is astounding on two fronts. First, I am amazed that Excel handles this correctly. Second, it is amazing that anyone would ever try this. Who would have thought that Excel would handle this correctly? Clearly, Derek from Springfield.

Bonus Tip: Fill in a Text Field on the Subtotal Rows

Say that each customer in a data set is assigned to a single sales rep. It would be great if you could bring the sales rep name down to the subtotal row. Here are the steps:

1. Collapse the data to the #2 view.

2. Select all of the sales rep cells, from the first subtotal row to the last customer subtotal row. Don't include the Grand Total row. At this point, you have both the visible and hidden rows selected. You need just the blank rows or just the visible rows.

3. At the right side of the Home tab, open the Find & Select dropdown. Choose Go To Special. In the Go To Special dialog, choose Blanks. Click OK.

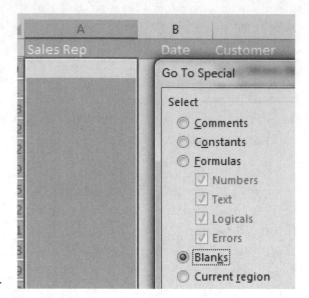

4. At this point, you've selected only the blank sales rep cells on the Subtotal rows. In my case, the active cell is A49. You need a formula here to point one cell up. Type =A48. Instead of pressing Enter, press Ctrl+Enter to enter a similar formula in all of the subtotal rows. In each case, it brings the sales rep from the previous row down.

The results: The subtotal rows show the sales rep name in addition to the numeric totals.

	A	B	C
1	Sales Rep	Date	Customer
49	Geoffrey G Lilley		Wag More Dog Store, San Antonio Total
91	Geoffrey G Lilley		BradEdgar.com Total
133	Kevin J Sullivan		CPASelfStudy.com Total
172	Michael Dietterick		F-Keys Ltd Total
222	P B Rayudu		Hybrid Software Total

Bonus Tip: An Easier Way to Fill in a Text Field on Subtotal Rows

Kimberly in Oklahoma City and Sarah in Omaha combined to provide a faster solution to getting the sales rep to appear on the Subtotal rows. Provided you only need the data in the #2 Summary View, this works amazingly well:

1. Click the #3 group and outline button to see all rows.

2. Select the first sales rep in A2.

3. Press Ctrl++ and press Enter. In other words, while holding down Ctrl, press the plus sign. This opens the Insert Cells dialog with "Shift Cells Down" selected. Pressing Enter is like pressing OK. This moves all of the sales reps down one row and leaves an ugly gap in A2 and the first row of every other customer.

But when you go back to the #2 view, the gaps disappear and the report is correct.

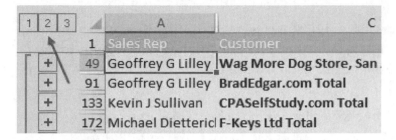

Bonus Tip: Format the Subtotal Rows

It is a little odd that Subtotals only bolds the customer column and not anything else in the subtotal row. Follow these steps to format the subtotal rows:

1. Collapse the data to the #2 view.

2. Select all data from the first subtotal to the grand totals.

3. Press Alt+; or select Home, Find & Select, Go To Special, Visible Cells Only).

4. Click OK. Format the subtotal rows by applying bold and a fill color.

Now, when you go back to the #3 view, the subtotal rows will be easy to spot.

Bonus Tip: Copy the Subtotal Rows

Once you've collapsed the data down to the #2 view, you might want to copy the subtotals to a new worksheet. If so, select all the data. Press Alt+; to select only the visible cells. Press Ctrl+C to copy. Switch to a new workbook and press Ctrl+V to paste. The pasted subtotal formulas are converted to values.

Thanks to Patricia McCarthy for suggesting to select visible cells. Thanks to Derek Fraley for his suggestion from row 6.

#31 Sort and Filter by Color or Icon

Conditional formatting got a lot of new features in Excel 2007, including icon sets and more than three levels of rules. This allows for some pretty interesting formatting over a large range. But once you format the cells, you might want to quickly see all the ones that are formatted a particular way. In Excel 2007, sorting and filtering were also updated to help you do just that!

This book analysis table has some highlighted rows to flag interesting books and an icon next to the price if the book is in the top 25% of prices in the list.

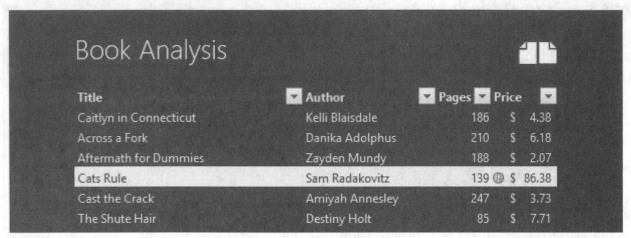

If you want to quickly view all the highlighted rows or cells that have icons, just drop down the filter for the column and choose Filter by Color (or Sort by Color to bubble them to the top).

Then you can pick the formatting you want to sort or filter by! This doesn't just work for conditional formatting; it also works for manually coloring cells. It is also available on the right-click menu of a cell under the Filter or Sort flyout, and in the Sort dialog.

This tip is from Sam Radakovitz, a project manager on the Excel team. He is more fond of cats than dogs.

#32 Consolidate Quarterly Worksheets

There are two ancient consolidation tools in Excel.

To understand them, say that you have three data sets. Each has names down the left side and months across the top. Notice that the names are different, and each data set has a different number of months.

Name	Jan	Feb	Mar
James WSLCB Tallman	75	75	69
Michael Seeley	98	90	83
David Colman	62	53	88
P B Rayudu	71	86	93
Fr. Tony Azzarto	71	84	70
Erik Svensen	62	91	81

Name	Apr	May	Jun	Jul	Aug
Michael Seeley	62	56	83	78	98
David Colman	92	58	83	81	67
P B Rayudu	84	97	69	58	60
Erik Svensen	71	69	65	91	68
Michael Karpfen	52	80	89	83	73
Victor E. Scelba II	93	70	54	90	81
Emily Mathews	80	57	51	62	69

Name	Sep	Oct	Nov	Dec
Michael Seeley	94	79	86	92
P B Rayudu	75	83	85	90
Erik Svensen	81	79	87	97
Michael Karpfen	78	86	93	91
Emily Mathews	64	93	92	90
Robert Mika	99	84	93	99
David Ringstrom	71	80	93	94

Illustration: Cartoon Bob D'Amico

3

You want to combine these into a single data set.

The first tool is the Consolidate command on the Data tab. Choose a blank section of the workbook before starting the command. Use the RefEdit button to point to each of your data sets and then click Add. In the lower left, choose Top Row and Left Column.

When you click OK, a superset of all three data sets is produced. The first column contains any name in any of the three data sets. Row 1 contains any month in any data set.

	A	B	C	D	E	F	G	H	I	J	K	L	M
1		Jan	Feb	Mar	Apr	May	Jun	Jul	Aug	Sep	Oct	Nov	Dec
2	James WSLCB Tallman	75	75	69									
3	Michael Seeley	98	90	83	62	56	83	78	98	94	79	86	92
4	David Colman	62	53	88	92	58	83	81	67				
5	P B Rayudu	71	86	93	84	97	69	58	60	75	83	85	90
6	Fr. Tony Azzarto	71	84	70									
7	Erik Svensen	62	91	81	71	69	65	91	68	81	79	87	97
8	Michael Karpfen				52	80	89	83	73	78	86	93	91
9	Victor E. Scelba II				93	70	54	90	81				
10	Emily Mathews				80	57	51	62	69	64	93	92	90
11	Robert Mika									99	84	93	99
12	David Ringstrom									71	80	93	94

In the above figure, notice three annoyances: Cell A1 is always left blank, the data in A is not sorted, and if a person was missing from a data set, then cells are left empty instead of being filled with 0.

Filling in cell A1 is easy enough. Sorting by name involves using Flash Fill to get the last name in column N. Here is how to fill blank cells with 0:

1. Select all of the cells that should have numbers: B2:M11.

2. Press Ctrl+H to display Find & Replace.

3. Leave the Find What box empty, and type a zero in the Replace With: box.

4. Click Replace All.

The result: a nicely formatted summary report, as shown below.

Name	Jan	Feb	Mar	Apr	May	Jun	Jul	Aug	Sep	Oct	Nov	Dec
Fr. Tony Azzarto	71	84	70	0	0	0	0	0	0	0	0	0
David Colman	62	53	88	92	58	83	81	67	0	0	0	0
Michael Karpfen	0	0	0	52	80	89	83	73	78	86	93	91
Emily Mathews	0	0	0	80	57	51	62	69	64	93	92	90

The other ancient tool is the Multiple Consolidation Range pivot table. Follow these steps to use it:

1. Press Alt+D, P to invoke the Excel 2003 Pivot Table and Pivot Chart Wizard.

2. Choose Multiple Consolidation Ranges in step 1 of the wizard. Click Next.

3. Choose I Will Create the Page Fields in step 2a of the wizard. Click Next.

4. In Step 2b of the wizard, use the RefEdit button to point to each table. Click Add after each.

5. Click Finish to create the pivot table, as shown below.

Sum of Value	C▼										
Row ▼	Jan	Feb	Mar	Apr	May	Jun	Jul	Aug	Sep	Oct	Nov
David Colman	62	53	88	92	58	83	81	67			
David Ringstrom									71	80	9
Emily Mathews				80	57	51	62	69	64	93	9
Erik Svensen	62	91	81	71	69	65	91	68	81	79	8
Fr. Tony Azzarto	71	84	70								
James WSLCB Tallman	75	75	69								

Thanks to CTroy for suggesting this feature.

#33 Create Your First Pivot Table

Pivot tables let you summarize tabular data to a one-page summary in a few clicks. Start with a data set that has headings in row 1. It should have no blank rows, blank columns, blank headings or merged cells.

	A	B	C	D	E	F	G	H
1	Region	Market	Rep	Date	Customer	Quantity	Product	Revenue
2	West	NoCal	Symons	1/5/2022	www.ExcelTricks.de	1000	Gizmo	22810
3	South	Houston	Kazmdav	1/6/2022	Wilde XL Solutions Ltd.	100	Gadget	2257
4	Northeast	New York	McGunigal	1/8/2022	Harlem Globetrotters	400	Gizmo	9152
5	Midwest	Cleveland	aBoBoBool	1/8/2022	Serving Brevard Realty	800	Gadget	18552
6	Northeast	New York	McGunigal	1/11/2022	We Report Space	400	Widget	8456

Select a single cell in your data and choose Insert, Pivot Table.

Excel will detect the edges of your data and offer to create the pivot table on a new worksheet. Click OK to accept the defaults.

Excel inserts a new blank worksheet to the left of the current worksheet. On the right side of the screen is the Pivot Table Fields pane. At the top, a list of your fields with checkboxes.

At the bottom are four drop zones with horrible names and confusing icons. Any fields that you drag to the Columns area will appear as headings across the top of your report. Any fields that you drag to the Rows area appear as headings along the left side of your report. Drag numeric fields to the Values area.

You can build some reports without dragging the fields. If you checkmark a text field, it will automatically appear in the Rows area. Checkmark a numeric field and it will appear in the Values area. By choosing Region and Revenue, you will create this pivot table:

	A	B
1		
2		
3	Region ▼	Sum of Revenue
4	West	840363
5	Midwest	2733471
6	South	2504958
7	Northeast	629020
8	**Grand Total**	**6707812**

To get products across the top of the report, drag the Product field and drop it in the Columns area:

3	Sum of Revenue	Product ▼				
4	**Region** ▼	**Doodads**	**Gadget**	**Gizmo**	**Widget**	**Grand Total**
5	West	4948	368928	202216	264271	840363
6	Midwest	45828	1003191	984901	699551	2733471
7	South	5859	727777	1018113	753209	2504958
8	Northeast	16924	241200	187790	183106	629020
9	**Grand Total**	**73559**	**2341096**	**2393020**	**1900137**	**6707812**

Note: your first pivot table might have the words "Column Labels" and "Row Labels" instead of headings like Product and Region. If so, choose Design, Report Layout, Show in Tabular Form. Later, in "#37 Specify Defaults for All Future Pivot Tables" on page 86, you will learn how to make Tabular Form the default for your pivot tables.

Bonus Tip: Rearrange fields in a pivot table

The power of pivot tables is the ability to rearrange the fields. If your manager decides you should put Regions across the top and products down the side, it is two drags to create the new report. Drag product to Rows. Drag Region to Columns.

You will have this report:

Sum of Revenue	Region				
Product	West	Midwest	South	Northeast	Grand Total
Doodads	4948	45828	5859	16924	73559
Gadget	368928	1003191	727777	241200	2341096
Gizmo	202216	984901	1018113	187790	2393020
Widget	264271	699551	753209	183106	1900137
Grand Total	840363	2733471	2504958	629020	6707812

To remove a field from the pivot table, drag the field tile outside of the Fields pane, or simply uncheck the field in the top of the Fields pane.

Bonus Tip: Format a Pivot Table

The Design tab has a gallery with 84 built-in formats for pivot tables. Choose a design from the gallery and the colors change.

One frustrating feature with a pivot table is that the numbers always start out as General format. Right-click any number and choose Number Format…. Any changes you make to the number formatting using this command will be remembered as long as Revenue stays in the pivot table. (Before Excel 2010, pivot tables would frequently forget the number formatting. This was fixed in Excel 2010.)

Bonus Tip: Format One Cell in a Pivot Table

This is new in Microsoft 365 starting in 2018. You can right-click any cell in a pivot table and choose Format Cell. Any formatting that you apply is tied to that data in the pivot table. In the figure below, Florida Figs have a yellow fill color.

	A	B	C
1	Category	(All)	
2			
3	Sum of Sales	Region	
4	Product	California	Florida	N
5	Apple	8479	6235
6	Banana	8287	2635
7	Cherry	4373	3590
8	Date	3004	1496
9	Elderberry	2307	0
10	Fig	0	9683
11	Cucumber	1881	9512
12	Grand Total	28331	33151
13			

If you change the pivot table, the yellow formatting follows the Florida Fig.

	A	B	C
3	Product	Region	Sum of Sales
26	Elderberry	Texas	1381
27	Elderberry	Washington	5901
28	Elderberry Total		19679
29	⊟ Fig	Florida	9683
30	Fig	Missouri	7531
31	Fig	New York	5650

If you add a new inner field, then multiple cells for Florida Fig will have the fill color.

	A	B	C	D
3	Product	Region	Rep	Sum of Sales
49	⊟ Fig	⊟ Florida	Sonny	6137
50	Fig	Florida	Fred	3546
51	Fig	Florida Total		9683
52	Fig	⊟ Missouri	Lewis	7531

The formatting will persist if you remove Florida or Fig due to a filter. If you filter to vegetables, Fig is hidden. Filter to fruit and Fig will still be formatted. However, if you completely remove either Product or Region from the pivot table, the formatting will be lost.

Bonus Tip: Fill in the Blanks in the Annoying Outline View

If your pivot table is in Tabular or Outline Form and you have more than one row field, the pivot table defaults to leaving a lot of blank cells in the outer row fields:

3	Region ▼	Market ▼	Sum of Revenue
4	⊟West	NoCal	521,373
5		SoCal	318,990
6	West Total		840,363
7	⊟Midwest	Chicago	520,176
8		Cincinnati	512,391
9		Cleveland	559,826

Starting in Excel 2010, use Design, Report Layout, Repeat all Item Labels to fill in the blanks in column A:

3	Region ▼	Market ▼	Sum of Revenue
4	⊟West	NoCal	521,373
5	West	SoCal	318,990
6	West Total		840,363
7			
8	⊟Midwest	Chicago	520,176
9	Midwest	Cincinnati	512,391
10	Midwest	Cleveland	559,826

There is another way to have blanks in the Values area of a pivot table. Say that you have a product which is only sold in a few regions. If there are no Doodad sales in Atlanta, Excel will leave that cell empty instead of putting a zero there. Right-click the pivot table and choose Pivot Table Options. On the Layout & Format tab, find the box For Empty Cells, Show: and type a zero.

Bonus Tip: Rearrange Fields Pane

Howie Dickerman is currently in charge of pivot tables at Microsoft. He inherited the product and suggests some of the defaults could have been different. For one, he suggests using the gear at the top right of the PivotTable Fields pane and changing the view to Fields Section and Areas Section side-by-side.

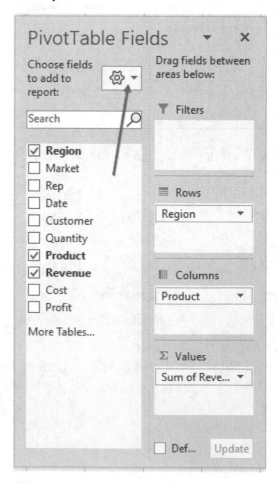

#34 Create a Year-over-Year Report in a Pivot Table

Let's say you have two years' worth of detail records. Each record has a daily date. When you build a pivot table from this report, you will have hundreds of rows of daily dates in the pivot table. This is not much of a summary.

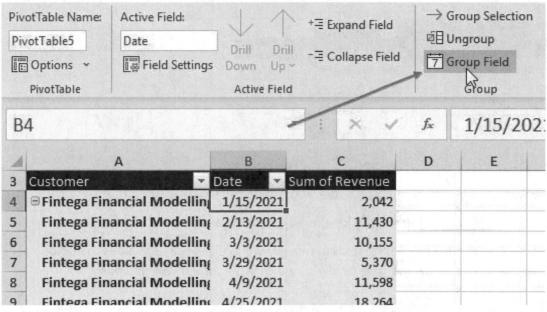

Choose one of those date cells in the pivot table. From the Analyze tab in the Ribbon, choose Group Field.

Because you are on a date field, you get *this* version of the Grouping dialog. In it, deselect Months and select Years.

The daily dates are rolled up to years. Move the Date field from Rows to Columns.

The result is almost perfect. But instead of a grand total in column D, you probably want a percentage variance. To get rid of the Grand Total column, right-click on the Grand Total heading and choose Remove Grand Total.)

To build the variance column as shown below, you need to write a formula outside the pivot table that points inside the pivot table. Do not touch the mouse or arrow keys while building the formula, or the often-annoying GETPIVOTDATA function will appear. Instead, simply type =C5/B5-1 and press Enter.

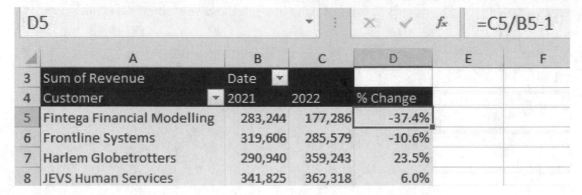

	A	B	C	D	E	F
3	Sum of Revenue	Date				
4	Customer	2021	2022	% Change		
5	Fintega Financial Modelling	283,244	177,286	-37.4%		
6	Frontline Systems	319,606	285,579	-10.6%		
7	Harlem Globetrotters	290,940	359,243	23.5%		
8	JEVS Human Services	341,825	362,318	6.0%		

Bonus Tip: Another Way to Calculate Year-Over-Year

Instead of creating a formula outside of the pivot table, you can do this inside the pivot table.

Start from the image with column D empty. Drag Revenue a second time to the Values area.

Look in the Columns section of the Pivot Table Fields panel. You will see a tile called Values that appears below Date. Drag that tile so it is below the Date field. Your pivot table should look like this:

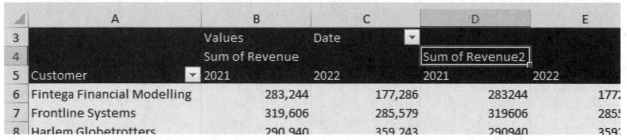

	A	B	C	D	E
3		Values	Date		
4		Sum of Revenue		Sum of Revenue2	
5	Customer	2021	2022	2021	2022
6	Fintega Financial Modelling	283,244	177,286	283244	177:
7	Frontline Systems	319,606	285,579	319606	285!
8	Harlem Globetrotters	290,940	359,243	290940	359:

Double-click the Sum of Revenue2 heading in D4 to display the Value Field Settings dialog. Click on the tab for Show Values As. Change the drop-down menu to % Difference From. Change the Base Field to Date. Change the Base Item to (Previous Item). Type a better name than Sum of Revenue2 - perhaps % Change. Click OK.

You will have a mostly blank column D (because the pivot table can't calculate a percentage change for the first year. Right-click the D and choose Hide.

Thanks to Tobias Ljung for this method.

#35 Change the Calculation in a Pivot Table

Pivot tables offer a myriad of calculations in the Field Settings dialog box. Here is a faster way to change a calculation:

1. Drag Revenue to the Values area twice.

2. Double-click on the heading Sum of Revenue2. Excel opens the Value Field Settings dialog.

3. Click on Show Values As and select % of Column Total from the dropdown.

4. Type a new name in the Custom Name field, such as % of Total.

Thanks to Александр Воробьев for suggesting this tip.

Bonus Tip: Why Do Pivot Tables Count Instead of Sum?

In almost every seminar, someone asks why pivot tables default to count instead of sum. This long-standing problem was fixed in May 2018 for Microsoft 365 subscribers. The Count was triggered if you had one revenue cell that contained text or an empty cell.

Someone wrote a letter to the Excel team complaining that a single empty cell should not be treated like text. If a cell is blank and you refer to that cell in a formula, Excel treats the cell as a zero. The letter-writer pointed out that a columns with mostly numbers and a few empty cells should not trigger a Count. The person on the Excel team agreed, and quietly pushed out a change.

If you are not using Microsoft 365, then you can avoid the Count issue by making sure that there are no blank cells in your revenue column. If you don't think that you have any blank cells, make sure you are selecting one cell in your data set and not the entire columns A:J. If your data is in A2:J999 and you select A:J, you are selecting 998 numbers and over a million empty cells.

#36 Find the True Top Five in a Pivot Table

Pivot tables offer a Top 10 filter. It is cool. It is flexible. But I hate it, and I will tell you why.

Here is a pivot table that shows revenue by customer. The revenue total is $6.7 million. Notice that the largest customer, Roto-Rooter, is 9% of the total revenue.

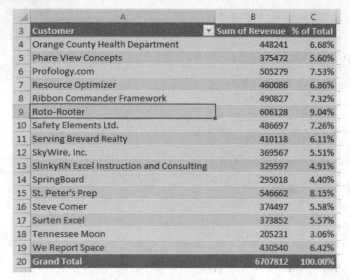

	A	B	C
3	Customer	Sum of Revenue	% of Total
4	Orange County Health Department	448241	6.68%
5	Phare View Concepts	375472	5.60%
6	Profology.com	505279	7.53%
7	Resource Optimizer	460086	6.86%
8	Ribbon Commander Framework	490827	7.32%
9	Roto-Rooter	606128	9.04%
10	Safety Elements Ltd.	486697	7.26%
11	Serving Brevard Realty	410118	6.11%
12	SkyWire, Inc.	369567	5.51%
13	SlinkyRN Excel Instruction and Consulting	329597	4.91%
14	SpringBoard	295018	4.40%
15	St. Peter's Prep	546662	8.15%
16	Steve Comer	374497	5.58%
17	Surten Excel	373852	5.57%
18	Tennessee Moon	205231	3.06%
19	We Report Space	430540	6.42%
20	Grand Total	6707812	100.00%

What if my manager has the attention span of a goldfish and wants to see only the top five customers? To start, open the dropdown in A3 and select Value Filters, Top 10.

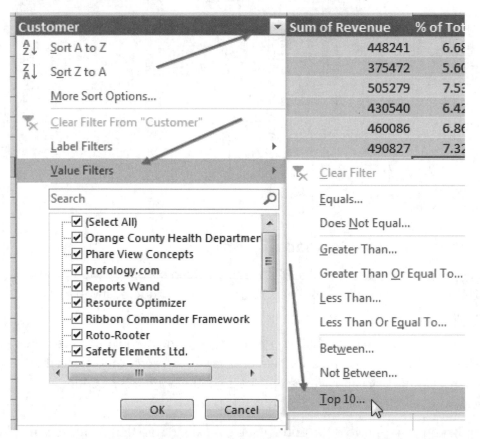

The super-flexible Top 10 Filter dialog allows Top/Bottom. It can do 10, 5, or any other number. You can ask for the top five items, top 80%, or enough customers to get to $5 million.

But here is the problem: The resulting report shows five customers and the total from those customers instead of the totals from everyone. Roto-Rooter, who was previously 9% of the total is 23% of the new total.

Customer	Sum of Revenue	% of Total
Profology.com	505279	19.17%
Ribbon Commander Framework	490827	18.62%
Roto-Rooter	606128	23.00%
Safety Elements Ltd.	486697	18.47%
St. Peter's Prep	546662	20.74%
Grand Total	2635593	100.00%

But First, a Few Important Words About AutoFilter

I realize this seems like an off-the-wall question. If you want to turn on the Filter dropdowns on a regular data set, how do you do it? Here are three really common ways:

- Select one cell in your data and click the Filter icon on the Data tab or press Ctrl+Shift+L.
- Select all of your data with Ctrl+* and click the Filter icon on the Data tab.
- Press Ctrl+T to format the data as a table.

These are three really good ways. As long as you know any of them, there is absolutely no need to know another way. But here's an incredibly obscure but magical way to turn on the filter:

- Go to your row of headers and then go to the rightmost heading cell. Move one cell to the right. For some unknown reason, when you are in this cell and click the Filter icon, Excel filters the data set to your left. I have no idea why this works. It really isn't worth talking about because there are already three really good ways to turn on the Filter dropdowns. I call this cell the magic cell.

And Now, Back to Pivot Tables

3

There is a rule that says you cannot use AutoFilter when you are in a pivot table. See below? The Filter icon is grayed out because I've selected a cell in the pivot table.

I don't know why Microsoft grays this out. It must be something internal that says AutoFilter and a pivot table can't coexist. So, there is someone on the Excel team who is in charge of graying out the Filter icon. That person has never heard of the magic cell. Select a cell in the pivot table, and the Filter gets grayed out. Click outside the pivot table, and Filter is enabled again.

But wait. What about the magic cell I just told you about? If you click in the cell to the right of the last heading, Excel forgets to gray out the Filter icon!

Sure enough, Excel adds AutoFilter dropdowns to the top row of your pivot table. And AutoFilter operates differently than a pivot table filter. Go to the Revenue dropdown and choose Number Filters, Top 10....

In the Top 10 AutoFilter dialog, choose Top 6 Items. That's not a typo...if you want five customers, choose 6. If you want 10 customers, choose 11.

To AutoFilter, the grand total row is the largest item in the data. The top five customers are occupying positions 2 through 6 in the data.

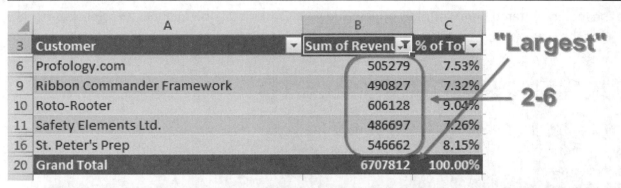

	A	B	C	
3	Customer ▼	Sum of Revenu ▼	% of Tot ▼	"Largest"
6	Profology.com	505279	7.53%	
9	Ribbon Commander Framework	490827	7.32%	2-6
10	Roto-Rooter	606128	9.04%	
11	Safety Elements Ltd.	486697	7.26%	
16	St. Peter's Prep	546662	8.15%	
20	Grand Total	6707812	100.00%	

Caution: Clearly, you are tearing a hole in the fabric of Excel with this trick. If you later change the underlying data and refresh your pivot table, Excel will not refresh the filter because, as far as Microsoft knows, there is no way to apply a filter to a pivot table!

Note: Our goal is to keep this a secret from Microsoft because it is a pretty cool feature. It has been "broken" for quite some time, so there are a lot of people who might be relying on it by now.

A Completely Legal Solution in Excel 2013+

If you want a pivot table showing you the top five customers but the total from all customers, you have to

move your data outside Excel. If you have Excel 2013 or newer running in Windows, there is a very convenient way to do this. To show you this, I've deleted the original pivot table. Choose Insert, Pivot Table. Before clicking OK, select the checkbox Add This Data To The Data Model.

Build your pivot table as normal. Use the dropdown in A3 to select Value Filters, Top 10, and ask for the top five customers. With one cell in the pivot table selected, go to the Design tab in the Ribbon and open the Subtotals dropdown. The final choice in the dropdown is Include Filtered Items in Totals. Normally, this choice is grayed out. But because the data is stored in the Data Model instead of a normal pivot cache, this option is now available.

3

Choose the Include Filtered Items in Totals option, and your Grand Total now includes an asterisk and the total of all of the data, as shown below.

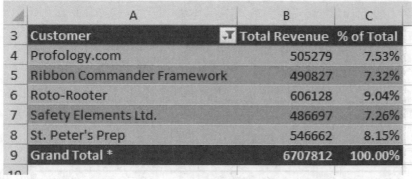

	A	B	C
3	Customer	Total Revenue	% of Total
4	Profology.com	505279	7.53%
5	Ribbon Commander Framework	490827	7.32%
6	Roto-Rooter	606128	9.04%
7	Safety Elements Ltd.	486697	7.26%
8	St. Peter's Prep	546662	8.15%
9	Grand Total *	6707812	100.00%

This magic cell trick originally came to me from Dan in my seminar in Philadelphia and was repeated 15 years later by a different Dan from my seminar in Cincinnati. Thanks to Miguel Caballero for suggesting this feature.

#37 Specify Defaults for All Future Pivot Tables

It took me six years, but I finally convinced the Excel team that a lot of people prefer Tabular layout for pivot tables to the Compact layout that became the default layout in Excel 2007. If you have Microsoft 365, you now have the ability to specify pivot table defaults.

Go to File, Options, Data. Click Edit Default Layout....

Change the Report Layout to Show in Tabular Form and choose the checkbox Repeat All Item Labels.

Tip: There are other settings that you can specify as the default. You can either click Pivot Table Options… and specify them or find a pivot table where you've already set up your favorite settings. Select one cell in that pivot table and click Import.

If you don't have Microsoft 365 and don't have access to pivot table defaults, you can get similar functionality by buying Pivot Power Premium from Debra Dalgleish at Contextures.com: mrx.cl/pppdebra.

Bonus Tip: Change What Drives You Crazy About Excel

I've managed to lobby the Excel team to get a few changes into Excel. It isn't always easy. It took me eight years of lobbying to get the Repeat All Item Labels feature added to Excel 2010. It took seven years to get the Pivot Table Defaults feature added.

But there is a new feedback mechanism that makes it possible for anyone to potentially get a favorite feature added to Excel. If you have a great idea of what would make Excel easier, write up a short post at https://Excel.UserVoice.com. Make sure to choose Excel for Windows (Desktop Application). Post your idea. And then get your friends and co-workers to vote for your idea. The great news is that the Excel team is listening to ideas posted at UserVoice. They key to getting the Excel team to respond is 20 votes. But I managed 200–300 votes for my Pivot Table Defaults before they started working on the feature.

#38 Make Pivot Tables Expandable Using Ctrl+T

If you choose all of columns A:J and you later want to add more records below the data, it takes only a simple Refresh to add the new data instead of having to find the Change Data Source icon. In the past, this made sense. But today, Change Data Source is right next to the Refresh button and not hard to find. Plus, there is a workaround in the Ctrl+T table.

When you choose your data set and select Format as Table by using Ctrl+T, the pivot table source will grow as the table grows. You can even do this retroactively, after the pivot table exists.

This figure below shows a data set and a pivot table. The pivot table source is A1:C16.

	A	B	C	D	E	F
1	Name	Region	Revenue			
2	Mike Mann	East	15100		Region	Revenue
3	Olga Kryuchkova	Central	13000		Central	$282,800
4	Graham Stent	West	20500		East	$176,500
5	Dennis P Jancsy	East	29800		West	$350,900
6	Diana McGunigale	Central	27800		Grand Total	$810,200
7	John Henning	West	39000			
8	Thomas Fries	East	7200			
9	Aiman Sadeq	Central	47700			
10	John Cockerill	West	36200			
11	Greg Heyman	East	39900			
12	Rick Grantham	Central	78600			
13	DeLisa Lee	West	100900			
14	Mark E Luhdorff	East	84500			
15	John T Lutz	Central	115700			
16	Mario Garcia	West	154300			
17						

Say that you want to be able to easily add new data below the pivot table, as shown below. Select one cell in the data and press Ctrl+T. Make sure that My Table Has Headers is checked in the Create Table dialog and click OK.

Some nice formatting is applied to the data set. But the formatting is not the important part.

	A	B	C
1	Name ▼	Region ▼	Revenue ▼
2	Mike Mann	East	15100
3	Olga Kryuchkova	Central	13000
4	Graham Stent	West	20500
5	Dennis P Jancsy	East	29800
6	Diana McGunigale	Central	27800

You have some new records to add to the table. Copy the records.

	A	B	C
1	Erik Svensen	East	42800
2	Melanie Breden	Central	98300
3	J Maltais	West	68400
4			
5			

Ctrl+c

Go to the blank row below the table and paste. The new records pick up the formatting from the table. The angle-bracket-shaped End-of-Table marker moves to C19. But notice that the pivot table has not updated yet.

	A	B	C	D	E	F
1	Name ▼	Region ▼	Revenue ▼			
2	Mike Mann	East	15100		Region ▼	Revenue
3	Olga Kryuchkova	Central	13000		Central	$282,800
4	Graham Stent	West	20500		East	$176,500
5	Dennis P Jancsy	East	29800		West	$350,900
6	Diana McGunigale	Central	27800		Grand Total	$810,200
7	John Henning	West	39000			
8	Thomas Fries	East	7200			
9	Aiman Sadeq	Central	47700			
10	John Cockerill	West	36200			
11	Greg Heyman	East	39900			
12	Rick Grantham	Central	78600			
13	DeLisa Lee	West	100900		**Pasted data**	
14	Mark E Luhdorff	East	84500			
15	John T Lutz	Central	115700		**No change yet**	
16	Mario Garcia	West	154300			
17	Erik Svensen	East	42800		**End of Table marker**	
18	Melanie Breden	Central	98300			
19	J Maltais	West	68400			
20					(Ctrl) ▼	

Click the Refresh button in the Pivot Table Tools Analyze tab. Excel adds the new rows to your pivot table.

Region ▼	Revenue
Central	$381,100
East	$219,300
West	$419,300
Grand Total	$1,019,700

Bonus Tip: Use Ctrl+T with VLOOKUP and Charts

In this figure, the VLOOKUP table is in E5:F9. Item A106 is missing from the table, and the VLOOKUP is returning #N/A. Conventional wisdom says to add A106 to the middle of your VLOOKUP table so you don't have to rewrite the formula.

	A	B	C	D	E	F	G
1	Qty	Item	Price?				
2	7	A104	37.95	=VLOOKUP(B2,$E$5:$F$9,2,0)			
3	8	A101	10.95				
4	2	A101	10.95		Item	Price	
5	9	A106	#N/A		A101	10.95	
6	7	A102	19.95		A102	19.95	
7	2	A103	28.95		A103	28.95	
8					A104	37.95	
9					A105	46.95	
10							

Instead, use Ctrl+T to format the lookup table. Note that the formula is still pointing to E5:F9; nothing changes in the formula.

	A	B	C	D	E	F
1	Qty	Item	Price?		**Ctrl+T**	
2	7	A104	37.95	=VLOOKUP(B2,$E$5:$F$9,2,0)		
3	8	A101	10.95			
4	2	A101	10.95		Item ▼	Price ▼
5	9	A106	#N/A		A101	10.95
6	7	A102	19.95		A102	19.95
7	2	A103	28.95		A103	28.95
8					A104	37.95
9		**No change**			A105	46.95
10		**in formula**				
11						
12						

But when you type a new row below the table, it becomes part of the table, and the VLOOKUP formula automatically updates to reflect the new range.

	A	B	C	D	E	F	G
1	Qty	Item	Price?	**Formula changes**			
2	7	A104	37.95	=VLOOKUP(B2,$E$5:$F$10,2,0)			
3	8	A101	10.95				
4	2	A101	10.95		Item ▼	Price ▼	
5	9	A106	24.95		A101	10.95	
6	7	A102	19.95		A102	19.95	
7	2	A103	28.95		A103	28.95	
8					A104	37.95	
9		**Add new row**			A105	46.95	
10					A106	24.95	
11							

The same thing happens with charts. The chart on the left is based on A1:B5, which is not a table. Format A1:B5 as a table by pressing Ctrl+T. Add a new row. The row is automatically added to the chart, as shown on the right.

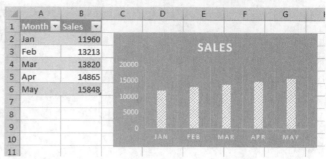

It is fairly cool that you can use Ctrl+T after setting up the pivot table, VLOOKUP, or chart, and Excel still makes the range expand.

When I asked readers to vote for their favorite tips, tables were popular. Thanks to Peter Albert, Snorre Eikeland, Nancy Federice, Colin Michael, James E. Moede, Keyur Patel, and Paul Peton for suggesting this feature. Four readers suggested using OFFSET to create expanding ranges for dynamic charts: Charley Baak, Don Knowles, Francis Logan, and Cecelia Rieb. Tables now do the same thing in most cases.

#39 Replicate a Pivot Table for Each Rep

Here is a great trick I learned from southern California–based Excel consultant Szilvia Juhasz.

The pivot table below shows products across the top and customers down the side. The pivot table is sorted so the largest customers are at the top. The Sales Rep field is in the report filter.

	A	B	C	D	E
1	Rep	(All) ▼			
2					
3	Sum of Revenue	Product ▼			
4	Customer	⤋ Gizmo	Gadget	WhatsIt	Grand Total
5	Harlem Globetrotters	382,878	414,502	402,311	1,199,691
6	MySpreadsheetLab	341,902	444,299	362,269	1,148,470
7	CPASelfStudy.com	335,541	267,607	285,829	888,977

If you open the Rep dropdown, you can filter the data to any one sales rep.

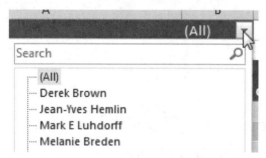

This is a great way to create a report for each sales rep. Each report summarizes the revenue from a particular salesperson's customers, with the biggest customers at the top. And you get to see the split between the various products.

The Excel team has hidden a feature called Show Report Filter Pages. Select any pivot table that has a field in the report filter. Go to the Analyze tab (or the Options tab in Excel 2007/2010). On the far left side is the large Options button. Next to the large Options button is a tiny dropdown arrow. Click this dropdown and choose Show Report Filter Pages....

Excel asks which field you want to use. Select the one you want (in this case the only one available) and click OK.

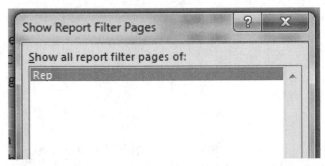

Over the next few seconds, Excel starts inserting new worksheets, one for each sales rep. Each sheet tab is named after the sales rep. Inside each worksheet, Excel replicates the pivot table but changes the name in the report filter to this sales rep.

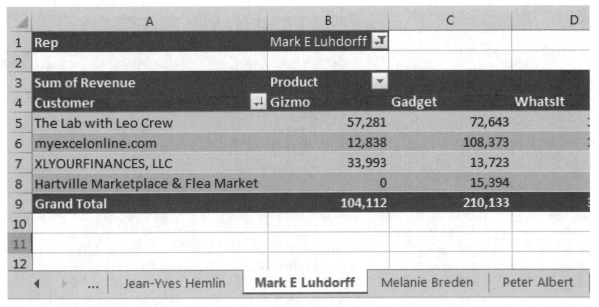

	A	B	C	D
1	Rep	Mark E Luhdorff		
2				
3	Sum of Revenue	Product		
4	Customer	Gizmo	Gadget	WhatsIt
5	The Lab with Leo Crew	57,281	72,643	
6	myexcelonline.com	12,838	108,373	
7	XLYOURFINANCES, LLC	33,993	13,723	
8	Hartville Marketplace & Flea Market	0	15,394	
9	Grand Total	104,112	210,133	
10				
11				
12				

◄ ► ... | Jean-Yves Hemlin | **Mark E Luhdorff** | Melanie Breden | Peter Albert

You end up with a report for each sales rep.

This would work with any field. If you want a report for each customer, product, vendor, or something else, add it to the report filter and use Show Report Filter Pages.

Thanks to Szilvia Juhasz for showing me this feature during a seminar I was teaching at the University of Akron many years ago. For the record, Szilvia was in row 1.

#40 Use a Pivot Table to Compare Lists

When you think of comparing lists, you probably think of VLOOKUP. If you have two lists to compare, you need to add two columns of VLOOKUP. In the figure below, you are trying to compare Tuesday to Monday and Wednesday to Tuesday and maybe even Wednesday to Monday. It is going to take a lot of VLOOKUP columns to figure out who was added to and dropped from each list.

	A	B	C	D	E	F	G	H
1	Monday			Tuesday			Weds	
2								
3	**Name**	**RSVP**		Name	RSVP		Name	RS
4	Carl Hjortsjö	2		Andrew Spain	3		Andrew Spain	3
5	Caroline Bonner	2		Caroline Bonner	2		Jean-Yves Hemlin	1
6	Dawn Kosmakos	2		Dawn Kosmakos	1		Jeffrey P. Coulson	2
7	Jeff Long	1		Kathryn Sullivan	2		John Durran	1
8	M.R. Rosenkrantz	1		M.R. Rosenkrantz	1		Kathryn Sullivan	1
9	Martin Lucas	2		Martin Lucas	2		Kevin Lehrbass	1
10	Paul Hannelly	2		Melissa Esquibel	2		M.R. Rosenkrantz	2
11	Roger Fisher	1		Michael Karpfen	2		Martin Lucas	1
12	Sabine Hanschitz	1		Peter Harvest	2		Melissa Esquibel	2
13	Ute Simon	2		Roger Fisher	1		Michael Karpfen	2
14	Yesenia Garcia	2		Sabine Hanschitz	1		Peter Harvest	1
15				Ute Simon	2		Roger Fisher	1
16				Yesenia Garcia	2		Sabine Hanschitz	2
17							Ute Simon	2
18								

You can use pivot tables to make this job far easier. Combine all of your lists into a single list with a new column called Source. In the Source column, identify which list the data came from. Build a pivot table from the combined list, with Name in rows, RSVP in values, and Source in columns. Turn off the Grand Total row, and you have a neat list showing a superset from day to day, as shown below.

	A	B	C
1	Combine all Lists		
2			
3	**Name**	**RSVP**	**Source**
13	Ute Simon	2	Monday
14	Yesenia Garcia	2	Monday
15	Andrew Spain	3	Tuesday
16	Caroline Bonner	2	Tuesday
17	Dawn Kosmakos	1	Tuesday
18	Kathryn Sullivan	2	Tuesday
19	M.R. Rosenkrantz	1	Tuesday
20	Martin Lucas	2	Tuesday
21	Melissa Esquibel	2	Tuesday
22	Michael Karpfen	2	Tuesday
23	Peter Harvest	2	Tuesday
24	Roger Fisher	1	Tuesday
25	Sabine Hanschitz	1	Tuesday
26	Ute Simon	2	Tuesday
27	Yesenia Garcia	2	Tuesday
28	Andrew Spain	3	Wednesday
29	Jean-Yves Hemlin	1	Wednesday

Sum of RSVP	Source		
Name	**Monday**	**Tuesday**	**Wednesday**
Andrew Spain		3	3
Carl Hjortsjö	2		
Caroline Bonner	2	2	
Dawn Kosmakos	2	1	
Jean-Yves Hemlin			1
Jeff Long	1		
Jeffrey P. Coulson			2
John Durran			1
Kathryn Sullivan		2	1
Kevin Lehrbass			1
M.R. Rosenkrantz	1	1	2
Martin Lucas	2	2	1
Melissa Esquibel		2	2
Michael Karpfen		2	2
Paul Hannelly	2		
Peter Harvest		2	1
Roger Fisher	1	1	1
Sabine Hanschitz	1	1	2
Ute Simon	2	2	2
Yesenia Garcia	2	2	
Grand Total	**18**	**23**	**22**

Bonus Tip: Show Up/Down Markers

There is a super-obscure way to add up/down markers to a pivot table to indicate an increase or a decrease.

Somewhere outside the pivot table, add columns to show increases or decreases. In the figure below, the difference between I6 and H6 is 3, but you just want to record this as a positive change. Use SIGN(I6-H6) to get either +1, 0, or -1.

Select the two-column range showing the sign of the change and then select Home, Conditional Formatting, Icon Sets, 3 Triangles. (I have no idea why Microsoft called this option 3 Triangles, when it is clearly 2 Triangles and a Dash, as shown below.)

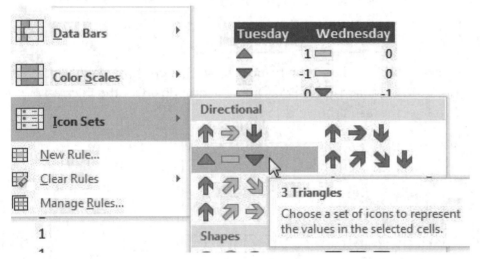

With the same range selected, now select Home, Conditional Formatting, Manage Rules, Edit Rule. Check the Show Icon Only checkbox.

With the same range selected, press Ctrl+C to copy. Select the first Tuesday cell in the pivot table. From the Home tab, open the Paste dropdown and choose Linked Picture. Excel pastes a live picture of the icons above the table.

At this point, adjust the column widths of the extra two columns showing the icons so that the icons line up next to the numbers in your pivot table, as shown below.

After seeing this result, I don't really like the thick yellow dash to indicate no change. If you don't like it either, select Home, Conditional Formatting, Manage Rules, Edit. Open the dropdown for the thick yellow dash and choose No Cell Icon, and you get the result shown below.

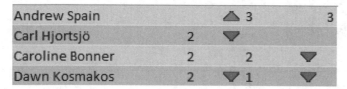

Bonus Tip: Compare Two Lists by Using Go To Special

This tip is not as robust as using a Pivot Table to Compare Two Lists, but it comes in handy when you have to compare one column to another column.

In the figure below, say that you want to find any changes between column A and column D.

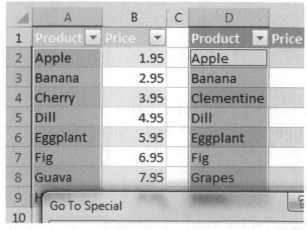

Select the data in A2:A9 and then hold down the Ctrl key while you select the data in D2:D9.

Select, Home, Find & Select, Go To Special. Then, in the Go To Special dialog, choose Row Differences. Click OK.

Only the items in column A that do not match the items in column D are selected. Use a red font to mark these items, as shown below.

	A	B	C	D	E
1	Product	Price		Product	Price
2	Apple	1.95		Apple	1.95
3	Banana	2.95		Banana	2.95
4	Cherry	3.95		Clementine	3.95
5	Dill	4.95		Dill	4.95
6	Eggplant	5.95		Eggplant	5.95
7	Fig	6.95		Fig	6.95
8	Guava	7.95		Grapes	7.95
9	Herbs	8.95		Herbs	8.95

Caution: This technique works only for lists that are mostly identical. If you insert one new row near the top of the second list, causing all future rows to be offset by one row, each of those rows is marked as a row difference.

Thanks to Colleen Young for this tip.

#41 Build Dashboards with Sparklines and Slicers

New tools debuted in Excel 2010 that let you create interactive dashboards that do not look like Excel. This figure shows an Excel workbook with two slicers, Region and Line, used to filter the data. Also in this figure, pivot charts plus a collection of sparkline charts illustrate sales trends.

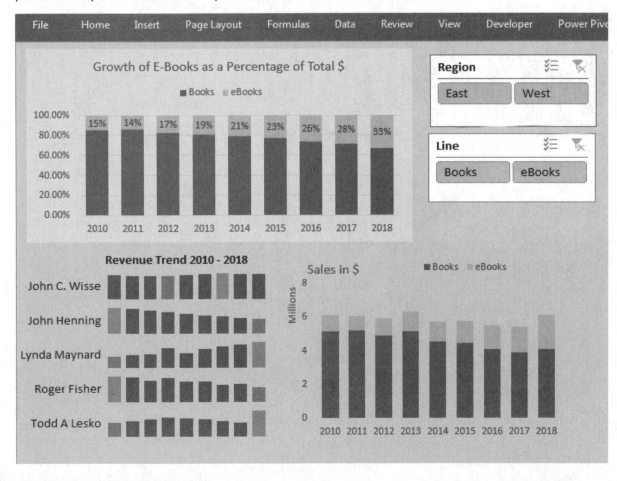

You can use a setup like this and give your manager's manager a touch screen. All you have to do is teach people how to use the slicers, and they will be able to use this interactive tool for running reports. Touch the East region and the Books line. All of the charts update to reflect sales of books in the East region.

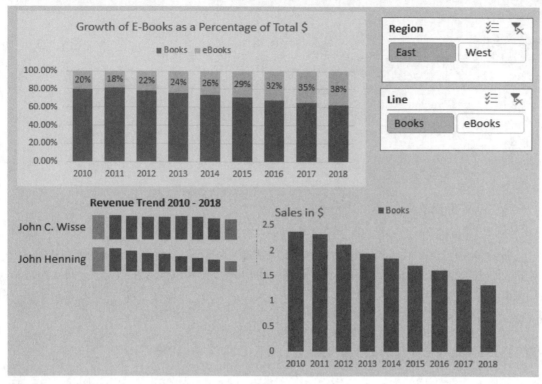

Switch to eBooks, and the data updates.

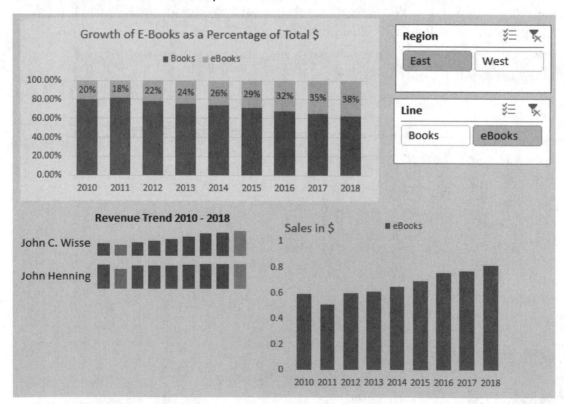

Pivot Tables Galore

Arrange your charts so they fit the size of your display monitor. Each pivot chart has an associated pivot table that does not need to be seen. Those pivot tables can be moved to another sheet or to columns outside of the area seen on the display.

Note: This technique requires all pivot tables share a pivot table cache. I have a video showing how to use VBA to synchronize slicers from two data sets at http://mrx.cl/syncslicer.

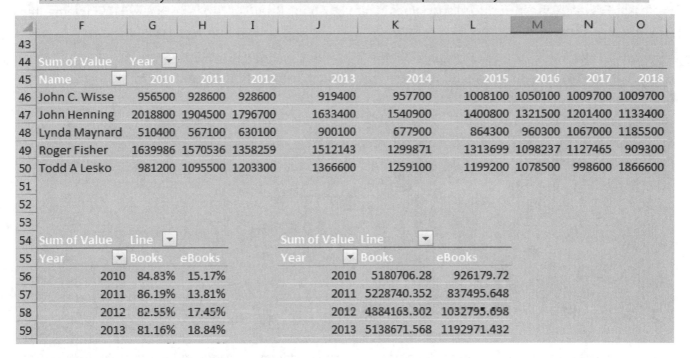

	F	G	H	I	J	K	L	M	N	O
44	Sum of Value	Year								
45	Name	2010	2011	2012	2013	2014	2015	2016	2017	2018
46	John C. Wisse	956500	928600	928600	919400	957700	1008100	1050100	1009700	1009700
47	John Henning	2018800	1904500	1796700	1633400	1540900	1400800	1321500	1201400	1133400
48	Lynda Maynard	510400	567100	630100	900100	677900	864300	960300	1067000	1185500
49	Roger Fisher	1639986	1570536	1358259	1512143	1299871	1313699	1098237	1127465	909300
50	Todd A Lesko	981200	1095500	1203300	1366600	1259100	1199200	1078500	998600	1866600

	Sum of Value	Line			Sum of Value	Line	
55	Year	Books	eBooks		Year	Books	eBooks
56	2010	84.83%	15.17%		2010	5180706.28	926179.72
57	2011	86.19%	13.81%		2011	5228740.352	837495.648
58	2012	82.55%	17.45%		2012	4884163.302	1032795.698
59	2013	81.16%	18.84%		2013	5138671.568	1192971.432

Filter Multiple Pivot Tables with Slicers

Slicers provide a visual way to filter. Choose the first pivot table on your dashboard and select Analyze, Slicers. Add slicers for region and line. Use the Slicer Tools tab in the Ribbon to change the color and the number of columns in each slicer. Resize the slicers to fit and then arrange them on your dashboard.

Initially, the slicers are tied to only the first pivot table. Select a cell in the second pivot table and choose Filter Connections (aka Slicer Connections in Excel 2010). Indicate which slicers should be tied to this pivot table. In many cases, you will tie each pivot table to all slicers. But not always. For example, in the chart showing how Books and eBooks add up to 100%, you need to keep all lines. The Filter Connections dialog box choices for that pivot table connect to the Region slicer but not the Line slicer.

3

Thanks to John Michaloudis from MyExcelOnline.com for the connecting multiple pivot tables to one slicer idea.

Sparklines: Word-Sized Charts

Professor Edward Tufte introduced sparklines in his 2007 book *Beautiful Evidence*. Excel 2010 implemented sparklines as either line, column, or win/loss charts, where each series fills a single cell.

Personally, I like my sparklines to be larger. In this example, I changed the row height to 30 and <gasp> merged B14:D14 into a single cell to make the charts wider. The labels in A14:A18 are formulas that point to the first column of the pivot table.

To change the color of the low and high points, choose these boxes in the Sparkline Tools tab:

Then change the color for the high and low points:

By default, sparklines are scaled independently of each other. I almost always go to the Axis settings and choose Same for All Sparklines for Minimum and Maximum. Below, I set Minimum to 0 for all sparklines.

Make Excel Not Look Like Excel

With several easy settings, you can make a dashboard look less like Excel:

- Select all cells and apply a light fill color to get rid of the gridlines.

- On the View tab, uncheck Formula Bar, Headings, and Gridlines.

- Collapse the Ribbon: at the right edge of the Ribbon, use the ^ to collapse. (You can use Ctrl+F1 or double-click the active tab in the Ribbon to toggle from collapsed to pinned.)

- Use the arrow keys to move the active cell so it is hidden behind a chart or slicer.

- Hide all sheets except for the dashboard sheet.

- In File, Options, Advanced, hide the scroll bars and sheet tabs.

Bonus Tip: Line Up Dashboard Sections with Different Column Widths

If you are anything like me, you often need to fit a lot of data into a small area in a dashboard. What if columns in one dashboard tile don't line up with columns in another tile? Using a linked picture will solve the problem. In the figure below, the report in A1:M9 requires 13 columns. But the report in Rows 11:13 needs that same space to be two columns. I am never one to recommend merged cells, so let's not broach that evil topic.

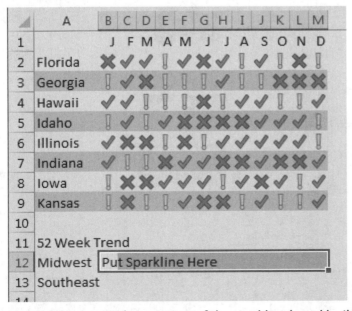

Instead, go to another section of the workbook and build the report tile. Copy the cells that encompass the tile.

Select where you want the tile to appear. On the Home tab, click on the lower half of the Paste dropdown to open the paste options. The last icon is Paste Picture Link. Click that icon. A live picture of the other cells appears.

Bonus Tip: Use Picture Lookup

I love this technique, which essentially does a VLOOKUP that returns a picture selected in response to a formula answer. In the image below, make sure that your lookup table starts in row 2 or below. It cannot start in row 1.

In cell C6, someone enters how many passengers need to be accommodated.

A cool new function called IFS in C7 figures out which row in the table contains the picture that you want to show. In this case, there are 7 passengers, which means you need a 12-passenger van.

Those icons are an Microsoft 365 feature found under Insert, Icons. But you could use any clipart or photos.

The table below appears on a worksheet called Icons. The OFFSET function in A10 tells Excel to start in Icons!$B$1, move down 3 rows, move over 0 columns, and select a range 1 row tall by 1 column wide.

	A	B	C
1	Capacity		
2		1	
3		4	
4		12	
5			
6	How Many People?		7
7	Which Row		3
8	=IFS(C6=1,1,C6<=4,2,C6<=12,3)		
9	Offset Function		0
10	=OFFSET(Icons!$B$1,Icons!$C$7,0,1,1)		
11	Assign Offset formula to a Name		

I always build the OFFSET function in a cell to ensure that I don't get any syntax errors. But when you use the technique described here, you cannot use OFFSET in a cell. You have to copy the formula and use Formulas, Define Name and create a name that refers to the OFFSET formula.

Copy the cell containing the first picture in your table. Go to the dashboard and use Paste Picture Link, as discussed in the previous topic. Look in the formula bar, and you see that this linked picture is coming from =$B$2, or =Icons$B$2 if you are on a different worksheet.

With the linked picture still selected, click in the formula bar. Change the formula for the linked picture to point to the name that you gave to the OFFSET formula. Amazingly, the picture will now update any time that the calculation in C7 points to a new vehicle.

Thanks to Ghaleb Bakri for suggesting a similar technique using dropdown boxes. Ryan Wilson suggested making Excel not look like Excel. Jon Wittwer of Vertex42 suggested the sparklines and slicers trick. Mynda Treacy taught me the picture lookup in her amazing dashboard course at mrx.cl/dashcourse.

Bonus Tip: Report Slicer Selections in a Title

Slicers are great, but they can take up a lot of space in your report.

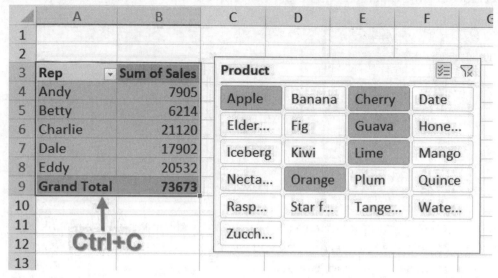

Here is an awesome way to get the selected slicers in a single cell. First, select your entire pivot table and copy with Ctrl+C.

Then, paste a new pivot table somewhere outside of your print range. Copying and pasting makes sure that both pivot tables react to the slicer. Change the pivot table so you have the slicer field in the Row area. Right-click the Grand Total and choose Remove Grand Total. You should end up with a pivot table that looks like this:

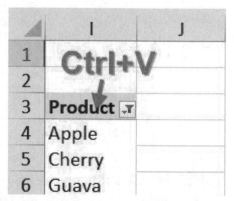

The list of products starts in I4 and might potentially extend to I26. Use the new TEXTJOIN function to join all of the selected products in a single cell. The first argument of TEXTJOIN is the delimiter. I use a comma followed by a space. The second argument tells Excel to ignore empty cells. This makes sure that Excel does not add a bunch of commas to the end of your formula result.

	A	B	C	D
1	Report for Apple, Cherry, Guava, Lime, Orange			
2	="Report for "&TEXTJOIN(", ",TRUE,I4:I26)			
3	**Rep** ▾	**Sum of Sales**		
4	Andy	7905		
5	Betty	6214		
6	Charlie	21120		
7	Dale	17902		
8	Eddy	20532		
9	**Grand Total**	**73673**		
10				

#42 See Why GETPIVOTDATA Might Not Be Entirely Evil

Most people first encounter GETPIVOTDATA when they try to build a formula outside a pivot table that uses numbers in the pivot table. For example, this variance percentage won't copy down to the other months due to Excel inserting GETPIVOTDATA functions.

	✗ ✓	f_x	=GETPIVOTDATA("Sales",$B$3,"Date",1, "Years",2019)/GETPIVOTDATA("Sales",$B$3, "Date",1,"Years",2018)-1

	B	C	D	E	F	G
	Sales	**Years** ▾				
	Date ▾	**2018**	**2019**	% Change		
	Jan	80772	77864	-3.6%		
	Feb	81151	84640	-3.6%		
	Mar	80773	77381	-3.6%		

Excel inserts GETPIVOTDATA any time you use the mouse or arrow keys to point to a cell inside the pivot table while building a formula outside the pivot table.

By the way, if you don't want the GETPIVOTDATA function to appear, simply type a formula such as =D5/C5-1 without using the mouse or arrow keys to point to cells. That formula copies without any problems.

	✗ ✓	f_x	=D5/C5-1

	B	C	D	E	F
	Sales	**Years** ▾			
	Date ▾	**2018**	**2019**	% Change	
	Jan	80772	77864	-3.6%	
	Feb	81151	84640	4.3%	
	Mar	80773	77381	-4.2%	

Here is a data set that contains one plan number per month per store. There are also actual sales per month per store for the months that are complete. Your goal is to build a report that shows actuals for the completed months and plan for the future months.

	A	B	C	D
1	Store	Month	Type	Sales
1727	Fair Oaks Mall	Dec	Plan	123700
1728	Bellevue Square	Dec	Plan	140500
1729	U Village	Dec	Plan	126600
1730	Park Place	Jan	Actual	13475
1731	Kierland Commons	Jan	Actual	11708
1732	Scottsdale Fashion Square	Jan	Actual	12415
1733	Chandler Fashion Center	Jan	Actual	12848

Build a pivot table with Store in Rows. Put Month and Type in Columns. You get the report shown below, with January Actual, January Plan, and the completely nonsensical January Actual+Plan.

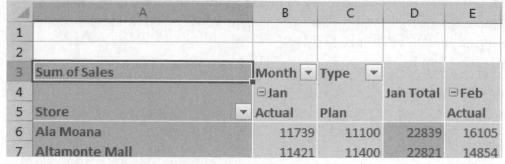

	A	B	C	D	E
1					
2					
3	Sum of Sales	Month ▾	Type ▾		
4		⊟ Jan		Jan Total	⊟ Feb
5	Store ▾	Actual	Plan		Actual
6	Ala Moana	11739	11100	22839	16105
7	Altamonte Mall	11421	11400	22821	14854

If you select a month cell and go to Field Settings, you can change Subtotals to None.

This removes the useless Actual+Plan. But you still have to get rid of the plan columns for January through April. There is no good way to do this inside the pivot table.

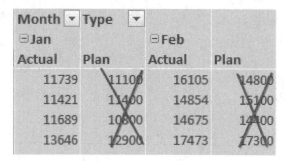

Month ▾	Type ▾		
⊟ Jan		⊟ Feb	
Actual	Plan	Actual	Plan
11739	~~11100~~	16105	~~14800~~
11421	~~11400~~	14854	~~15100~~
11689	~~10800~~	14675	~~14400~~
13646	~~12900~~	17473	~~17300~~

So, your monthly workflow becomes:

1. Add the actuals for the new month to the data set.

2. Build a new pivot table from scratch.

3. Copy the pivot table and paste as values so it is not a pivot table anymore.

4. Delete the columns that you don't need.

There is a better way to go. The following very compressed figure shows a new Excel worksheet added to the workbook. This is all just straight Excel, no pivot tables. The only bit of magic is an IF function in row 4 that toggles from Actual to Plan, based on the date in cell P1.

| E4 | | | | fx | =IF((1+MONTH($P1))>COLUMN(A1),"Actual","Plan") | | | | | | | | | | | |

	A	B	C	D	E	F	G	H	I	J	K	L	M	N	O	P	Q	R
1	**XYZ Company Super Report**														Actuals Through:	4/30		
2																		
3					Jan	Feb	Mar	Apr	May	Jun	Jul	Aug	Sep	Oct	Nov	Dec		
4					Actual	Actual	Actual	Actual	Plan	Plan	Plan	Plan	Plan	Plan	Plan	Plan	Total	
5			Houston Area															
6				Baybrook													$0K	
7				Highland Village													0K	
8				Willowbrook													0K	
9				The Woodlands Mall													0K	
10			Houston Total		$0K	$0K	$0K	$0K	$0K	$0K	$0K	$0K	$0K	$0K	$0K	$0K	$0K	
11																		
12			Dallas/Forth Worth Area															
13				Firewheel													$0K	
14				Galleria													0K	
15				Hulen Mall													0K	
16				Northeast Mall													0K	
17				Northpark Center													0K	
18				The Parks													0K	
19				Southlake Town Square													0K	
20				Stonebriar Mall													0K	
21				Willowbend													0K	
22			Dallas Total		$0K	$0K	$0K	$0K	$0K	$0K	$0K	$0K	$0K	$0K	$0K	$0K	$0K	
23																		
24			Other															
25				Huebner Oaks													$0K	
26				La Cantera													0K	
27				Northstar Mall													0K	
28				Cielo Vista Mall													0K	
29				The Domain													0K	
30				Lakeline													0K	
31			Other Total		$0K	$0K	$0K	$0K	$0K	$0K	$0K	$0K	$0K	$0K	$0K	$0K	$0K	
32																		
33			Grand Total		$0K	$0K	$0K	$0K	$0K	$0K	$0K	$0K	$0K	$0K	$0K	$0K	$0K	
34																		

The very first cell that needs to be filled in is January Actual for Baybrook. Click in that cell and type an equal sign.

Using the mouse, navigate back to the pivot table. Find the cell for January Actual for Baybrook. Click on that cell and press Enter. As usual, Excel builds one of those annoying GETPIVOTDATA functions that cannot be copied.

But today, let's study the syntax of GETPIVOTDATA.

The first argument below is the numeric field "Sales". The second argument is the cell where the pivot table resides. The remaining pairs of arguments are field name and value. Do you see what the auto-generated formula did? It hard-coded "Baybrook" as the name of the store. That is why you cannot copy these auto-generated GETPIVOTDATA formulas. They actually hard-code names into formulas. Even though you can't copy these formulas, you can edit them. In this case, it would be better if you edited the formula to point to cell $D6.

	D	E	F	G	H	I	J	K	L	M	N
1	**uper Report**										A
2											
3		Jan	Feb	Mar	Apr	May	Jun	Jul	Aug	Sep	
4		Actual	Actual	Actual	Actual	Plan	Plan	Plan	Plan	Plan	
5	rea										
6	Baybrook	=GETPIVOTDATA("Sales",Sheet3!$A$3,"Store","Baybrook","Month","Jan","Type","Actual")									
7	Highland Village										

The figure below shows the formula after you edit it. Gone are "Baybrook", "Jan", and "Actual". Instead, you are pointing to $D6, E$3, and E$4.

	D	E	F	G	H	I	J	K	L
1	ny **Super Report**								
2									
3		Jan	Feb	Mar	Apr	May	Jun	Jul	Aug
4		Actual	Actual	Actual	Actual	Plan	Plan	Plan	Plan
5	rea								
6	Baybrook	=GETPIVOTDATA("Sales",Sheet3!$A$3,"Store",$D6,"Month",E$3,"Type",E$4)							
7	Highland Village								
8	v	GETPIVOTDATA(data_field, pivot_table, [field1, item1], [field2, item2], [field3, **item3**], [field4, item4],							

Copy this formula and then choose Paste Special, Formulas in all of the other numeric cells.

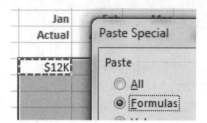

Now here's your monthly workflow:

1. Build an ugly pivot table that no one will ever see.

2. Set up the report worksheet.

Each month, you have to:

1. Paste new actuals below the data.

2. Refresh the ugly pivot table.

3. Change cell P1 on the report sheet to reflect the new month. All the numbers update.

	C	D	E	F	G	H	I	J	K	L	M	N	O	P	Q
1	ompany **Super Report**													Actuals Through:	5/31	
2															
3			Jan	Feb	Mar	Apr	May	Jun	Jul	Aug	Sep	Oct	Nov	Dec	
4			Actual	Actual	Actual	Actual	Actual	Plan	Plan	Plan	Plan	Plan	Plan	Plan	Total
5	Houston Area														
6		Baybrook	$12K	$17K	$22K	$25K	$24K	$32K	$28K	$24K	$20K	$32K	$49K	$121K	$406K
7		Highland Village	13K	17K	20K	24K	23K	33K	29K	24K	20K	33K	49K	122K	406K
8		Willowbrook	15K	19K	24K	30K	30K	37K	32K	28K	23K	37K	55K	138K	467K
9		The Woodlands Mall	14K	19K	24K	28K	27K	36K	32K	27K	23K	36K	54K	135K	453K
10	Houston Total		$54K	$71K	$90K	$106K	$103K	$138K	$120K	$103K	$86K	$138K	$207K	$516K	$1,732K
11															
12	Dallas/Forth Worth Area														
13		Firewheel	$11K	$15K	$18K	$23K	$22K	$29K	$25K	$22K	$18K	$29K	$43K	$108K	$364K

You have to admit that using a report that pulls numbers from a pivot table gives you the best of both worlds. You are free to format the report in ways that you cannot format a pivot table. Blank rows are fine. You can have currency symbols on the first and last rows but not in between. You get double-underlines under the grand totals, too.

Thanks to @iTrainerMX for suggesting this feature.

#43 Eliminate VLOOKUP or XLOOKUP with the Data Model

Say that you have a data set with product, date, customer, and sales information.

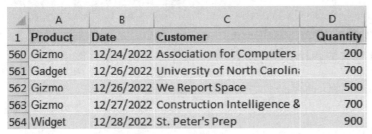

	A	B	C	D
1	Product	Date	Customer	Quantity
560	Gizmo	12/24/2022	Association for Computers	200
561	Gadget	12/26/2022	University of North Carolin:	700
562	Gizmo	12/26/2022	We Report Space	500
563	Gizmo	12/27/2022	Construction Intelligence &	700
564	Widget	12/28/2022	St. Peter's Prep	900

The IT department forgot to put sector in there. Here is a lookup table that maps customer to sector. Time for a VLOOKUP, right?

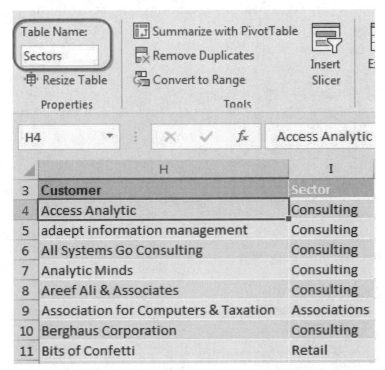

	H	I
3	Customer	Sector
4	Access Analytic	Consulting
5	adaept information management	Consulting
6	All Systems Go Consulting	Consulting
7	Analytic Minds	Consulting
8	Areef Ali & Associates	Consulting
9	Association for Computers & Taxation	Associations
10	Berghaus Corporation	Consulting
11	Bits of Confetti	Retail

There is no need to do VLOOKUPs to join these data sets if you have Excel 2013 or newer. These versions of Excel have incorporated the Power Pivot engine into the core Excel. (You could also do this by using the Power Pivot add-in for Excel 2010, but there are a few extra steps.)

In both the original data set and the lookup table, use Home, Format as Table. On the Table Tools tab, rename the table from Table1 to something meaningful. I've used Data and Sectors.

Select one cell in the data table. Choose Insert, Pivot Table. Starting in Excel 2013, there is an extra box, Add This Data to the Data Model, that you should select before clicking OK.

3

The Pivot Table Fields list appears, with the fields from the Data table. Choose Revenue. Because you are using the Data Model, a new line appears at the top of the list, offering Active or All. Click All.

Surprisingly, the PivotTable Fields list offers all the other tables in the workbook. This is ground-breaking. You haven't done a VLOOKUP yet. Expand the Sectors table and choose Sector. Two things happen to warn you that there is a problem.

First, the pivot table appears with the same number in all the cells.

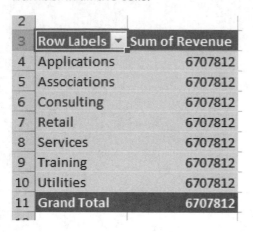

Perhaps the more subtle warning is a yellow box that appears at the top of the PivotTable Fields list, indicating that you need to create a relationship. Choose Create. (If you are in Excel 2010 or 2016, try your luck with Auto-Detect - it often succeeds.)

In the Create Relationship dialog, you have four dropdown menus. Choose Data under Table, Customer under Column (Foreign), and Sectors under Related Table. Power Pivot will automatically fill in the matching column under Related Column (Primary). Click OK.

The resulting pivot table is a mash up of the original data and the data in the lookup table. No VLOOKUPs required.

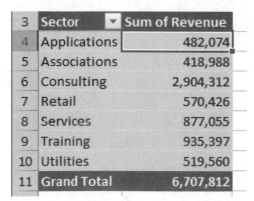

Bonus Tip: Count Distinct

To see an annoyance with pivot tables, drag the Customer column from the Data table to the VALUES area. The field says Count of Customer, but it is really a count of the invoices belong to each sector. What if you really want to see how many unique customers belong to each sector?

3	Sector ▼	Sum of Revenue	Count of Customer
4	Applications	482,074	44
5	Associations	418,988	32
6	Consulting	2,904,312	238
7	Retail	570,426	49
8	Services	877,055	79
9	Training	935,397	75
10	Utilities	519,560	46
11	Grand Total	6,707,812	563

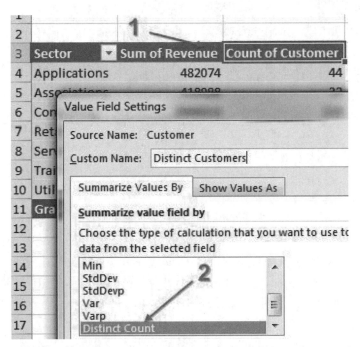

Double-click the Count of Customer heading. At first, the Summarize Values By offers choices such as Sum, Average, and Count. Scroll down to the bottom. Because the pivot table is based on the Data Model, you now have Distinct Count.

After you select Distinct Count, the pivot table shows a distinct count of customers for each sector. This was very hard to do in regular pivot tables.

Sector ▼	Revenue	Distinct Customers
Applications	482,074	6
Associations	418,988	5
Consulting	2,904,312	30
Retail	570,426	5
Services	877,055	10
Training	935,397	11
Utilities	519,560	6
Grand Total	6,707,812	73

Thanks to Colin Michael and Alejandro Quiceno for suggesting Power Pivot.

#44 Compare Budget Versus Actual via Power Pivot

Budgets are done at the top level – revenue by product line by region by month. Actuals accumulate slowly over time – invoice by invoice, line item by line item. Comparing the small Budget file to the voluminous Actual data has been a pain forever. I love this trick from Rob Collie, aka PowerPivotPro.com.

To set up the example, you have a 54-row budget table: 1 row per month per region per product.

The invoice file is at the detail level: 422 rows so far this year.

	Product	Region	Date	Budget
1	**Budget - Top Level**			
2				
3	Product	Region	Date	Budget
52	Whatsit	West	1/31/2018	10,300
53	Whatsit	West	2/28/2018	10,600
54	Whatsit	West	3/31/2018	10,900
55	Whatsit	West	4/30/2018	11,200
56	Whatsit	West	5/31/2018	11,500
57	Whatsit	West	6/30/2018	11,800

	Invoice	Date	Region	Product	Revenue
1	**Invoice Detail**				
2					
3	Invoice	Date	Region	Product	Revenue
417	1414	6/26/2015	Central	Widget	1728
418	1415	6/29/2015	West	Gadget	1719
419	1416	6/29/2015	East	Widget	2199
420	1417	6/29/2015	Central	Widget	2087
421	1418	6/29/2015	East	WhatsIt	2309
422	1419	6/29/2015	Central	Widget	1652
423	1420	6/30/2015	Central	Gadget	1994
424	1421	6/30/2015	Central	WhatsIt	2055
425	1422	6/30/2015	East	Gadget	1931

There is no VLOOKUP in the world that will ever let you match these two data sets. But, thanks to Power Pivot (aka the Data Model in Excel 2013+), this becomes easy.

You need to create tiny little tables that I call "joiners" to link the two larger data sets. In my case, Product, Region, and Date are in common between the two tables. The Product table is a tiny four-cell table. Ditto for Region. Create each of those by copying data from one table and using Remove Duplicates.

Illustration: George Berlin

"Joiners"			
Product	Region	Date	Month
Gadget	Central	1/2/2018	2018-01
WhatsIt	East	1/5/2018	2018-01
Widget	West	1/6/2018	2018-01
		1/7/2018	2018-01
		1/8/2018	2018-01
		1/9/2018	2018-01

The calendar table on the right was actually tougher to create. The budget data has one row per month, always falling on the end of the month. The invoice data shows daily dates, usually weekdays. So, I had to copy the Date field from both data sets into a single column and then remove duplicates to make sure that all dates are represented. I then used =TEXT(J4,"YYYY-MM") to create a Month column from the daily dates.

If you don't have the full Power Pivot add-in, you need to create a pivot table from the Budget table and select the checkbox for Add This Data to the Data Model.

Choose whether you want to analyze multiple tables
☑ Add this data to the Data Model

As discussed in the previous tip, as you add fields to the pivot table, you will have to define six relationships. While you could do this with six visits to the Create Relationship dialog, I fired up my Power Pivot add-in and used the diagram view to define the six relationships.

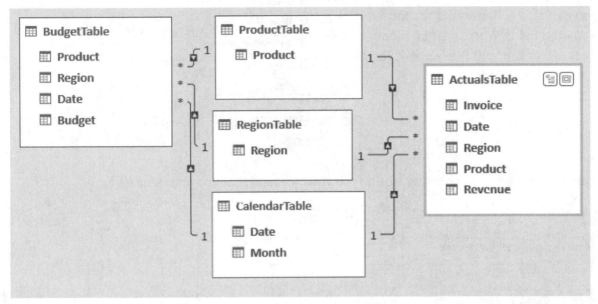

Here is the key to making all of this work: You are free to use the numeric fields from Budget and from Actual. But if you want to show Region, Product, or Month in the pivot table, they must come from the joiner tables!

Here is a pivot table with data coming from five tables. Column A is coming from the Region joiner. Row 2 is coming from the Calendar joiner. The Product slicer is from the Product joiner. The Budget numbers come from the Budget table, and the Actual numbers come from the Invoice table.

	A	B	C	D	E	F	G	H	I
1			Month ▼						
2	Regio ▼	Values	2018-01	2018-02	2018-03	2018-04	2018-05	2018-06	Grand Total
3	Central	Budget	15450	15900	16350	16800	17250	17700	99450
4	Central	Actuals	24203	24703	19815	28208	27555	26961	151445
5	East	Budget	10300	10600	10900	11200	11500	11800	66300
6	East	Actuals	17949	23174	17538	25180	29175	17967	130983
7	West	Budget	20600	21200	21800	22400	23000	23600	132600
8	West	Actuals	24378	11971	14170	11162	11229	10501	83411
9	Total Budget		46350	47700	49050	50400	51750	53100	298350
10	Total Actuals		66530	59848	51523	64550	67959	55429	365839
11									
12		Product			≟ ▼ᵪ				
13									
14		Gadget		WhatsIt	Widget				

This works because the joiner tables apply filters to the Budget and Actual table. It is a beautiful technique and shows that Power Pivot is not just for big data.

3

Bonus Tip: Portable Formulas

If you have the full version of Power Pivot, you can use the DAX formula language to create new calculated fields. From the Power Pivot tab in the Ribbon, choose Measures, New Measure.

Give the field a name, such as Variance. When you go to type the formula, type =[. As soon as you type the square bracket, Excel gives you a list of fields to choose from.

Note that you can also assign a numeric format to these calculated fields. Wouldn't it be great if regular pivot tables brought the numeric formatting from the underlying data?

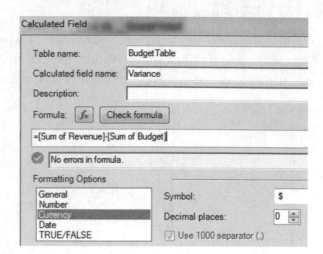

In the next calculation, VariancePercent is reusing the Variance field that you just defined.

So far, you've added several calculated fields to the pivot table, as shown below.

Region	Values	Month 2018-01	2018-02
Central	Sum of Budget	7730	7950
Central	Sum of Revenue	10539	13909
Central	Variance	$2,809	$5,959
Central	VariancePercent	36.3 %	75.0 %

But you don't have to leave any of those fields in the pivot table. If your manager only cares about the variance percentage, you can remove all of the other numeric fields.

VariancePercent	Central	East	West	Grand Total
Month				
2018-01	▲ 36.3 %	▲ 27.8 %	▼ -76.8 %	▼ -15.8 %
2018-02	▲ 75.0 %	▲ 9.8 %	▼ -83.0 %	▼ -9.7 %
2018-03	▼ -22.6 %	▲ 120.9 %	▼ -56.4 %	▼ -5.7 %
2018-04	▲ 187.3 %	▲ 2.7 %	▼ -66.9 %	▲ 33.3 %
2018-05	▲ 158.9 %	▲ 191.4 %	▼ -33.4 %	▲ 80.7 %
2018-06	▲ 7.1 %	▲ 108.9 %	▼ -48.5 %	▲ 5.0 %
Grand Total	▲ 74.4 %	▲ 78.8 %	▼ -60.2 %	▲ 15.6 %

Note that the DAX in this bonus tip is barely scratching the surface of what is possible. If you want to explore Power Pivot, you need to get a copy of *Power Pivot and Power BI* by Rob Collie.

Thanks to Rob Collie for teaching me this feature. Find Rob at www.PowerPivotPro.com.

Bonus Tip: Text in the Values of a Pivot Table

Another amazing use for a measure in a Data Model pivot table is to use the CONCATENATEX function to move text into the values area of a pivot table.

In this data set, there is an original and revised value for each sales rep.

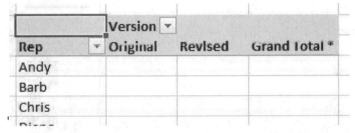

	A	B	C	D	E
1	Region	Market	Rep	Version	Code
2	East	NYC	Andy	Original	Guava
3	East	NYC	Andy	Revised	Date
4	Central	ORD	Barb	Original	Guava
5	Central	ORD	Barb	Revised	Melon
6	West	LAX	Chris	Original	Apple
7	West	LAX	Chris	Revised	Fig

Insert a pivot table and check the box for Add This Data To The Data Model. Drag Rep to the Rows and Version to Columns.

	Version		
Rep	Original	Revised	Grand Total *
Andy			
Barb			
Chris			

The Grand Totals get really ugly, so you should remove them now. On the Design tab, use Grand Totals, Off For Rows and Columns.

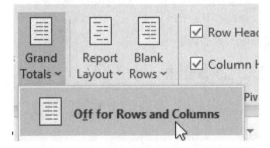

In the Pivot Table Fields panel, right-click the Table name and choose Add Measure.

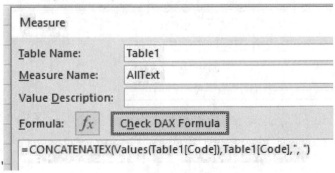

The formula for the measure is =CONCATENATEX(Values(Table1[Code]),Table1[Code],", "). The VALUES function makes sure that you don't get duplicate values in the answer.

Measure

Table Name: Table1

Measure Name: AllText

Value Description:

Formula: *fx*   [Check DAX Formula]

=CONCATENATEX(Values(Table1[Code]),Table1[Code],", ")

After defining the measure, drag the measure to the Values area. In this case, each cell only has one value.

AllText Version ▾		
Rep ▾	Original	Revised
Andy	Guava	Date
Barb	Guava	Melon
Chris	Apple	Fig
Diane	Fig	Fig
Ed	Cherry	Guava

However, if you rearrange the pivot table, you might have multiple values joined in a cell.

AllText	Version ▾	
Market ▾	Original	Revised
ATL	Fig, Cherry	Fig, Orange
LAX	Apple, Elderberry	Fig, Lime
MSP	Date, Cherry	Guava, Date
NYC	Guava	Date
ORD	Guava, Banana	Melon, Banana
PHL	Date, Fig	Date, Fig
SFO	Honeydew, Elderberry	Honeydew, Iceberg

Caution: A cell may not contain more than 32,768 characters. If you have a large data set, it is possible that this Grand Total of this measure will be more than 32,768 characters. The Excel team never anticipated that a pivot table cell would contain more than this many characters, but thanks to DAX and CONCATENATEX, it can happen. When it does happen, Excel can not draw the pivot table. But - there is no error message - the pivot table simply stops updating until you get rid of the Grand Total or somehow make the largest cell be less than 32,768 characters.

#45 Slicers for Pivot Tables From Two Data Sets

Say that you have two different data sets. You want a pivot table from each data set and you want those two pivot tables to react to one slicer.

This really is the holy grail of Excel questions. Lots of Excel forums have many complicated ways to attempt to make this work. But the easiest way is loading all of the data into the workbook data model.

Both of the tables have to have one field in common. Make a third table with the unique list of values found in either column.

Store Name ▾	Sum of Sales 2019	Store Name ▾	Sum of
Brea Mall	309467	Brea Mall	
Corona Del Mar Plaza	325574	Chino Hills Shoppes	
Fashion Valley	307504	Corona Del Mar Plaza	
Irvine Spectrum	254090	Dos Lagos Center	
Jordan Creek Mall	246447	Fashion Valley	

If the two tables are shown above, the third table has to have Store Names that are found in either table: Brea, Chino Hills, Corona Del Mar, Dos Lagos, Fashion Valley, Irvine, and so on.

Format all three of your tables using Ctrl+T.

Use the Relationships icon on the Data tab to set up a relationship from each of the two original tables to the third table.

If you have access to the Power Pivot grid, the diagram view would look like this:

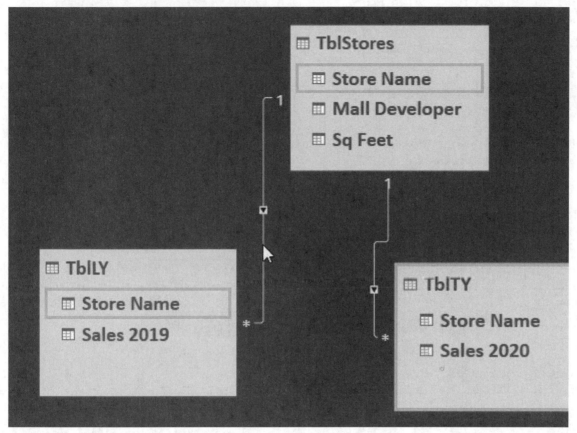

If not, the Relationships diagram should show two relationships, although certainly not as pretty as above.

From either pivot table, choose Insert Slicer. Initially, that slicer will only show one table. Click on the All tab and choose Mall Developer from your third table.

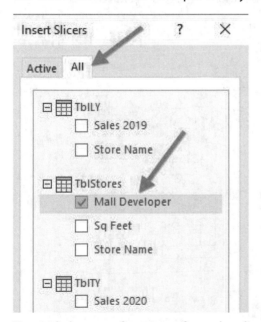

Try and choose a few items from the slicer. Watch your hopes get dashed as only one pivot table reacts. Once you recover, click on the Slicer. In the Slicer Tools Design tab of the Ribbon, choose Report Connections. Add the other pivot table to this slicer:

Report Connections (Mall Developer)

Select PivotTable and PivotChart reports to connect

	Name	Sheet
☑	PivotTable5	Sheet1
☑	PivotTable6	Sheet1

Finally, both pivot tables will react to the slicer.

Store Name ▾	Sum of Sales 2019	Store Name ▾	Sum of Sales 2020
Paseo	310198	Paseo	341218
Simi Valley Town Center	317889	Simi Valley Town Center	349678
The Galleria Edina	271106	The Galleria Edina	298217
Victoria Gardens	328199	Victoria Gardens	361019
Grand Total *	**1227392**	**Grand Total ***	**1350132**

Mall Developer

Caruso Affiliated ...	Developers Divers...	Forest City Manag...	Gabbert & Gabbe...
Investec	Irvine Retail Group	Poag & McEwen L...	Shops At Chino Hi...
Simon Property G...	Westfield	General Growth P...	

#46 Use F4 for Absolute Reference or Repeating Commands

The mighty F4 key should be in your Excel arsenal for two completely different reasons:

- Use F4 to add dollar signs in formula references to make them absolute, mixed, or relative.

- When you are not editing a formula, use F4 to repeat the last command.

Illustration: Cartoon Bob D'Amico

Make a Reference Absolute

In the following figure, the tax in C2 is B2 times F1.

C2	▾	⋮	✕	✓	*fx*	=B2*F1

◢	A	B	C	D	E	F
1	Customer	Merchandise $	Tax $		Rate	6.25%
2	Robert Jelen	24.95	1.56			
3	Sam Radakovitz	114.95				
4	Judy A Glaser	69.95				
5	Diana McGunigale	34.95				
6	Edwin Deo	9.95				
7	Mario Garcia	169.95				
8	Anne Troy	129.95				
9	Robert S. McClellan	154.95				
10	David Gainer	199.95				
11	David Haggarty	109.95				

But when you copy this formula down, none of the sales tax calculations are working. As you copy the formula down the column, the B2 reference automatically changes to B3, B4, and so on. That is what you want. But unfortunately, the reference to the sales tax in F1 is changing as well. That is not what you want.

SUM	▾	⋮	✕	✓	*fx*	=B5*F4

◢	A	B	C	D	E	F	G
1	Customer	Merchandise $	Tax $		Rate	6.25%	
2	Robert Jelen	24.95	1.56				
3	Sam Radakovitz	114.95	0.00				
4	Judy A Glaser	69.95	0.00				
5	Diana McGunigale	34.95	=B5*F4				
6	Edwin Deo	9.95	0.00				
7	Mario Garcia	169.95	0.00				
8	Anne Troy	129.95	0.00				

The solution? Edit the original formula and press F4. Two dollar signs are added to the final element of the formula. The $F$1 says that no matter where you copy this formula, that part of the formula always needs to point to F1. This is called an absolute reference. Pressing F4 while the insertion point is touching the F1 reference is a fast way to add both dollar signs.

SUM	▾	⋮	✕	✓	*fx*	=B2*$F$1

◢	A	B	C	D	E	F
1	Customer	Merchandise $	Tax $		Rate	6.25%
2	Robert Jelen	24.95	=B2*$F$1	**F4**		
3	Sam Radakovitz	114.95	7.18			
4	Judy A Glaser	69.95	4.37			
5	Diana McGunigale	34.95	2.18			

There are other times when you need only part of the reference to be locked. In the following example, you need to multiply H2 by A3 by C1. The H1 will always point to H1, so you need both dollar signs in

4

$H$1. The A3 will always point back to column A, so you need $A3. The C1 will always point to row 1, so you need C$1.

	A	B	C	D	E	F	G	H
1			105%	107%	103%	115%		Base
2		Name	Q1	Q2	Q3	Q4		10000
3	113%	Micheal Reynolds	=$H$2*$A3*C$1					
4	112%	John Cockerill						
5	115%	Adam Weaver						
6	112%	Michael Dietterick						
7	113%	Ryan Wilson						
8	113%	James Williams						
9	112%	Mike Dolan Fliss						
10	112%	Paul Hannelly						
11	115%	Dawn Kosmakos						
12	112%	Jeff Long						

To enter the above formula, you would press F4 once after clicking on H1, three times after clicking on A3, and twice after clicking on C1. What if you screw up and press F4 too many times? Keep pressing F4: It will toggle back to relative then absolute, then row absolute, then column absolute.

The result? A single formula that can be copied to C3:F12.

F12		fx	=$H$2*$A12*F$1

	A	B	C	D	E	F	G	H
1			105%	107%	103%	115%		Base
2		Name	Q1	Q2	Q3	Q4		10000
3	113%	Micheal Reynolds	11865	12091	11639	12995		
4	112%	John Cockerill	11760	11984	11536	12880		
5	115%	Adam Weaver	12075	12305	11845	13225		
6	110%	Michael Dietterick	11550	11770	11330	12650		
7	113%	Ryan Wilson	11865	12091	11639	12995		
8	113%	James Williams	11865	12091	11639	12995		
9	114%	Mike Dolan Fliss	11970	12198	11742	13110		
10	112%	Paul Hannelly	11760	11984	11536	12880		
11	115%	Dawn Kosmakos	12075	12305	11845	13225		
12	112%	Jeff Long	11760	11984	11536	12880		

Tip: If you forget to put dollar signs in the formula, you can edit the formula, click inside any cell reference and press F4 the appropriate number of times. If you have a cell reference such as C3:C12, select the colon with the mouse and press F4 to change both C3 and C12 to $C$3:$C$12.

Caution: There is a special type of reference called an Expanding Range. In this instance, you might lock down the start of the range using F$3 but let the end of the range be relative. The reference starts out as F$3:F3 but will expand as you copy it down, such as F$3:F12. Using F4 will never toggle through an expandable reference. You have to click inside the first F3 in the formula bar and press F4 to change just that part of the reference. See an Expanding Range in use in "#60 Preview What Remove Duplicates Will Remove" on page 153.

Repeat the Last Command

Keyboard shortcuts are great. For example, Alt+E, D, C Enter deletes a column. But even if you are really fast at doing Alt+E, D, C Enter, it can be a pain to do this many times in a row.

	A	B	C	D	E	F	G	H	I
1	Name		Q1		Q2		Q3		Q4
2	Jeffrey P. Coulson		161		153		136		163
3									
4	Robert Phillips		150		143		198		161
5									
6	Peter Harvest		132		185		167		150
7									
8	Trace Cordell		149		140		167		176
9									

Alt+EDC

After deleting column B, press the Right Arrow key to move to the next column that needs to be deleted. Instead of doing Alt+E, D, C Enter again, simply press F4. This beautiful command repeats the last command that you invoked.

	A	B	C	D	E
1	Name	Q1		Q2	
2	Jeffrey P. Coulson	161		153	
3					
4	Robert Phillips	150		143	
5					
6	Peter Harvest	132		185	
7					

Rt Arrow
F4

To delete the remaining columns, keep pressing Right Arrow and then F4.

	A	B	C	D	E	F	G
1	Name	Q1	Q2		Q3		Q4
2	Jeffrey P. Coulson	161	153		136		163
3							
4	Robert Phillips	150	143		198		161
5							
6	Peter Harvest	132	185		167		150
7							

Rt Arrow
F4

Next, you need to delete a row, so use Alt+E, D, R Enter to delete the row.

	A	B	C	D	E
1	Name	Q1	Q2	Q3	Q4
2	Jeffrey P. Coulson	161	153	136	163
3					
4	Robert Phillips	150	143	198	161
5					
6	Peter Harvest	132	185	167	150

Alt+EDR Enter

4

To keep deleting rows, press the Down Arrow key followed by F4 until all the blank rows are gone.

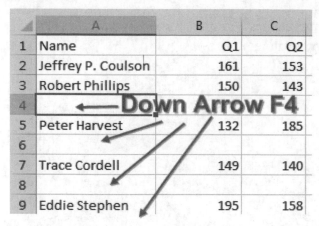

The F4 trick works for a surprising number of commands. Perhaps you just built a custom format to display numbers in thousands: #,##0,K. If you see a few more cells that need the same format, select the cells and press F4.

Annoyingly, a few commands do not work with F4. For example, going into Field Settings in a pivot table and changing the number format and calculation is one that would be nice to repeat. But it does not work.

Bonus Tip: Use a Named Range Instead of Absolute References

If you want to avoid using $ in references to make them absolute, you can use named ranges instead. Select the tax rate cell in F1 and click in the name box to the left of the formula bar.

Type a name for this cell or range of cells. You cannot use spaces in the name, but TaxRate (or Tax_Rate) will work.

When you type the formula, use =B2*TaxRate.

Tip: To see all of the named ranges in a worksheet, reduce the zoom to 39% or lower.

Thanks to Myles Arnott, Glen Feechan, Shelley Fishel, Colin Legg, and Nathan Zelany for suggesting this feature. Bob Umlas sent in the tip about seeing names below 39% zoom.

#47 Quickly Convert Formulas to Values

I always say there are five ways to do anything in Excel. Converting live formulas to values is a task that has far more than five ways. But I will bet that I can teach you two ways that are faster than what you are using now.

The goal is to convert the formulas in column D to values.

You are probably using one of the ways shown below.

Some Ways to Paste Values

Ctrl+C, Paste Dropdown, Values

Ctrl+C, Alt+E, S, V Enter

Ctrl+C, Ctrl+Alt+V, V, Enter

Ctrl+C, Ctrl+V, Ctrl, V

Ctrl+C, Alt, H, V, V

Rt-Click, Copy, Rt-Click, Paste Options Values

For Those Who Prefer Using the Mouse

If you prefer to use the mouse, nothing is faster than this trick I learned from Dave in Columbus, Indiana. You don't even have to copy the cells using this technique:

1. Select the data.

2. Go to the right edge of the selection box.

3. Hold down the right mouse button while you drag the box to the right.

4

4. Keep holding down the right mouse button while you drag the box back to the original location.

5. When you release the right mouse button, in the menu that pops up, select Copy Here As Values Only.

How does anyone ever randomly discover right-click, drag right, drag left, let go? It is not something that you would ever accidentally do.

It turns out the menu is called the Alternate Drag-and-Drop menu. You get this menu any time you right-drag a selection somewhere.

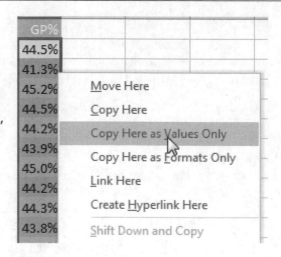

In this case, you want the values to cover the original formulas, so you have to drag right and then back to the left.

For Those Who Prefer Using Keyboard Shortcuts

I love keyboard shortcuts. I can Ctrl+C, Alt+E, S, V, Enter faster than you can blink. But starting in Excel 2010, there is a faster way. Look at the bottom row of your keyboard. To the left of the Spacebar, you usually have Ctrl, Windows, Alt. To the right of the Spacebar is Alt, *Something*, and Ctrl.

What is that key between the right Alt and the right Ctrl? It has a picture of a mouse pointer and a pop-up menu. Its official name is the Application key. I've heard it called the Program key, the Menu key, the Context Menu key, and the Right-Click key. I don't care what you call it, but here is a picture of it:

Here is the fastest keyboard shortcut for copying and pasting values. Press Ctrl+C. Press and release the Program/Application/Right-Click key. Press V.

Again, this only works in Excel 2010 or newer.

And, if you have a Lenovo laptop, it is likely that you don't even have this key. On a keyboard without this key, you can press Shift+F10 instead.

Bonus Tip: Skip Blanks While Pasting

A mysterious part of the Paste Special dialog is the Skip Blanks feature. What does it do? Say that you have a list of existing values. In another column, you have updates for some of those values but not all of them. In the next figure, select D2:D10 and Copy.

	A	B	C	D
1	State	Rate		Updated Rate
2	Alabama	92		87
3	Alaska	51		
4	Arizona	10		14
5	Arkansas	13		
6	California	21		
7	Colorado	17		16
8	Connecticut	51		
9	Delaware	39		
10	Florida	20		15

Select the original values in B2:B10. Do a Paste Special and select Skip Blanks.

The 87 in D2 overwrites the 92 in B2, but Excel does not clear out the 51 in B3.

	A	B
1	State	Rate
2	Alabama	87
3	Alaska	51
4	Arizona	14
5	Arkansas	13
6	California	21
7	Colorado	16
8	Connecticut	51
9	Delaware	39
10	Florida	15

Thanks to Ed Bott, Ken McLean, Melih Met, and Bryony Stewart-Seume for suggesting this feature. Laura Lewis suggested the Skip Blanks trick.

4

#48 See All Formulas at Once

You inherit a spreadsheet from a former co-worker and you need to figure out how the calculations work. You could visit each cell, one at a time, and look at the formula in the formula bar. Or you could quickly toggle between pressing F2 and Esc to see the formula right in the cell.

	A	B	C	D
1	Vendor	Last Year	Growth	Next Year
2	adaept information management	190,716	7%	204,100
3	Orange County Health Department	188,874	8%	204,000
4	MrExcel.com	188,173	5%	197,600
5	Access Analytic	177,972	7%	190,400
6	Excelerator BI	185,529	4%	193,000
7	MyOnlineTrainingHub.com	181,901	6%	192,800
8	Cambia Factor	153,609	6%	162,800
9	data2impact	154,605	8%	117,000
10	Blockhead Data Consultants	121,751	8%	131,500
11	Bits of Confetti	100,308	8%	108,300
12	Total	1,643,438		1,701,500

But there is a faster way. On most U.S. keyboards, just below the Esc key is a key with two accent characters: the tilde from Spanish and the grave accent from French. It is an odd key. I don't know how I would ever use this key to actually type piñata or frère .

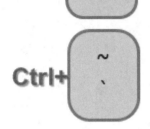

If you hold down Ctrl and the grave accent, you toggle into something called Show Formulas mode. Each column gets wider, and you see all of the formulas.

B	C	D
Last Year	Growth	Next Year
190716	=RANDBETWEEN(4,8)/100	=ROUND(B2*(1+C2),-2)
188874	=RANDBETWEEN(4,8)/100	=ROUND(B3*(1+C3),-2)
188173	=RANDBETWEEN(4,8)/100	=ROUND(B4*(1+C4),-2)
177972	=RANDBETWEEN(4,8)/100	=ROUND(B5*(1+C5),-2)
185529	=RANDBETWEEN(4,8)/100	=ROUND(B6*(1+C6),-2)
181901	=RANDBETWEEN(4,8)/100	=ROUND(B7*(1+C7),-2)
153609	=RANDBETWEEN(4,8)/100	=ROUND(B8*(1+C8),-2)
154605	=RANDBETWEEN(4,8)/100	=ROUND(B9*(1+C9),-2)-50000
121751	=RANDBETWEEN(4,8)/100	=ROUND(B10*(1+C10),-2)
100308	=RANDBETWEEN(4,8)/100	=ROUND(B11*(1+C11),-2)
1643438		=SUM(D2:D11)

This gives you a view of all the formulas at once. It is great for spotting "plug" numbers (D9) or when someone added the totals with a calculator and typed the number instead of using =SUM(). You can see that the co-worker left RANDBETWEEN functions in this model.

Note: Here is another use for the Tilde key. Say you need to use the Find dialog to search for a wildcard character (such as the * in "Wal*Mart" or the ? in "Hey!?" Precede the wildcard with a tilde. Search for Wal~*Mart or Hey!~?.

Tip: To type a lowercase n with a tilde above, hold down Alt while pressing 164 on the number keypad. Then release Alt.

Bonus Tip: Highlight All Formula Cells

If you are going to be auditing the worksheet, it would help to mark all of the formula cells. Here are the steps:

1. Select any blank cell in the worksheet.

2. Choose Home, Find & Select, Formulas.

3. All of the formula cells will be selected. Mark them in a different font color, or, heck, use Home, Cell Styles, Calculation.

To mark all of the input cells, use Home, Find & Select, Go To Special, Constants. I prefer to then uncheck Text, Logical, and Errors, leaving only the numeric constants. Click OK in the Go To Special dialog.

Why Is the F1 Key Missing from Your Keyboard?

Twice I have served as a judge for the ModelOff Financial Modeling Championships in New York. On my first visit, I was watching contestant Martijn Reekers work in Excel. He was constantly pressing F2 and Esc with his left hand. His right hand was on the arrow keys, swiftly moving from cell to cell. F2 puts a cell in Edit mode so you can see the formula in the cell. Esc exits Edit mode and shows you the number. Martijn would press F2 and Esc at least three times every second.

But here is the funny part: What dangerous key is between F2 and Esc? F1. If you accidentally press F1, you will have a 10-second delay while Excel loads online Help. If you are analyzing three cells a second, a 10-second delay is a disaster. You might as well go to lunch. So, Martijn had pried the F1 key from his keyboard so he would never accidentally press it.

Photo Credit: Mary Ellen Jelen

Bonus Tip: Trace Precedents to See What Cells Flow into a Formula

If you need to see which cells flow into a formula, you can use the Trace Precedents command in the Formula Auditing group on the Formulas tab. In the following figure, select D6. Choose Trace Precedents. Blue lines will draw to each cell referenced by the formula in D6.

The dotted line leading to a symbol in B4 means there is at least one precedent on another worksheet. If you double-click the dotted line, Excel shows you a list of the off-sheet precedents.

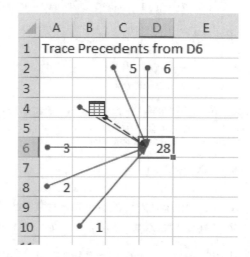

If you stay in cell D6 and choose Trace Precedents a few more times, you will see the second-level precedents, then the third-level precedents, and so on. When you are done, click Remove Arrows.

Bonus Tip: See Which Cells Depend on the Current Cell

Sometimes you have the opposite problem: You want to see which cells rely on the value in the current cell. Choose any cell and click Trace Dependents to see which cells directly refer to the active cell.

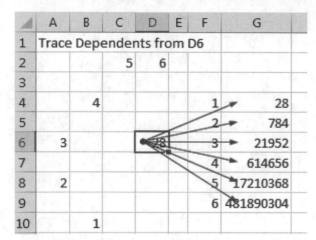

#49 Audit a Worksheet With Spreadsheet Inquire

There is about a 20% chance that you have some amazing tools in your Excel that you've never seen. Well, wait…there is a 100% chance that you've never seen everything in Excel; there are things in Excel that I have never seen, I consider knowing everything Excel to be my job. The 20% that I mentioned before refers to one particular set of tools, called Spreadsheet Inquire.

Inquire was developed by a company called Prodiance that offered the slick Spreadsheet Compare tool for $145 per person per year. The Excel team liked it so much that Microsoft bought out Prodiance and gave the tool for free to anyone who is on Pro Plus, Professional Plus, or Enterprise Level E3.

In classic Microsoft fashion, they kept the tool hidden so even if you have it, you don't know that it is there. If you've ever seen a Power Pivot tab in your Ribbon, you likely have Inquire. It is at least worth the minute to figure out if you have it.

If you have the Developer tab in the Ribbon, click the COM Add-Ins button and continue to step 3 below. Otherwise, follow these steps:

1. Go to File, Options. In the left bar of Excel Options, choose Add-ins (near the bottom of the list).

2. Go all the way to the bottom of the dialog, next to Manage. Open the dropdown and change from Excel Add-Ins to COM Add-ins. After choosing COM Add-ins, click Go….

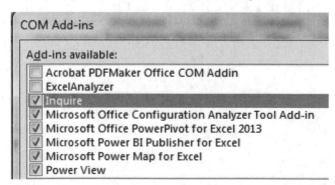

3. If you have Inquire in the list, check the box next to it, click OK, and keep reading. If you don't have Inquire in your list, jump ahead to "#50 Discover New Functions by Using fx" on page 127.

Once you enable Inquire, you have a new tab in the Ribbon called Inquire that provides the following options.

- The Workbook Analysis takes from a few seconds to a few minutes to build a report about your worksheet. It tells you the number of formulas, hidden sheets, linked workbooks, external data connections, and array formulas, as well as how many formulas result in errors. Click any category for a list of the various items.

- The next three icons allow you to draw diagrams showing relationships between workbooks, worksheets, or cells. The diagram below shows all inbound and outbound dependencies for cell D6. You can see the second-level precedents. Each node can be collapsed or expanded.

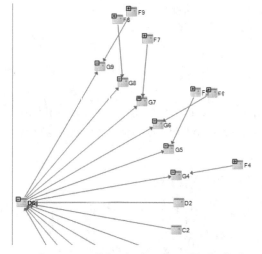

- Compare Files helps you find all changes between two open files. It does a really good job. You can foil most comparison tools by deleting a row in the second file. But Inquire detects that row 8 was deleted and keeps comparing row 9 in one file to row 8 in the other file.

- Clean Excess Cell Formatting locates the last non blank cell in a worksheet and deletes all conditional formatting beyond that cell. You might want to do this, for example, if someone selects an entire row or column and applies conditional formatting.

Thanks to Ron Armstrong, Olga Kryuchkova, and Sven Simon for suggesting this feature.

#50 Discover New Functions by Using fx

There are 400+ functions in Excel. I have room for only 120 tips this book, so there is no way I can cover them all. But instead of taking 450 pages to describe every function, I am going to teach you how to find the function that you need.

The Excel 2007 formulas tab introduced a huge *fx* Insert Function icon. But you don't need to use the one on the Formulas tab; the same icon has been to the left of the formula bar ever since I can remember.

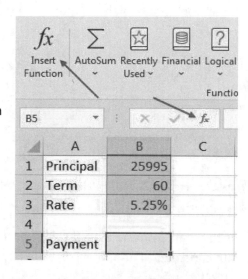

If you are trying to figure out how to calculate a loan payment, the Insert Function dialog will help. Click the icon next to the formula bar. In the Search for a Function box, type what you are trying to do. Click Go. The Select a Function box shows functions related to your search term. Click on a function in that box to see the description at the bottom of the dialog.

Caution: A change in Excel Help caused the search to return less results starting in 2019.

When you find the correct function and click OK, Excel takes you into the Function Arguments dialog. This is an amazing tool when you are new to a function. As you click in each argument box, help appears at the bottom of the window, with specifics on that argument.

Personally, I could never get the PMT function to work correctly because I always forgot that the rate had to be the interest rate per period. Instead of pointing to the 5.25% in B3, you have to point to B3/12. Below, the help for Nper explains that it is the total number of payments for the loan, also known as the term, from B2.

PV is the loan amount. Since I never write a check for negative $493, I want the answer from PMT to be positive instead of negative. That is why I always use –B1 for the PV argument. If you use B1 instead, you will get the correct $493.54065 answer, but it will appear as negative in your worksheet. Think of the original $25,995 as money leaving the bank; that is why the PV is negative.

Notice in the above figure that three argument names are bold. These are the required arguments. Once you finish the required arguments, the Function Arguments dialog shows you the answer in two places. I always use this as a sanity check. Does this answer sound like a typical car payment?

This one topic really covered three things: how to calculate a loan payment, how to use the *fx* icon to discover new functions, and how to use the Function Arguments dialog to get help on any function.

If you are in a situation where you remember the function name but still want to use the Function Arguments dialog, type =PMT(with the opening parenthesis and then press Ctrl+A. If you press Ctrl+Shift+A, Excel will insert the names of the arguments into the formula.

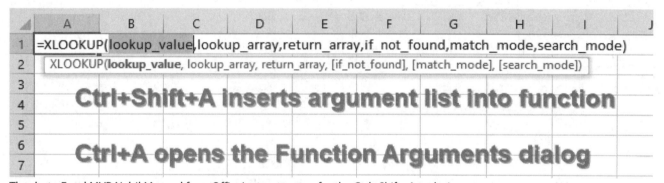

Thanks to Excel MVP Nabil Mourad from OfficeInstructor.com for the Ctrl+Shift+A technique.

#51 Use Function Arguments for Nested Functions

The Function Arguments dialog shown above is cool, but in real life, when you have to nest functions, how would you use this dialog?

Say that you want to build a formula to do a two-way lookup:

=INDEX(B2:E16,MATCH(G2,A2:A16,0),MATCH(H2,B1:E1,0))

	A	B	C	D	E	F	G	H	I
1		Jan	Feb	Mar	Apr		Acct	Month	Result
2	C221	4	6	8	10		E106	Apr	20
3	C236	6	9	12	15				
4	E106	8	12	16	20				
5	C116	10	15	20	25				

You would start out using the Function Arguments dialog box for INDEX. In the Row_num argument box, type MATCH(. Using the mouse, go up to the formula bar and click anywhere inside the word MATCH.

Caution: Don't click the formula in the cell. You have to click the formula in the formula bar.

The Function Arguments dialog switches over to MATCH. When you are finished building the MATCH function, go up to the formula bar and click anywhere in the word INDEX.

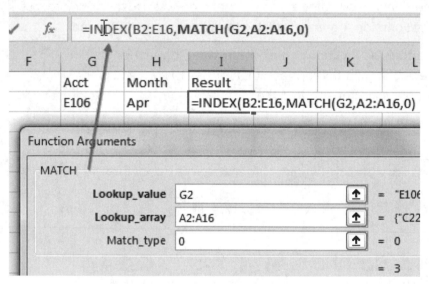

Repeat these steps to build the MATCH in the third argument of INDEX. Make sure to click back in the word INDEX in the formula bar when you are done with the second MATCH.

It turns out that the Function Arguments dialog can be fooled into building an invalid function. Type a well-formed but nonsensical function in the formula bar. Using the mouse, click inside the fake function name in the formula bar and click the fx icon.

Thanks to Tony DeJonker, Cat Parkinson, & Geoff in Huntsville for suggesting the Function Arguments dialog trick.

#52 Calculate Nonstandard Work Weeks

In my live Power Excel seminars, it is pretty early in the day when I show how to right-click the Fill Handle, drag a date, and then choose Fill Weekdays. This fills Monday through Friday dates. I ask the audience, "How many of you work Monday through Friday?" A lot of hands go up. I say, "That's great. For everyone else, Microsoft clearly doesn't care about you." Laughter.

It certainly seems that if you work anything other than Monday through Friday or have a year ending any day other than December 31, a lot of things in Excel don't work very well.

However, two functions in Excel show that the Excel team does care about people who work odd work weeks: NETWORKDAYS.INTL and WORKDAY.INTL.

But let's start with their original Monday–Friday antecedents. The following figure shows a start date in column B and an end date in column C. If you subtract =C5-B5, you will get the number of days between the two dates. To figure out the number of weekdays, you use =NETWORKDAYS(B2,C2).

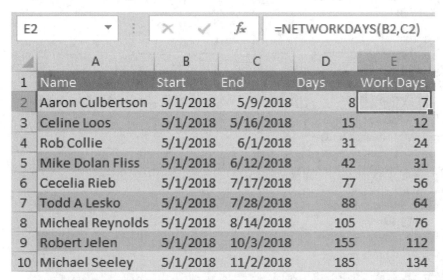

Note: If you subtract Monday August 14 from Friday August 18, Excel will tell you that there are 4 days between the two dates. Excel does not count the end date. But, NETWORKDAYS counts both the first and last date in the range.

It gets even better. NETWORKDAYS allows for an optional third argument where you specify work holidays. In the next figure, the list of holidays in H3:H15 allows the Work Days Less Holidays calculation in column F.

`=NETWORKDAYS(B4,C4,$H$3:$H$15)`

	D	E	F	G	H
	Days	Work Days	Work Days less Holidays		
2018	8	7	7		Holidays
2018	15	12	12		5/28/2018
2018	31	24	23		7/4/2018
2018	42	31	30		9/3/2018
2018	77	56	54		10/8/2018
2018	88	64	62		11/12/2018
2018	105	76	74		11/22/2018
2018	155	112	109		11/23/2018
2018	185	134	130		12/24/2018
2018	192	139	135		12/25/2018
2018	206	149	142		1/1/2019
2019	350	251	239		1/21/2019
					2/18/2019
					5/27/2019

Prior to Excel 2007, the NETWORKDAYS and WORKDAY functions were available if you enabled the Analysis ToolPak add-in that shipped with every copy of Excel. For Excel 2007, those add-ins were made a core part of Excel. In Excel 2007, Microsoft added INTL versions of both functions with a new Weekend argument. This argument allowed for any two consecutive days as the weekend and also allowed for a one-day weekend.

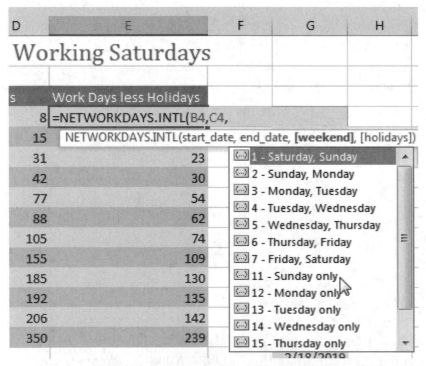

Plus, there are several countries with weekends that don't fall on Saturday and Sunday. Those countries gained functionality with NETWORKDAYS.INTL and WORKDAY.INTL.

However, there are still cases where the weekend does not meet any of the 14 weekend definitions added in Excel 2007.

For example, the Hartville Marketplace is open Monday, Thursday, Friday, and Saturday. That means their weekend is Tuesday, Wednesday, and Sunday.

Starting in Excel 2010, instead of using 1-7 or 11-17 as the weekend argument, you can pass 7-digit binary text to indicate whether a company is open or closed on a particular day. It seems a bit unusual, but you use a 1 to indicate that the store is closed for the weekend and a 0 to indicate that the store is open. After all, 1 normally means On and 0 normally means Off. But the name of the argument is Weekend, so 1 means it is a day off, and 0 means you don't have the day off.

Thus, for the Monday, Thursday, Friday, Saturday schedule at the Hartville Marketplace, you would use "0110001". Every time I type one of these text strings, I have to silently say in my head, "Monday, Tuesday, Wednesday…" as I type each digit.

Marion Coblentz at the Hartville Marketplace could use the following formula to figure out how many Marketplace days there are between two dates.

C8			f_x	=NETWORKDAYS.INTL(A8,B8,"0110001")		

	A	B	C	D	E	F	G
1	Hartville Marketplace and Flea Market						
2	Open Monday, Thursday, Friday, Saturday						
3	Closed Tuesday, Wednesday, Sunday						
4	7 Binary Digits, starting with Monday						
5	1=Weekend, 0=Open						
6							
7	Start	End	Work Days				
8	5/1/2018	5/9/2018	4	=NETWORKDAYS.INTL(A8,B8,"0110001")			
9	5/1/2018	5/16/2018	8				
10	5/1/2018	6/1/2018	18				
11	5/1/2018	6/12/2018	24				
12	5/1/2018	7/17/2018	44				
13	5/1/2018	7/28/2018	51				

By the way, I did not use the optional Holidays argument above because Memorial Day, July 4, and Labor Day are the biggest customer days in Hartville.

If you are ever in northeastern Ohio, you need to stop by Hartville to see the 100% American-Made house inside of the Hartville Hardware and to try the great food at the Hartville Kitchen.

Bonus Tip: Use WORKDAY.INTL for a Work Calendar

While NETWORKDAYS calculates the work days between two dates, the WORKDAY function takes a starting date and a number of days, and it calculates the date that is a certain number of work days away.

One common use is to calculate the next work day. In the following figure, the start date is the date on the previous row. The number of days is always 1. To generate a class schedule that meets on Monday, Wednesday, and Friday, specify a weekend of "0101011".

1	Fill Monday, Wednesday, Friday Dates	
2	Mon, 1/4/2021	
3	Wed, 1/6/2021	=WORKDAY.INTL(A2,1,"0101011")
4	Fri, 1/8/2021	=WORKDAY.INTL(A3,1,"0101011")
5	Mon, 1/11/2021	=WORKDAY.INTL(A4,1,"0101011")

#53 Turn Data Sideways with a Formula

Someone built this lookup table sideways, stretching across C1:N2. I realize that I could use HLOOKUP instead of VLOOKUP, but I prefer to turn the data back to a vertical orientation.

Copy C1:N2. Right-click in A4 and choose the Transpose option under the Paste Options. Transpose is the fancy Excel word for "turn the data sideways."

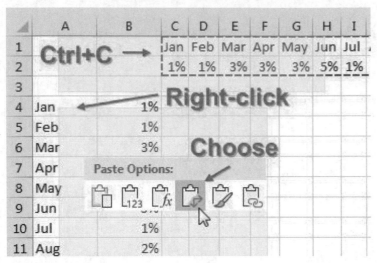

I transpose a lot. But I use Alt+E,S,E,Enter to transpose instead of the right-click.

There is a problem, though. Transpose is a one-time snapshot of the data. What if you have formulas in the horizontal data? Is there a way to transpose with a formula?

The first way is a bit bizarre. If you are trying to transpose 12 horizontal cells, you need to select 12 vertical cells in a single selection. Start typing a formula such as =TRANSPOSE(C2:N2) in the active cell but do not press Enter. Instead, hold down Ctrl+Shift and then press Enter. This puts a single array formula in the selected cells. This TRANSPOSE formula is going to return 12 answers, and they will appear in the 12 selected cells, as shown below.

⊿	A	B	C	D	E	F	G	H	I	J	K	L	M	N
1			Jan	Feb	Mar	Apr	May	Jun	Jul	Aug	Sep	Oct	Nov	Dec
2			2%	3%	1%	1%	4%	5%	4%	4%	3%	2%	4%	1%
3														
4	Jan	=TRANSPOSE(C2:N2)												
5	Feb													
6	Mar			**1. Select B4:B15**										
7	Apr			**2. Type formula**										
8	May			**3. Ctrl+Shift+Enter**										
9	Jun													
10	Jul													
11	Aug													
12	Sep			**(enters a single formula**										
13	Oct			**in 12 cells at one time)**										
14	Nov													
15	Dec													
16														

As the data in the horizontal table changes, the same values appear in your vertical table, as shown below.

Tip: If your version of Excel has the SORT, FILTER, and UNIQUE functions, you can simply enter =TRANSPOSE(C2:N2) in cell B4 without pressing Ctrl+Shift+Enter.

But array formulas are not well known. Some spreadsheet rookie might try to edit your formula and forget to press Ctrl+Shift+Enter.

To avoid using the array formula, use a combination of INDEX and ROW, as shown in the figure below. =ROW(1:1) is a clever way of writing the number 1. As you copy this formula down, the row reference changes to 2:2 and returns a 2.

The INDEX function says you are getting the answers from C2:N2, and you want the *n*th item from the range.

	A	B	C	D	E	F	G	H	I
1			Jan	Feb	Mar	Apr	May	Jun	Jul
2			1%	1%	4%	4%	1%	2%	2%
3									
4	Jan	1%	=INDEX($C$2:$N$2,ROW(1:1))						
5	Feb								

In the figure below, =FORMULATEXT in column C shows how the formula changes when you copy down.

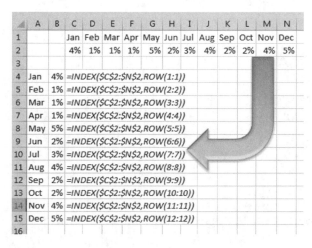

Bonus Tip: Protect Rows with an Array Formula

Here is an odd use for an array formula: Say that you don't want anyone to delete or insert any rows in one section of a worksheet. Scroll far to the right, off the screen, and build an array in those rows. Select Z1:Z9. Type =2 and press Ctrl+Shift+Enter. You can use any number, =0, =1, =2, and so on.

If someone tries to delete a row, Excel prevents it and shows a cryptic message about arrays, shown below.

Thanks to Excel Ace and Tracia Williams for suggesting this feature.

#54 Handle Multiple Conditions in IF

When you need to do a conditional calculation, the IF function is the answer. It works like this: If <something is true>, then <this formula>; otherwise <that formula>. In the following figure, a simple IF calculates a bonus for your sales of more than $20,000.

	A	B	C	D	E
D4			f_x	=IF(B4>=20000,0.02*B4,0)	
1	Pay a 2% bonus for sales > 20000				
2					
3	Sales Rep	Revenue	GP%	Bonus	
4	Richard B Lanza	22810	45.9%	456.2	
5	David Haggarty	2257	54.0%	0	
6	Anthony J. LoBello Jr.	18552	46.3%	0	
7	Jon Higbed	9152	50.5%	0	
8	David Colman	8456	46.1%	0	
9	Eddie Stephen	21730	54.4%	434.6	

But what happens when two conditions need to be met? Most people will nest one IF statement inside another, as shown below:

1	Bonus for sales > 20000 + GP%>50%			
2	=IF(B4>20000,IF(C4>0.5,0.02*B4,0),0)			
3	Sales Rep	Revenue	GP%	Bonus
4	Richard B Lanza	22810	45.9%	0
5	David Haggarty	2257	54.0%	0
6	Anthony J. LoBello Jr.	18552	46.3%	0
7	Jon Higbed	9152	50.5%	0
8	David Colman	8456	46.1%	0

But this nesting gets out of hand if you have many conditions that have to be met. Use the AND function to shorten and simplify the formula. =AND(Test,Test,Test,Test) is True only if all of the logical tests evaluate to True. The following example shows a shorter formula with the same results.

◢	A	B	C	D
1	Bonus for sales > 20000 + GP%>50%			
2	=IF(AND(B4>20000,C4>0.5),0.02*B4,0)			
3	Sales Rep	Revenue	GP%	Bonus
4	Richard B Lanza	22810	45.9%	0
5	David Haggarly	2257	54.0%	0
6	Anthony J. LoBello Jr.	18552	46.3%	0
7	Jon Higbed	9152	50.5%	0
8	David Colman	8456	46.1%	0
9	Eddie Stephen	21730	54.4%	434.6
10	Mike excelisfun Girvir	16416	48.2%	0

If you like AND, you might find a use for OR and NOT. =OR(Test,Test,Test,Test) is True if any one of the logical tests are True. NOT reverses an answer, so =NOT(True) is False, and =NOT(False) is True. If you ever have to do something fancy like a NAND, you can use NOT(AND(Test,Test,Test,Test)).

> **Caution**: Although Excel 2013 introduced XOR as an Exclusive Or, it does not work the way that accountants would expect. =XOR(True,False,True,True) is True for reasons that are too complicated to explain here. XOR counts whether you have an odd number of True values. Odd. Really odd.

Bonus Tip: Use Boolean Logic

I always cover IF in my seminars. And I always ask how people would solve the two-conditions problem. The results are often the same: 70–80% of people use nested IF, and 20–30% use AND. Just one time, in Virginia, a woman from Price Waterhouse offered the formula shown below:

◢	A	B	C	D
1	Bonus for sales > 20000 + GP%>50%			
2	=B4*0.02*(B4>20000)*(C4>0.5)			
3	Sales Rep	Revenue	GP%	Bonus
4	Richard B Lanza	22810	45.9%	0
5	David Haggarty	2257	54.0%	0
6	Anthony J. LoBello Jr.	18552	46.3%	0
7	Jon Higbed	9152	50.5%	0
8	David Colman	8456	46.1%	0
9	Eddie Stephen	21730	54.4%	434.6
10	Mike excelisfun Girvir	16416	48.2%	0

4

It works. It gives the same answer as the other formulas. Calculate the bonus .02*B4. But then multiply that bonus by logical tests in parentheses. When you force Excel to multiply a number by True or False, the True becomes 1, and the False becomes 0. Any number times 1 is itself. Any number times 0 is 0. Multiplying the bonus by the conditions ensures that only rows that meet both conditions are paid.

It is cool. It works. But it seems confusing when you first see it. My joke in my seminar is, "If you are leaving your job next month and you hate your co-workers, start using this formula."

#55 Troubleshoot VLOOKUP

VLOOKUP is my favorite function in Excel. If you can use VLOOKUP, you can solve many problems in Excel. But there are things that can trip up a VLOOKUP. This topic talks about a few of them.

But first, the basics of VLOOKUP in plain English.

The data in A:C came from the IT department. You asked for sales by item and date. They gave you item number. You need the item description. Rather than wait for the IT department to rerun the data, you find the table shown in column F:G.

	A	B	C	D	E	F	G	H
1	Item	Date	Qty	Description				
2	W25-6	8/1/2018	878			SKU	Description	
3	CR 50-4	8/1/2018	213			BG33-3	14K Gold Bangle Bracelet with Vin
4	CR 50-4	8/2/2018	744			CR50-3	14K Gold Cross with Onyx
5	BR26-3	8/3/2018	169			RG75-3	14K Gold RAY OF LIGHT Onyx Me
6	CR50-6	8/3/2018	822			RG78-25	14K Gold Ballerina Ring w/ Blue &
7	ER46-14	8/3/2018	740			W25-6	18K Italian Gold Women's Watch
8	DC70 25	0/2/2010	620			DD26 2	10K Italian Cold Man's Bracolot

You want VLOOKUP to find the item in A2 while it searches through the first column of the table in $F$3:$G$30. When VLOOKUP finds the match in F7, you want VLOOKUP to return the description found in the second column of the table. Every VLOOKUP that is looking for an exact match has to end in False (or zero, which is equivalent to False). The formula below is set up properly.

D2	▼	:	×	✓	fx	=VLOOKUP(A2,$F$3:$G$30,2,FALSE)

	A	B	C	D	E	F	
1	Item	Date	Qty	Description			
2	W25-6	8/1/2018	878	18K Italian Gold Women's Watch	SKU	Descri
3	CR 50-4	8/1/2018	213	14K Gold Onyx Cross		BG33-3	14K G
4	CR 50-4	8/2/2018	744	14K Gold Onyx Cross		CR50-3	14K G
5	BR26-3	8/3/2018	169	18K Italian Gold Men's Bracelet	RG75-3	14K G
6	CR50-6	8/3/2018	822	14K Gold Onyx Cross with White	RG78-25	14K G
7	ER46-14	8/3/2018	740	14K Gold Fish Hoop Earrings	W25-6	18K Ita

Notice that you use F4 to add four dollar signs to the address for the lookup table. As you copy the formula down column D, you need the address for the lookup table to remain constant. There are two common alternatives: You could specify the entire columns F:G as the lookup table. Or, you could name F3:G30 with a name such as ItemTable. If you use =VLOOKUP(A2,ItemTable,2,False), the named range acts like an absolute reference.

Any time you do a bunch of VLOOKUPs, you need to sort the column of VLOOKUPs. Sort ZA, and any #N/A errors come to the top. In this case, there is one. Item BG33-9 is missing from the lookup table. Maybe it is a typo. Maybe it is a brand-new item. If it is new, insert a new row anywhere in the middle of your lookup table and add the new item.

	A	B	C	Sort⫰ZA	E	F
1	Item	Date	Qty	Description		
2	BG33-9	8/19/2018	87	#N/A		SKU
3	W25-6	8/1/2018	878	18K Italian Gold Women's Watch		BG33-3
4	W25-6	8/21/2018	254	18K Italian Gold Women's Watch		CR50-3
5	W25-6	8/22/2018	832	18K Italian Gold Women's Watch		RG75-3
6	W25-6	8/29/2018	581	18K Italian Gold Women's Watch		RG78-25
7	BR26-3	8/3/2018	169	18K Italian Gold Men's Bracelet		W25-6
8	BR26-3	8/5/2018	541	18K Italian Gold Men's Bracelet		BR26-3
9	BR26-3	8/6/2018	849	18K Italian Gold Men's Bracelet		BR15-3
10	BR26-3	8/10/2018	881	18K Italian Gold Men's Bracelet		BG33-8
11	BR26-3	8/12/2018	737	18K Italian Gold Men's Bracelet		BG33-17

It is fairly normal to have a few #N/A errors. But in the figure below, exactly the same formula is returning nothing but #N/A. When this happens, see if you can solve the first VLOOKUP. You are looking up the BG33-8 found in A2. Start cruising down through the first column of the lookup table. As you can see, the matching value clearly is in F10. Why can you see this, but Excel cannot see it?

D2 · : × ✓ *fx* =VLOOKUP(A2,$F$3:$G$30,2,FALSE)

	A	B	C	D	E	F	G
1	Item	Date	Qty	Description			
2	BG33-8	8/1/2018	580	#N/A		SKU	Description
3	Cross50-5	8/1/2018	422	#N/A		BG33-3	14K Gold Bar
4	RG78-25	8/2/2018	638	#N/A		CR50-3	14K Gold Cro
5	BG33-8	8/3/2018	775	#N/A		RG75-3	14K Gold RA'
6	BG33-8	8/3/2018	331	#N/A		RG78-25	14K Gold Bal
7	ER46-7	8/3/2018	140	#N/A		W25-6	18K Italian Go
8	RG75-3	8/3/2018	231	#N/A		BR26-3	18K Italian Go
9	W25-6	8/4/2018	878	#N/A		BR15-3	14K Gold Ony
10	CR50-6	8/4/2018	571	#N/A		BG33-8	14K Gold Bar
11	ER41-4	8/4/2018	208	#N/A		BG33-17	14K Gold Bar

Go to each cell and press the F2 key. The figure below shows F10. Note that the insertion cursor appears right after the 8.

W25-6	1ο
BR26-3	18ŀ
BR15-3	14ŀ
BG33-8	14ŀ
BG33-17	14ŀ
CR 50-4	14ŀ
CR50-2	14ŀ

The following figure shows cell A2 in Edit mode. The insertion cursor is a couple of spaces away from the 8. This is a sign that at some point, this data was stored in an old COBOL data set. Back in COBOL, if the Item field was defined as 10 characters and you typed only 6 characters, COBOL would pad it with 4 extra spaces.

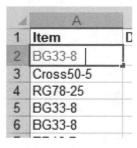

	A	
1	Item	D
2	BG33-8	
3	Cross50-5	
4	RG78-25	
5	BG33-8	
6	BG33-8	

4

The solution? Instead of looking up A2, look up TRIM(A2).

| D2 | ▼ | : | × | ✓ | fx | =VLOOKUP(TRIM(A2),$F$3:$G$30,2,FALSE) |

	A	B	C	D	E	F	G
1	Item	Date	Qty	Description			
2	BG33-8	8/1/2018	580	14K Gold Bangle	SKU		Description
3	Cross50-5	8/1/2018	422	14K Gold Onyx C	BG33-3		14K Gold Bangle Br
4	RG78-25	8/2/2018	638	14K Gold Ballerin	CR50-3		14K Gold Cross with

The TRIM() function removes leading and trailing spaces. If you have multiple spaces between words, TRIM converts them to a single space. In the figure below there are spaces before and after both names in A1. =TRIM(A1) removes all but one space in A3.

| A3 | ▼ | : | × | ✓ | fx | =TRIM(A1) |

	A	B	C
1	John Durran		
2	* John Durran *	="*"&A1&"*"	
3	John Durran	=TRIM(A1)	
4	*John Durran*	="*"&A3&"*"	

By the way, what if the problem had been trailing spaces in column F instead of column A? Add a column of TRIM() functions to E, pointing to column F. Copy those and paste as values in F to make the lookups start working again.

The other very common reason that VLOOKUP won't work is shown here. Column F contains real numbers. Column A holds text that looks like numbers.

| D2 | ▼ | : | × | ✓ | fx | =VLOOKUP(A2,$F$3:$G$30,2,FALSE) |

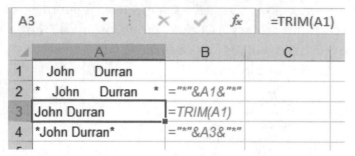

	A	B	C	D	E	F	G
1	Item	Date	Qty	Description			
2	4399	8/1/2018	80	#N/A		SKU	Description
3	4250	8/1/2018	422	#N/A		6041	14K Gold Ban
4	3712	8/2/2018	638	#N/A		2304	14K Gold Cros
5	4399	8/3/2018	775	#N/A		1242	14K Gold RAY
6	4399	8/3/2018	331	#N/A		3712	14K Gold Ball
7	3363	8/3/2018	140	#N/A		5805	18K Italian Go
8	1242	8/3/2018	231	#N/A		1995	18K Italian Go
9	5805	8/4/2018	878	#N/A		2619	14K Gold Ony
10	2925	8/4/2018	571	#N/A		4399	14K Gold Ban
11	3270	8/4/2018	208	#N/A		4101	14K Gold Ban
12	3270	8/5/2018	429	#N/A		5403	14K Gold Ony

Select all of column A. Press Alt+D, E, F. This does a default Text to Columns operation and converts all text numbers to real numbers. The lookup starts working again.

Alt+D, E, F

	A	B	C	D	E
1	Item	Date	Qty	Description	
2	4399	8/1/2018	580	14K Gold Bangle Bra	
3	4250	8/1/2018	422	14K Gold Onyx Cross	
4	3712	8/2/2018	638	14K Gold Ballerina Ri	

If you want the VLOOKUP to work without changing the data, you can use =VLOOKUP(1*A2,...) to handle numbers stored as text or =VLOOKUP(A2&"",...) when your lookup table has text numbers.

#56 Use a Wildcard in VLOOKUP

You can use a wildcard in VLOOKUP or XLOOKUP. If you aren't sure if your lookup table will contain Apple, Apple Computer, or Apple Computer Inc, you can use =VLOOKUP("Apple*",Table,2,False), and Excel will find the first item in the lookup table that starts with Apple. (Thanks to -Khalif John Clark)

Bonus Tip: VLOOKUP to Two Tables

You want to try to find a match in Table1. If a match is not found, then do a lookup to Table2. You can use =IFNA(Formula,Value if NA). =IFNA(VLOOKUP(A2,Table1,3,False),VLOOKUP(A2,Table2,3,False)).

#57 Replace Columns of VLOOKUP with a Single MATCH

The following figure shows a situation in which you have to do 12 VLOOKUP functions for each account number.

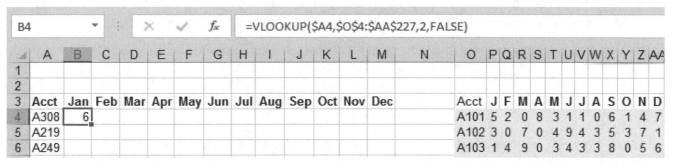

VLOOKUP is powerful, but it takes a lot of time to do calculations. Plus, the formula has to be edited in each cell as you copy across. The third argument has to change from 2 to 3 for February, then 4 for March, and so on.

C4				fx	=VLOOKUP($A4,$O$4:$AA$227,3,FALSE)									
	A	B	C	D	E	F	G	H	I	J	K	L	M	N	O
1														
2														
3	Acct	Jan	Feb	Mar	Apr	May	Jun	Jul	Aug	Sep	Oct	Nov	Dec		Acct
4	A308	6	1												A10·
5	A219														A10:

One workaround is to add a row with the column numbers. Then, the third argument of VLOOKUP can point to this row, as shown below. At least you can copy the same formula from B4 and paste to C4:M4 before copying the 12 formulas down.

G4				fx	=VLOOKUP($A4,$O$4:$AA$227,G$1,FALSE)									
	A	B	C	D	E	F	G	H	I	J	K	L	M	N	O	P
1		2	3	4	5	6	7	8	9	10	11	12	13		
2															
3	Acct	Jan	Feb	Mar	Apr	May	Jun	Jul	Aug	Sep	Oct	Nov	Dec		Acct	J
4	A308	6	1	9	2	9	1	5	4	4	4	7	3		A101	5
5	A219	0	0	5	0	2	8	8	7	8	3	0	0		A102	3

But here is a much faster approach: add a new column B with Where? as the heading. Column B contains a MATCH function. This function is very similar to VLOOKUP: You are looking for the value in A4 in the column P4:P227. The 0 at the end is like the False at the end of VLOOKUP. It specifies that you want an exact match. Here is the big difference: MATCH returns where the value is found. The answer 208 says

4

that A308 is the 208th cell in the range P4:P227. From a recalc time perspective, MATCH and VLOOKUP are about equal.

Formula bar: **=MATCH(A4,$P$4:$P$227,0)** — cell B4

	Acct	Where?	Jan	Feb	Mar	Apr	May	Jun	Jul	Aug	Sep	Oct	No
4	A308	208											
5	A219	119											
6	A249	149											
7	A154	54											

I can hear what you are thinking: "What good is it to know where something is located? I've never had a manager call up and ask, 'What row is that receivable in?'"

While humans rarely ask what row something is in, it can be handy for the INDEX function to know that position. The formula in the following figure tells Excel to return the 208th item from Q4:Q227.

Formula bar: **=INDEX(Q$4:Q$227,$B4)**

	Acct	Where?	Jan	...	Dec		Acct	J	F	M	A
4	A308	208	=INDEX(Q$4:Q$227,$B4)				A101	5	2	0	8
5	A219	119					A102	3	0	7	0
6	A249	149					A103	1	4	9	0
7	A154	54					A104	0	4	2	5
8	A128	28					A105	9	4	8	1
9	A229	129					A106	6	3	6	2

As you copy this formula across, the array of values moves across the lookup table as shown below. For each row, you are doing one MATCH and 12 INDEX functions. The INDEX function is incredibly fast compared to VLOOKUP. The entire set of formulas will calculate 85% faster than 12 columns of VLOOKUP.

Formula bar: **=INDEX(Y$4:Y$227,$B4)**

	Acct	Where?	Jan	Feb	Mar	Apr	May	Jun	Jul	Aug	Sep	Oct	Nov	Dec		Acct	J	F	M	A	M	J	J	A	S	O	N	D
4	A308	208	6	1	9	2	9	1	5	4	=INDEX(Y$4:Y$227,$B4)						5	2	0	8	3	1	1	0	6	1	4	7
5	A219	119	0	0	5	0	2	8	8	7	8	3	0	0		A102	3	0	7	0	4	9	4	3	5	3	7	1
6	A249	149	1	7	1	3	2	9	6	7	1	2	9	5		A103	1	4	9	0	3	4	3	3	8	0	5	6
7	A154	54	2	5	8	0	3	3	5	5	2	8	9	3		A104	0	4	2	5	0	0	9	7	6	8	8	5
8	A128	28	4	1	8	6	2	5	7	8	4	0	9	5		A105	9	4	8	1	3	4	5	7	7	7	9	7

Note: In late 2018, Microsoft 365 introduced new logic for VLOOKUP that makes the calculation speed as fast as the INDEX/MATCH shown here. Late in 2019, the new XLOOKUP function will solve this problem. See "XLOOKUP Benefit 12: Sum all lookup values in a single formula" on page 152.

#58 Lookup to the Left with INDEX/MATCH

What if your lookup value is to the right of the information that you want VLOOKUP to return? Conventional wisdom says VLOOKUP cannot handle a negative column number in order to go left of the key.

	A	B	C	D	E
1	Name	Department			
2	Alex Pilar	=VLOOKUP(A2,$D$4:$E$11,-1,FALSE)			
3	Gary Kane			Department	Name
4	Leonard LaFrenier			Accounting	Allan Matz
5	Allan Matz	Won't		Finance	Gary Kane
6	Alex Pilar	Work!		Accounting	Alex Pilar
7	Alex Pilar			Finance	Larry Vance
8	Larry Vance			Tax	Leonard LaFrenier
9	Larry Vance			Finance	Lorna Banuilos
10	Alex Pilar			Accounting	Erik Svensen
11	Larry Vance			Finance	Victor E. Scelba II
12	Lorna Banuilos				

One solution is =VLOOKUP(I7,CHOOSE({1,2},G1:G5,F1:F5),2,0). If you have Microsoft 365, see "XLOOKUP Benefit 4: No problem looking to the left of the key field" on page 147.

However, I prefer to use MATCH to find where the name is located and then use INDEX to return the correct value.

			fx	=INDEX($D$4:$D$11,MATCH(A2,$E$4:$E$11,0))			

	A	B	C	D	E	F	G
1	Name	Department					
2	Alex Pilar	=INDEX($D$4:$D$11,MATCH(A2,$E$4:$E$11,0))					
3	Gary Kane	Finance		Department	Name		
4	Leonard LaFrenier	Tax		Accounting	Allan Matz		
5	Allan Matz	Accounting		Finance	Gary Kane		
6	Alex Pilar	Accounting		Accounting	Alex Pilar		
7	Alex Pilar	Accounting		Finance	Larry Vance		
8	Larry Vance	Finance		Tax	Leonard LaFrenier		
9	Larry Vance	Finance		Finance	Lorna Banuilos		
10	Alex Pilar	Accounting		Accounting	Erik Svensen		
11	Larry Vance	Finance		Finance	Victor E. Scelba II		
12	Lorna Banuilos	Finance					
13	Alex Pilar	Accounting					

VLOOKUP was suggested by Rod Apfelbeck, Patty Hahn, John Henning, @ExcelKOS, and @tomatecaolho. The INDEX/MATCH trick came from Mark Domeyer, Jon Dow, Justin Fishman, Donna Gilliland, Alex Havermans, Jay Killeen, Martin Lucas, Patrick Matthews, Mike Petry, Michael Tarzia, and @beatexcel. Thanks to all of you.

4

Poster Credit: Bobby Rosenstock
justAjar Design Press, http://www.justajar.com/

#59 Twelve Benefits of XLOOKUP

The new XLOOKUP function is rolling out to Microsoft 365 starting in November 2019. Joe McDaid of the Excel team designed XLOOKUP to unify the people who use VLOOKUP and the people who use INDEX/ MATCH. This section will discuss the 12 benefits of XLOOKUP:

1. Exact match is the default.

2. Integer-based third argument of VLOOKUP is now a proper reference.

3. IFNA is built-in to handle missing values.

4. XLOOKUP has no problem going to the left.

5. Find next-smaller or next-larger match without sorting the table.

6. XLOOKUP can do HLOOKUP.

7. Find the last match by searching from the bottom.

8. Wildcards are "off" by default, but you can turn them back on.

9. Return all 12 months in a single formula.

10. Can return a cell reference if the XLOOKUP is next to a colon such as XLOOKUP();XLOOKUP()

11. Can do a two-way match like INDEX(,MATCH,MATCH) can do.

12. Can sum all lookups in a single formula like LOOKUP could do.

Here is the syntax:

=XLOOKUP(Lookup_Value, Lookup_Array, Results_Array, [if_not_found], {match_mode}, [search_mode]).

XLOOKUP Benefit 1: Exact Match by Default

99% of my VLOOKUP formulas end in ,FALSE or ,0 to indicate an exact match. If you always use the exact match version of VLOOKUP, you can start leaving the match_mode off of your XLOOKUP function.

In the following figure, you are looking up W25-6 from cell A4. You want to look for that item in L8:L35. When it is found, you want the corresponding price from column N. There is no need to specify False as the match_mode because XLOOKUP defaults to an exact match.

4

	A	B	C	D	K	L	M	N	O
1	**XLOOKUP Benefit #1: Exact Match is Automatic**								
2						where to look	what to return		
3	Item	Date	Qty	Price					
4	W25-6	8/1/2019	878	=XLOOKUP(A4,$L$8:$L$35,$N$8:$N$35)					
5	CR 50-4	8/1/2019	213	14.95					
6	CR 50-4	8/2/2019	744	14.95					
7	BR26-3	8/3/2019	169	39.95		SKU	Description	Price	Category
8	CR50-6	8/3/2019	822	19.95		BG33-3	14K Gold Bangle Bracelet	29.95	Wrist
9	ER46-14	8/3/2019	740	15.95		CR50-3	14K Gold Cross with Ony	19.95	Charm
10	RG78-25	8/3/2019	638	89.95		RG75-3	14K Gold RAY OF LIGHT	79.95	Ring
11	BR15-3	8/4/2019	817	39.95		RG78-25	14K Gold Ballerina Ring w	89.95	Ring
12	Cross50-5	8/4/2019	871	19.95		W25-6	18K Italian Gold Women's	69.95	Wrist
13	CR50-2	8/4/2019	686	14.95		BR26-3	18K Italian Gold Men's Br	39.95	Wrist
14	BR26-3	8/5/2019	541	39.95		BR15-3	14K Gold Onyx Men's Bra	39.95	Wrist
15	ER41-4	8/5/2019	208	15.95		BG33-8	14K Gold Bangle Bracelet	39.95	Wrist

XLOOKUP Benefit 2: the Results_Array is a reference instead of an integer

Think about the VLOOKUP formula that you would use before XLOOKUP. The third argument would've been a 3 to indicate that you wanted to return the 3rd column. There was always a danger that a clueless co-worker would've inserted (or deleted) a column in your table. With an extra column in the table, the VLOOKUP that had been returning a price would start returning a description. Because XLOOKUP was pointing to a cell reference, the formula rewrites itself to keep pointing to the price that is now in column O.

	A	B	C	D	K	L	M	N	O	P
2						=VLOOKUP(A4,L8:P35,3,FALSE) **breaks!**				
3	Item	Date	Qty	Price		18K Italian Gold Women's Watch				
4	W25-6	8/1/2019	878	=XLOOKUP(A4,$L$8:$L$35,$O$8:$O$35)						
5	CR 50-4	8/1/2019	213	14.95				**keeps**		
6	CR 50-4	8/2/2019	744	14.95				**working!**		
7	BR26-3	8/3/2019	169	39.95		SKU		Description	Price	Category
8	CR50-6	8/3/2019	822	19.95		BG33-3		14K Gold Bar	29.95	Wrist
9	ER46-14	8/3/2019	740	15.95		CR50-3	x	14K Gold Cro	19.95	Charm
10	RG78-25	8/3/2019	638	89.95		RG75-3		14K Gold RAY	79.95	Ring
11	BR15-3	8/4/2019	817	39.95		RG78-25	x	14K Gold Bal	89.95	Ring

XLOOKUP Benefit 3: IFNA is built in as an optional argument

The dreaded #N/A error is returned when your lookup value is not found in the table. In the past, to replace #N/A with something else, you would have to use IFERROR or IFNA wrapped around the VLOOKUP.

	A	B	C	D
3	Item	Date	Qty	Price
4	W25-6	8/1/2019	878	69.95
5	CR 50-4	8/1/2019	213	14.95
6	X999	8/2/2019	744	#N/A
7	BR26-3	8/3/2019	169	39.95
8	CR50-6	8/3/2019	822	19.95
9	ER46-14	8/3/2019	740	15.95
10	X999	8/3/2019	638	#N/A

Thanks to a suggestion from Rico S. on my YouTube channel, the Excel team incorporated an optional fourth argument for if_not_found. If you want to replace those #N/A errors with zero, simply add ,0 as the fourth argument. Or, you could use some text, such as "Value not found".

MID	▼	⋮	×	✓	*fx*	=XLOOKUP(A4,$L$8:$L$35,$N$8:$N$35,0	

	A	B	C	D	K	L	M
3	Item	Date	Qty	Price			
4	W25-6	8/1/2019	878	=XLOOKUP(A4,$L$8:$L$35,$N$8:$N$35,0			
5		XLOOKUP(lookup_value, lookup_array, return_array, [if_not_found], [match_mode], [search_mode])					
6	X999	8/2/2019	744	0			
7	BR26-3	8/3/2019	169	39.95		SKU	Description
8	CR50-6	8/3/2019	822	19.95		BG33-3	14K Gold Bangle Brace
9	ER46-14	8/3/2019	740	15.95		CR50-3	14K Gold Cross with Or
10	X999	8/3/2019	638	0		RG75-3	14K Gold RAY OF LIGH
11	BR15-3	8/4/2019	817	39.95		RG78-25	14K Gold Ballerina Ring

XLOOKUP Benefit 4: No problem looking to the left of the key field

VLOOKUP can not look to the left of the key field without resorting to VLOOKUP(A4, CHOOSE({1,2}, G7:G34,F7:F34),2,False). With XLOOKUP, there is no problem having the Results_array to the left of the Lookup_array.

	A	B	C	D	E	F	G
3	Item	Date	Qty	Category?			
4	W25-6	8/1/2019	878	=XLOOKUP(A4,$G$7:$G$34,$F$7:$F$34)			
5	CR 50-4	8/1/2019	213	Charm			
6	CR 50-4	8/2/2019	744	Charm		Category	Item
7	BR26-3	8/3/2019	169	Wrist		Wrist	BG33-3
8	CR50-6	8/3/2019	822	Charm		Charm	CR50-3
9	ER46-14	8/3/2019	740	Ear		Ring	RG75-3
10	RG78-25	8/3/2019	638	Ring		Ring	RG78-25
11	BR15-3	8/4/2019	817	Wrist		Wrist	W25-6

XLOOKUP Benefit 5: Next-smaller or next-larger match without sorting

VLOOKUP had an option to look for the exact match or just smaller value. You could either leave the fourth argument out of VLOOKUP, or change the False to True. For this to work, the lookup table had to be sorted in ascending sequence.

	Invoice	Rep	Amount	Bonus			
3							
4	1001	Carole	12835	12			
5	1002	Andy	19634	12			
6	1003	Carole	898	0		Sale	Bonus
7	1004	Hector	7747	5		0	0
8	1005	Andy	6239	5		5000	5
9	1006	Gary	19867	12		10000	12
10	1007	Andy	27537	100		20000	50
11	1008	Dale	679	0		25000	100
12	1009	Flo	24240	50			

But VLOOKUP did not have the ability to return the exact match or next larger item. For that, you had to switch over to using MATCH with a -1 as the match_mode and you had to be careful that the lookup table was sorted descending.

XLOOKUP's optional fifth argument match_mode can look for only the exact match, equal to or just smaller, equal to or just larger. Note that the values in XLOOKUP make more sense than in MATCH:

- -1 finds the value equal to or just smaller
- 0 find an exact match
- 1 finds the value equal to or just larger.

But, the most amazing part: the lookup table does not have to be sorted and any match_mode will work.

4

Below, a match_mode of -1 find the next-smaller item.

	Amount	Bonus					Reservation	Passengers	Recon
ole	12835	=XLOOKUP(C4,$F$7:$F$11,$G$7:$G$11,,-1						2	Car
ly	19634	XLOOKUP(lookup_value, lookup_array, return_array, [if_not_found], **[match_mode]**, [search_m
ole	898	0		Sale	Bonus		💬 0 - Exact match
ctor	7747	5		0	0		💬 -1 - Exact match or next smaller item
ly	6239	5		5000	5		💬 1 - Exact match or next larger item
y	19867	12		10000	12		💬 2 - Wildcard character match
ly	27537	100		20000	50		A100		2	Car
e	679	0		25000	100		A107		20	Bus
	24240	50					A108		40	Bus
							A100		12	Tour V

Here, a match_mode of 1, finds what vehicle is needed depending on the number of people in the party. Note that the lookup table is not sorted by passengers and the vehicle name is to the left of the key.

	I	J	K	L	M	N
3	Reservation	Passengers	Recommended			
4	A101	2	=XLOOKUP(J4,$N$6:$N$10,$M$6:$M$10,,1)			
5	A102	5	Van		Vehicle	Capacity
6	A103	12	Tour Van		Bus	64
7	A104	1	Motorcycle		Car	4
8	A105	11	Tour Van		Motorcycle	1
9	A106	2	Car		Tour Van	12
10	A107	20	Bus		Van	6
11	A108	40	Bus			
12	A109	12	Tour Van			

XLOOKUP Benefit 6: Sideways XLOOKUP replaces HLOOKUP

The lookup_array and results_array can be horizontal with XLOOKUP, making it simple to replace HLOOKUP.

	A	B	C	D	E	F	G	H	I
3						Jan	Feb	Mar	Apr
4	Item	Month	Sales	Bonus		1.5%	2.4%	3.0%	1.2%
5	BG33-8	Jan	17753	=XLOOKUP(B5,$F$3:$Q$3,$F$4:$Q$4)					
6	Cross50-5	Feb	16500	2.4%					
7	RG78-25	Mar	26648	3.0%					
8	BG33-8	Oct	10564	1.6%					

XLOOKUP Benefit 7: Search from the bottom for latest match

I have an old video on YouTube answering a question from a British horse farm. They had a fleet of vehicles. Every time a vehicle came in for fuel or service, they logged vehicle, date, and mileage in a spreadsheet. They wanted to find the latest known mileage for each vehicle. While the Excel-2017 era MAXIFS might solve this today, the solution many years ago was an arcane formula using LOOKUP and involved division by zero.

Today, XLOOKUP's optional sixth argument lets you specify that the search should start from the bottom of the data set.

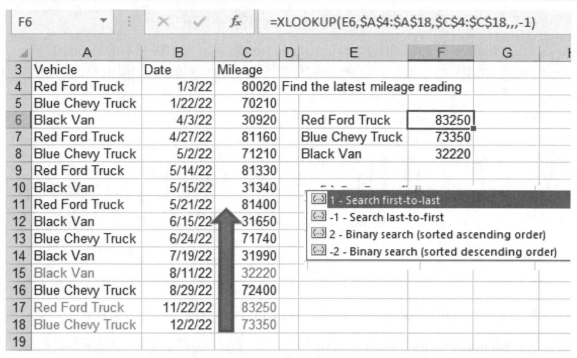

Note: While this is a great improvement, it only lets you find the first or last match. Some people hoped this would let you find the second or third match, but that is not the intention of the search_mode argument.

Caution: The figure above shows that there are search modes using the old binary search. Joe McDaid advises against using these. First, the improved lookup algorithm from 2018 is fast enough that there is no significant speed benefit. Second, you run the risk of a clueless co-worker sorting the lookup table and introducing wrong answers.

XLOOKUP Benefit 8: Wildcards are "turned off" by default

Most people did not realize that VLOOKUP is treating asterisk, question mark, and tilde as wildcard characters as described in "#56 Use a Wildcard in VLOOKUP" on page 141. With XLOOKUP, wildcards are turned off by default. If you want XLOOKUP to treat these characters as a wildcard, use 2 as the Match_Mode.

	A	B	C	D	E	F	G	H	I	J	K
4		Wal*Mart		Sears	10						
5				Target	20						
6				Wallboard Mart	30						
7				WalMart	40						
8				Wal*Mart	50						
9											
10		30	Wallboard Mart	=VLOOKUP(B4,$D$4:$E$8,2,0) VLOOKUP treats * ? ~ as Wildcard							
11		50	Wal*Mart	=XLOOKUP(B4,D4:D8,E4:E8) XLOOKUP gets this right							
12		30	Wallboard Mart	=XLOOKUP(B4,D4:D8,E4:E8,,2) you can force XLOOKUP to use wildcards with match_type of 2							
13											
14											
15				⌐0 - Exact match							
16				⌐-1 - Exact match or next smaller item							
17				⌐1 - Exact match or next larger item							
18				⌐2 - Wildcard character match							
19											

4

XLOOKUP Benefit 9: Return All 12 Months in a Single Formula!

This is really a benefit of Dynamic Arrays, but it is my favorite reason to love XLOOKUP. When you have to return all 12 months in a lookup, a single formula entered in B6 with a rectangular return_array will return multiple results. Those results will spill into adjacent cells.

In the figure below, a single formula entered in B7 returns all 12 answers shown in B7:M7.

| MID | ▼ | : | × | ✓ | fx | =XLOOKUP(A6,$O$6:$O$229,$P$6:$AA$229) |

	A	B	C	D	E	F	G	H	I	J	K	L	M	N		O	P	Q	R	S	T	U	V	W	X	Y	Z	AA
5	Acct	Jan	Feb	Mar	Apr	May	Jun	Jul	Aug	Sep	Oct	Nov	Dec			Acct	J	F	M	A	M	J	J	A	S	O	N	D
6	A308	=XLOOKUP(A6,$O$6:$O$229,$P$6:$AA$229)								4	7	3			A101	5	2	0	8	3	1	1	0	6	1	4	7
7	A219	0	0	5	0	2	8	8	7	8	3	0	0			A102	3	0	7	0	4	9	4	3	5	3	7	1
8	A249	1	7	1	3	2	9	6	7	1	2	9	5			A103	1	4	9	0	3	4	3	3	8	0	5	6
9	A154	2	5	8	0	3	3	5	5	2	8	9	3			A104	0	4	2	5	0	0	9	7	6	8	8	5
10	A128	4	1	8	6	2	5	7	8	4	0	9	5			A105	9	4	8	1	3	4	5	7	7	7	9	7

Benefit 10: XLOOKUP Can Return a Cell Reference If Adjacent to Colon

This one is complex but beautiful. In the past, there were seven functions that would change from return-ing a cell value to returning a cell reference if the function was touching a colon. For an example, see "#80 Use A2:INDEX() as a Non-Volatile OFFSET" on page 185. XLOOKUP is the eights function to offer this be-havior, joining CHOOSE, IF, IFS, INDEX, INDIRECT, OFFSET, and SWITCH.

Consider the following figure. Someone select Cherry in E4 and Fig in E5. You want a formula that will sum everything from B6 to B9.

	A	B	C	D	E	F	G	H	I
4	Apple	5		From:	Cherry				
5	Banana	10		To:	Fig				
6	Cherry	15							
7	Date	20		90	=SUM(XLOOKUP(E4,A4:A29,B4:B29):XLOOKUP(E5,A4:A29,B4:B29))				
8	Elderberry	25							
9	Fig	30		15	=XLOOKUP(E4,A4:A29,B4:B29)				
10	Guava	35		30	=XLOOKUP(E5,A4:A29,B4:B29)				

In the figure above, you can see that an XLOOKUP of E4 will return the 15 from cell B6. An XLOOKUP of E5 will return the 30 from B9. However, if you take the two XLOOKUP functions from cells D9 and D10 and put them together with a colon in-between, the behavior of XLOOKUP changes. Instead of returning 15, the first XLOOKUP returns the cell address B6!

To prove this, I've selected D7 and use Formulas, Evaluate Formula. After pressing Evaluate two times, the next part to be calculated is XLOOKUP("Cherry",A4:A29,B4:B29), as shown here.

Evaluate Formula	?

Reference:		Evaluation:
Reference!$D$7	=	SUM(XLOOKUP(*"Cherry"*,A4:A29,B4:B29):XLOOKUP(E5,A4:A29, B4:B29))

Press Evaluate again and amazingly, the XLOOKUP formula returns $B$6 instead of the 15 stored in B6. This happens because there is a colon immediately following this XLOOKUP formula.

Evaluation:
= SUM($B$6:XLOOKUP(E5,A4:A29,B4:B29))

Press Evaluate two more times, and the interim formula will be =SUM(B6:B9).

▲	A	B	C	D	E	F	G
4	Apple	5		From:	Cherry		
5	Banana	10		To:	Fig		
6	Cherry	15					
7	Date	20		90	=SUM(XLOOKUP(E4,A4:A29,B4:B29		
8	Elderberry	25					
9	Fig	30		Evaluate Formula			
10	Guava	35					
11	Honeydew	40		Reference:		Evaluation:	
12	Iceberg	45		Reference!$D$7	=	SUM($B$6:$B$9)	

This is amazing behavior that most people don't know about. Excel MVP Charles Williams tells me that it can be triggered with any of these three operators next to XLOOKUP: Colon, Space (Intersection operator), or a Comma (Union operator).

XLOOKUP Benefit 11: Two-way match like INDEX(,MATCH,MATCH)

For all of my VLOOKUP friends, the INDEX/MATCH people have been waiting to see if XLOOKUP can handle a two-way match. The great news: it can do it. The bad news: the methodology is a little different than the INDEX/MATCH fans would expect. It might be a little over their heads. But I am sure they can come around to this method.

For a two-way match, you want to find which row contains the account number A621 shown in J3. So, the XLOOKUP starts out easy enough: =XLOOKUP(J3,A5:A15. But then you have to provide a results_array. You can use the same trick as in "XLOOKUP Benefit 9: Return All 12 Months in a Single Formula!" on page 150, but use it to return a vertical vector. An inner XLOOKUP looks for the J4 month in the month headings in B4:G4. The return_array is specified as B5:G15. The result is that the inner XLOOKUP returns an array like the one shown in I10:I20 below. Since A621 is found in the fifth cell of the lookup_array and 104 is found in the fifth cell of the results_array, you get the correct answer from the formula. Below, J6 shows the old way. J7 returns the new way.

▲	A	B	C	D	E	F	G	H	I	J	K	L	M	N	O	P
1	**The Two-Way Match with XLOOKUP is Tricky**															
2																
3									Acct:	A621						
4	Acct	Jan	Feb	Mar	Apr	May	Jun		Month:	May						
5	A302	99	41	31	114	90	1									
6	A397	10	56	3	7	44	50		Old way	104	=INDEX(B5:G15,MATCH(J3,$A$5:$A$15,0),MATCH(J4,$B$4:$G$4,0))					
7	A552	55	26	28	85	111	81		New way	104	=XLOOKUP(J3,A5:A15,XLOOKUP(J4,B4:G4,B5:G15)					
8	A628	40	87	88	47	107	60									
9	A621	74	57	103	33	104	64		Why it works: the inner XLOOKUP returns a vertical range as the results_array:							
10	A211	93	92	84	61	112	79			90	=XLOOKUP(J4,B4:G4,B5:G15)					
11	A563	53	15	8	42	24	46			44						
12	A547	94	12	77	38	22	39			111						
13	A940	48	100	102	97	66	45			107						
14	A339	25	72	73	113	21	6			104						
15	A673	17	89	82	65	5	109			112						
16										24						
17										22						
18										66						
19										21						
20										5						
21																

XLOOKUP Benefit 12: Sum all lookup values in a single formula

The ancient LOOKUP function offered two strange tricks. First, if you are trying to figure out the total amount of bonus expense to accrue, you could ask LOOKUP to lookup all of the values in a single formula. In the image below, LOOKUP(C4:C14 is doing 11 lookups. But the LOOKUP function did not offer an exact match and required the lookup table to be sorted.

	A	B	C	D	E	F	G	H	I
3	Inv #	Rep	Amount		Sale	Bonus			
4	1001	Carole	12835		0	0			
5	1002	Andy	19634		5000	5			
6	1003	Carole	898		10000	12			
7	1004	Hector	7747		20000	50			
8	1005	Andy	6239		25000	100			
9	1006	Gary	19867						
10	1007	Andy	27537		Total Bonus				
11	1008	Dale	679		308	=SUM(LOOKUP(C4:C14,E4:E8,F4:F8))			
12	1009	Flo	24240		308	=SUM(XLOOKUP(C4:C14,E4:E8,F4:F8,,-1))			
13	1010	Kevin	25314						
14	1011	Larry	12375						
15									

With XLOOKUP, you can specify a range as the lookup_value and XLOOKUP will return all of the answers. The benefit is that XLOOKUP can do exact matches.

	K	L	M	N	O	P	Q	R
3	Shift	Name		Name	Rate			
4	AM Manager	Ed		Barb	96			
5	AM Asst	Barb		Diane	72			
6	AM Grill	Kelly		Ed	120			
7	AM Grill	Jared		Flo	72			
8	AM Front	Gary		Gary	56			
9	AM Front	Flo		Hank	72			
10	PM Manager	Ed		Ike	70			
11	PM Grill	Diane		Jared	78			
12	PM Grill	Ike		Kelly	80			
13	PM Front	Gary						
14	PM Front	Hank		892	=SUM(XLOOKUP(L4:L14,N4:N12,O4:O12))			
15								

Bonus Tip: What about a Twisted LOOKUP?

Excel MVP Mike Girvin often shows a trick of the LOOKUP function where the Lookup_Vector is vertical and the Result_Vector is horizontal. XLOOKUP will not natively support this trick. But, if you cheat a little bit and wrap the results_array in the TRANSPOSE function, you can manage a twisted lookup.

▲	A	B	C	D	E	F	G	H
3	A		Andy	Betty	Charlie	Dale	Eddy	Flo
4	B							
5	C							
6	D		Letter:					
7	E		C	Charlie	=LOOKUP(C7,A3:A8,C3:H3)			
8	F		C	Charlie	=XLOOKUP(C8,A3:A8,TRANSPOSE(C3:H3))			
9								

#60 Preview What Remove Duplicates Will Remove

The Remove Duplicates tool added in Excel 2010 was a nice addition.

Data Tools

However, the tool does remove the duplicates. Sometimes, you might want to see the duplicates before you remove them. And the Home, Conditional Formatting, Highlight Cells, Duplicate Values marks both instances of Andy instead of just the one that will be removed. The solution is to create a conditional formatting rule using a formula. Select A2:B14. Home, Conditional Formatting, New Rule, Use a Formula. The formula should be: =COUNTIF($A$1:$A1,$A2)>0.

It is hard to visualize why this will work. Notice that there is a dollar sign missing from $A$1:$A1. This creates an expanding range. In English the formula says "Look at all of the values from A1 to A just above the current cell and see if they are equal to the current cell". Only cells that return >0 will be formatted.

I've added the formula to column C below so you can see how the range expands. In Row 5, the COUNTIF checks how many times Andy appears in A1:A4. Since there is one match, the cell is formatted.

	A	B	C
1	Name	Amount	Formula
2	Andy	36.80	=COUNTIF($A$1:$A1,$A2)>0
3	Barb	36.90	=COUNTIF($A$1:$A2,$A3)>0
4	Chris	92.25	=COUNTIF($A$1:$A3,$A4)>0
5	Andy	85.15	=COUNTIF($A$1:$A4,$A5)>0
6	Diane	85.65	=COUNTIF($A$1:$A5,$A6)>0
7	Ed	78.35	=COUNTIF($A$1:$A6,$A7)>0
8	Chris	69.75	=COUNTIF($A$1:$A7,$A8)>0
9	Hank	62.90	=COUNTIF($A$1:$A8,$A9)>0
10	Gary	95.60	=COUNTIF($A$1:$A9,$A10)>0
11	Chris	47.25	=COUNTIF($A$1:$A10,$A11)>0
12	Flo	91.80	=COUNTIF($A$1:$A11,$A12)>0
13	Flo	94.35	=COUNTIF($A$1:$A12,$A13)>0
14	Hank	61.90	=COUNTIF($A$1:$A13,$A14)>0

#61 Replace Nested IFs with a Lookup Table

A long time ago, I worked for the vice president of sales at a company. I was always modeling some new bonus program or commission plan. I became pretty used to commission plans with all sorts of conditions. The one shown in this tip is pretty tame.

The normal approach is to start building a nested IF formula. You always start at either the high end or the low end of the range. "If sales are over $500K, then the discount is 20%; otherwise,…." The third argument of the IF function is a whole new IF function that tests for the second level: "If sales are over $250K, then the discount is 15%; otherwise,…."

These formulas get longer and longer as there are more levels. The toughest part of such a formula is remembering how many closing parentheses to put at the end of the formula.

Bonus Tip: Match the Parentheses

Excel cycles through a variety of colors for each new level of parentheses. While Excel reuses the colors, it uses black only for the opening parenthesis and for the matching closing parenthesis. As you are finishing the formula below, just keep typing closing parentheses until you type a black parenthesis.

	A	B	C	D
1	**Next Year Discount Level Rules**			
2	*Based on last year's revenue:*			
3	*Anyone over $500K: 20% discount*		=IF(B10>500000,20%,	
4	*Anyone over $250K: 15% discount*		IF(B10>250000,15%,	
5	*Anyone over $100K: 10% discount*		IF(B10>100000,10%,	
6	*Anyone over $50K: 5% discount*		IF(B10>50000,5%,	
7	*Anyone over $10K: 1% Discount*		IF(B10>10000,1%,0)))))	
9	Customer	Revenue	Future Discount	
10	SpringBoard	550000	20%	
11	LaFrenier Sons Septic	503500	20%	

Tip: In Microsoft 365, you could use the following formula to solve the discount presented above:
=IFS(B10>500000,20%,B10>250000,15%,B10>100000,10%,B10>50000,5%,B10>10000,1%,TRUE,0)

Back to the Nested Formula Tip

If you're using Excel 2003, your formula is already nearing the limit. With that version, you cannot nest more than 7 IF functions. It was an ugly day when the powers that be changed the commission plan and you needed a way to add an eighth IF function. Today, you can nest 64 IF functions. You should never nest that many, but it is nice to know there is no problem nesting 8 or 9.

Rather than use the nested IF function, try using the VLOOKUP function. When the fourth argument of VLOOKUP changes from False to True, the function is no longer looking for an exact match. Well, first VLOOKUP tries to find an exact match. But if an exact match is not found, Excel settles into the row just less than what you are searching for.

Consider the table below. In cell C13, Excel will be looking for a match for $28,355 in the table. When it can't find 28355, Excel will return the discount associated with the value that is just less—in this case, the 1% discount for the $10K level.

When you convert the rules to the table in E13:F18, you need to start from the smallest level and proceed to the highest level. Although it was unstated in the rules, if someone is below $10,000 in sales, the discount will be 0%. You need to add this as the first row in the table.

	A	B	C	D	E	F
5						
6	=VLOOKUP(B10,$E$13:$F$18,2,TRUE					
7						
8						
9	Customer	Revenue	Future Discount			
10	SpringBoard	550000	20%		Lookup Table	
11	LaFrenier Sons Septic	503500	20%			
12	myexcelonline.com	18699	1%		Sales	Discount
13	California Blazing Chile Farms	28355	1%		0	0%
14	Cambia Factor	4860	0%		10000	1%
15	All Systems Go Consulting	123750	10%		50000	5%
16	Vertex42	201250	10%		100000	10%
17	Mary Maids	255750	15%		250000	15%
18	leanexcelbooks.com	328250	15%		500000	20%
19	MN Excel Consulting	444050	15%			

Caution: When you are using the "True" version of VLOOKUP, your table has to be sorted ascending. Many people believe that all lookup tables have to be sorted. But a table needs to be sorted only for an approximate match.

What if your manager wants a completely self-contained formula and does not want to see the bonus table off to the right? After building the formula, you can embed the table right into the formula. Put the formula in Edit mode by double-clicking the cell or by selecting the cell and pressing F2. Use the cursor to select the entire second argument: $E$13:$F$18.

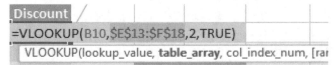

Discount
=VLOOKUP(B10,$E$13:$F$18,2,TRUE)
  VLOOKUP(lookup_value, **table_array**, col_index_num, [rar

4

Press the F9 key. Excel embeds the lookup table as an array constant. In the array constant, a semicolon indicates a new row, and a comma indicates a new column. See "Bonus Tip: Understanding Array Constants" on page 178

> P(B10,{0,0;10000,0.01;50000,0.05;100000,0.1;250000,0.15;500000,0.2},

Press Enter. Copy the formula down to the other cells.

You can now delete the table. The final formula is shown below.

Thanks to Mike Girvin for teaching me about the matching parentheses. The VLOOKUP technique was suggested by Danny Mac, Boriana Petrova, Andreas Thehos, and @mvmcos.

#62 Suppress Errors with IFERROR

Formula errors are common. If you have a data set with hundreds of records, a divide-by-zero and an #N/A errors are bound to pop up now and then.

In the past, preventing errors required Herculean efforts. Nod your head knowingly if you've ever knocked out =IF(ISNA(VLOOKUP(A2,Table,2,0)),"Not Found",VLOOKUP(A2,Table,2,0)). Besides being really long to type, that solution requires twice as many VLOOKUPs. First, you do a VLOOKUP to see if the VLOOKUP is going to produce an error. Then you do the same VLOOKUP again to get the non-error result.

Excel 2010 introduced the greatly improved =IFERROR(Formula,Value If Error). I know that IFERROR sounds like the old ISERROR, ISERR, and ISNA functions, but it is completely different.

This is a brilliant function: =IFERROR(VLOOKUP(A2,Table,2,0),"Not Found"). If you have 1,000 VLOOKUPs and only 5 return #N/A, then the 995 that worked require only a single VLOOKUP. Only the 5 VLOOKUPs returned #N/A that need to move on to the second argument of IFERROR.

Oddly, Excel 2013 added the IFNA() function. It is just like IFERROR but only looks for #N/A errors. One might imagine a strange situation where the value in the lookup table is found, but the resulting answer is a division by 0. If you want to preserve the divide-by-zero error for some reason, you can use IFNA() to do this.

B4	▼	:	×	✓	f_x	=IFNA(VLOOKUP(A4,Table,4,0),"Not Found")		

◢	A	B	C	D	E	F	G
1	Handle	Average					
2	Bluefeather8989	539		Handle	Qty	Revenue	Avg Price
3	MikeAsHimself	582		aBoBoBook	895	521785	583
4	MrExcel	#DIV/0!		Bluefeather8989	989	533071	539
5	ExcelisFun	Not Found		INDZARA	1124	611456	544
6	Bluefeather8989	539		Kazmdav	1019	507462	498
7	McGunigales	527		McGunigales	921	485367	527
8				MikeAsHimself	843	490626	582
9				MrExcel	0	0	#DIV/0!
10				Symons	972	562788	579

Of course, the person who built the lookup table should have used IFERROR to prevent the division by zero in the first place. In the figure below, the "n.m." is a former manager's code for "not meaningful."

	×	✓	*fx*	=IFERROR(F9/E9,"n.m.")	

D	E	F	G
Handle	Qty	Revenue	Avg Price
aBoBoBook	895	521785	583
Bluefeather8989	989	533071	539
INDZARA	1124	611456	544
Kazmdav	1019	507462	498
McGunigales	921	485367	527
MikeAsHimself	843	490626	582
MrExcel	0	0	n.m.
Symons	972	562788	579

Thanks to Justin Fishman, Stephen Gilmer, and Excel by Joe.

#63 Handle Plural Conditions with SUMIFS

Did you notice the "S" that got added to the end of SUMIF starting in Excel 2007? While SUMIF and SUMIFS sound the same, the new SUMIFS can run circles around its elder sibling.

The old SUMIF and COUNTIF have been around since Excel 97. In the figure below, the formula tells Excel to look through the names in B2:B22. If a name is equal to the name in F4, then sum the corresponding cell from the range starting in D2:D22. (While the third argument could be the first cell of the sum range D2, it will make the function volatile, causing the worksheet to calculate more slowly.)

SUMIF and COUNTIF were great with only one condition. But with two or more things to check, you had to switch over to SUMPRODUCT, as shown below. (I realize most people would replace my multiplication signs with commas and add a double-minus before the first two terms, but my version works, too.)

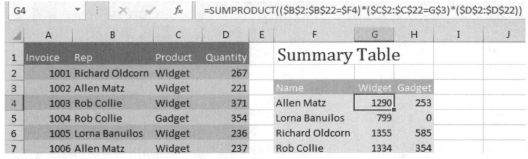

SUMIFS allows for up to 127 conditions. Because you might have an indeterminate number of conditions in the function, the numbers that you are adding up move from the third argument to the first argument.

In the following formula, you are summing D2:D22, but only the rows where column B is Allen Matz and column C is Widget. The logic of "Sum this if these conditions are true" is logical in SUMIFS.

| G4 | | | | f_x | =SUMIFS($D$2:$D$22,$B$2:$B$22,$F4,$C$2:$C$22,G$3) |

	A	B	C	D	E	F	G	H	I
1	Invoice	Rep	Product	Quantity		Summary Table			
2	1001	Richard Oldcorn	Widget	267					
3	1002	Allen Matz	Widget	221		Name	Widget	Gadget	
4	1003	Rob Collie	Widget	371		Allen Matz	1290	253	
5	1004	Rob Collie	Gadget	354		Lorna Banuilos	799	0	
6	1005	Lorna Banuilos	Widget	236		Richard Oldcorn	1355	585	
7	1006	Allen Matz	Widget	237		Rob Collie	1334	354	

Excel 2007 also added plural versions of COUNTIFS and AVERAGEIFS. In February 2017, Microsoft 365 added MAXIFS and MINIFS. All these "S" functions are very efficient and fast.

Thanks to Nathi Njoko, Abshir Osman, Scott Russell, and Ryan Sitoy.

#64 Geography, Exchange Rate & Stock Data Types in Excel

In the past, Excel did not really handle data types. Yes, you could format some cells as Date or Text, but the new data types provide a whole new entry point for new data types now and in the future.

Start with a column of City names. For large cities like Madison Wisconsin, you can just put Madison. For smaller towns, you might enter Madison, FL.

	A	B
1	City	
2	El Paso	
3	Madison	
4	Madison, AL	
5	Madison, FL	
6	Paris, KY	
7	Springfield, MO	
8	Houston	
9		

From the Data tab, select Geography.

Excel searches the Internet and finds a city for each cell. A folded map appears next to each cell. Notice that you lose the state that was in the original cell.

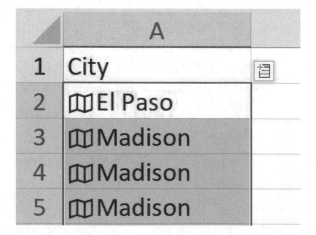

Click on the Map icon and a data card appears with information about the city.

	A	B	C
1	🗺 Springfield	**Springfield**	
2	🗺 Houston	Learn more on Bing	
3			
4		Admin Division 2 (County	
5		🗺 Greene County	
6			
7		Admin Division 1 (State/p	
8		🗺 Missouri	
9			
10		Country/region	
11		🗺 United States	
12		Population • 2018	
13		168,122	

The best part: for any data in the card, you can use a formula to pull that data into a cell. Enter =A2.Population in cell B2 and Excel returns the population of El Paso. Double click the Fill Handle in B2 and Excel returns the population for each city.

	A	B
1	City	Population
2	🗺 El Paso	683,080
3	🗺 Madison	2,853
4	🗺 Madison	47,959
5	🗺 Madison	2,853
6	🗺 Paris	9,840
7	🗺 Springfield	167,319
8	🗺 Houston	2,303,482

Caution: These new formulas might return a #FIELD! error. This means, Excel (or more correctly Bing), does not know the answer to this yet, but it may do so at some time in the future. It is not an error with the formula or the table, just a lack of knowledge currently.

Here is a great tip: Excel uses the context of other cells around the value to try to figure out ambiguous entries. In the following image, because Madison is in the middle of other Wisconsin cities, Excel will automatically choose Madison Wisconsin.

		f_x	=F2.[Admin Division 1 (State/province/other)]	
	D	E	F	G
	Green Bay		🗺 Green Bay	Wisconsin
	Milwaukee		🗺 Milwaukee	Wisconsin
	Madison	→	🗺 Madison	Wisconsin
	Appleton		🗺 Appleton	Wisconsin
	Stevens Point		🗺 Stevens Poi	Wisconsin

4

If you type Madison in a column that has Florida cities, Excel will correctly figure out that you want Madison Florida, even though it is smaller than the capital city of Wisconsin.

Miami		🗺 Miami	Florida	463,347
Orlando		🗺 Orlando	Florida	280,257
Jacksonville		🗺 Jacksonville	Florida	880,619
Madison	➡	🗺 Madison	Florida	2,853
Christmas		🗺 Christmas	Florida	1,146
Daytona Beach		🗺 Daytona Beach	Florida	66,645

If you simply type Madison in a cell without any other values above or below it, Excel won't choose any of the towns named Madison. Instead of a map icon, you will have a circled question mark. The Data Selector pane will appear to allow you to choose which Madison you want.

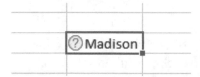

The Geography and Stock data types have extra features if you format as a table using Ctrl+T.

A new Add Data icon appears to the right of the heading. Use this drop-down menu to add fields without having to type the formulas. Clicking the icon will enter the formula for you.

	A	B	C
1	**City** ▾	**Population** ▾	
2	🗺 El Paso	683,080	
3	🗺 Madison	2,853	
4	🗺 Madison	47,959	

You can also sort the data by any field, even if it is not in the Excel grid. Open the drop-down menu for the City column. Use the new Display Field drop-down to choose Longitude.

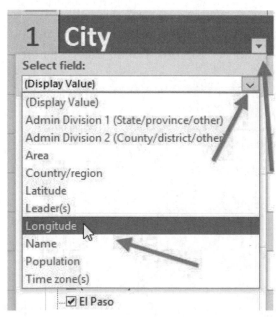

With Longitude selected, choose sort Smallest to Largest.

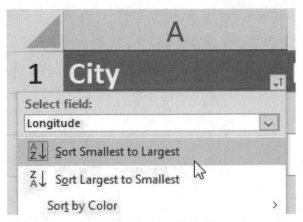

The result: data is sorted west to east.

	A	B	C	D
1	City	Population	Admin Di	Admin Division 2 (Ce
2	🗺 El Paso	683,080	Texas	El Paso County
3	🗺 Houston	2,303,482	Texas	Harris County
4	🗺 Springfield	167,319	Missouri	Greene County
5	🗺 Madison	252,551	Wisconsin	Dane County
6	🗺 Madison	47,959	Alabama	Madison County
7	🗺 Paris	9,840	Kentucky	Bourbon County
8	🗺 Madison	2,853	Florida	Madison County

Support for exchange rates appeared in early 2019. While it initially was accessed by using the Stocks icon, it now has it's own Currency icon in the gallery. Enter currency pairs such as USD-CAD for U.S. Dollar to Canadian Dollar. Use the Price field for the current exchange rate.

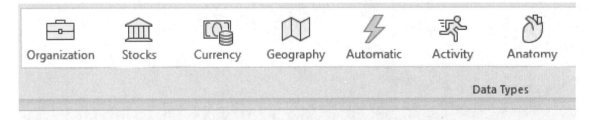

	Y	Z	AA	AB	AC	AD
			Currency	Price	52-Week Low	52-Week High
	USD-CAD		🏛 USD/CAD	$ 1.33	$ 1.30	$ 1.37
	CAD-USD		🏛 CAD/USD	$ 0.75	$ 0.73	$ 0.77
	USD-EUR		🏛 USD/EUR	$ 0.91	$ 0.86	$ 0.92
	EUR-USD		🏛 EUR/USD	$ 1.10	$ 1.09	$ 1.16
	USD-GBP	➡	🏛 USD/GBP	$ 0.78	$ 0.75	$ 0.84
	GBP-USD		🏛 GBP/USD	$ 1.29	$ 1.20	$ 1.34
	USD-AUD		🏛 USD/AUD	$ 1.47	$ 1.35	$ 1.50
	AUD-USD		🏛 AUD/USD	$ 0.68	$ 0.67	$ 0.74
	USD-BTC		🏛 USD/BTC	$ 0.0001398	$ 0.00	$ 0.00
	BTC-USD		🏛 BTC/USD	$ 7,133.76	$ 3,122.67	$ 13,895.10

4

Bonus Tip: Use Data, Refresh All to Update Stock Data

The other data type available is Stock data. Enter some publicly held companies:

	A
1	Company
2	Microsoft
3	Netflix
4	Southwest Airlines
5	Coca Cola

Choose, Data, Stocks. An icon of a building with Roman columns should appear next to each company You can add fields such as CEO, Price, Volume, High, Low, Previous Close.

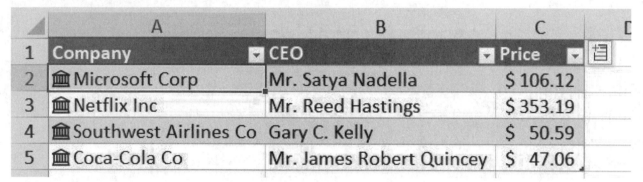

	A	B	C
1	Company	CEO	Price
2	🏛 Microsoft Corp	Mr. Satya Nadella	$ 106.12
3	🏛 Netflix Inc	Mr. Reed Hastings	$ 353.19
4	🏛 Southwest Airlines Co	Gary C. Kelly	$ 50.59
5	🏛 Coca-Cola Co	Mr. James Robert Quincey	$ 47.06

In contrast to Geography, where population might only be updated once a year, the stock price will be constantly changing throughout the trading day. Rather than go out to the Internet with every recalc, Excel will only updated the data from these Linked Data Types when you choose Refresh.

One easy way to update the stock prices is to use the Refresh All icon on the Data tab.

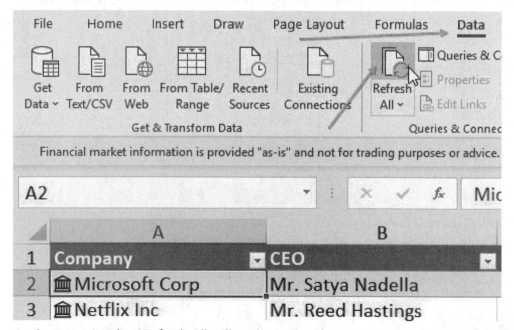

As the name implies, Refresh All will update everything in your workbook, including any Power Query data connections which might take a long time to update. If you want to only refresh the current block of linked data, right-click on A2, choose Data Types, Refresh.

The Stock data type only delivers the current day's stock price. For stock history, see the STOCKHISTORY function, discussed next.

#65 Get Historical Stock History from STOCKHISTORY

In June 2020, Microsoft 365 added the new STOCKHISTORY function. It will pull historical stock data after the market has closed. The syntax is as follows:

=STOCKHISTORY(stock,start_date,end_date,interval,headers,properties1,...)

For the stock, use any ticker symbol. The start date can be a cell containing a date or text such as "1-1-2021". The end date is assumed to be today, or you can enter another date. For the interval, use 0 for daily, 1 for weekly, 2 for monthly. The headers argument can be 0 for no headers, 1 for a single row of headers or 2 for the stock name and then headers. Properties1 through Properties6 specify which fields and the order they should appear: 0 is Date, 1 is Close, 2 is Open, 3 is High, 4 is Low, 5 is Volume. You can specify from 1 to 6 properties in any order.   …

=STOCKHISTORY(B1,"1-11-2021",TODAY(),0,2,0,1,5)				

B	C	D	E	F
GME				
XNYS:GME				
Date	Close	Volume		
1/11/2021	$ 19.94	14,927,612		
1/12/2021	$ 19.95	7,060,665		
1/13/2021	$ 31.40	143,595,555		
1/14/2021	$ 39.91	93,717,410		
1/15/2021	$ 35.50	46,866,358		
1/19/2021	$ 39.36	74,721,924		
1/20/2021	$ 39.12	33,471,789		
1/21/2021	$ 43.03	57,079,754		
1/22/2021	$ 65.01	197,157,946		
1/25/2021	$ 76.79	177,874,000		
1/26/2021	$147.98	178,587,974		
1/27/2021	$347.51	93,396,666		
1/28/2021	$193.60	58,815,805		
1/29/2021	$325.00	50,566,055		
2/1/2021	$225.00	37,382,152		
2/2/2021	$ 90.00	78,183,071		

Note that the stock data is updated once a day, a few hours after the market closes.

4

#66 More Data Types from Wolfram Alpha

During 2020, Microsoft licensed more data from the Wolfram Alpha database. There are now data types for Activity, Anatomy, Animal, Chemistry, City, Food, Location, Medical, Movie, Music, Nature, People, Plant, Space, University, and Yoga.

Data types now support arrays. The card view becomes an important way to browse the data available.

In the figure below, convert banana to a food data type. Click the icon to the left of Banana to open the data card. As you browse through the card, if you find something that you want to add to the grid, click the Extract to Grid icon.

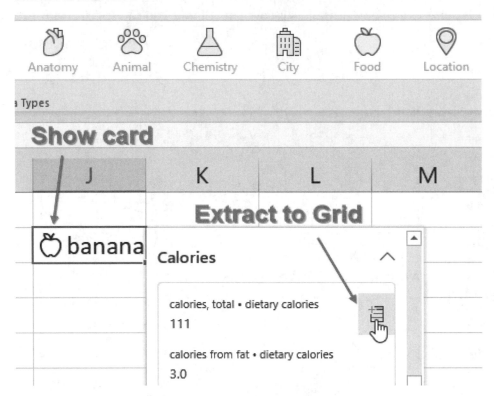

Bonus Tip: The Data Card is now Expandable and Supports Arrays

When data types first debuted, I was not a fan of the tiny Data Card that would appear. In 2020, the Excel team improved the data card. First, you can use a handle in the lower right to make the card wider. Second, you can use the card to explore and jump to other data types. Third, the data card now supports arrays.

Let's start in Springfield Missouri. Type Springfield MO in a cell and declare it as a Location. (Location is the new Wolfram Alpha data type and has more information than the old Geography field.)

Scroll down to Notable People. Initially, you can see Kathleen Turner, Lucas Grabeel, and someone who's name starts with Payn.... To the left of that list, there is an Array icon.

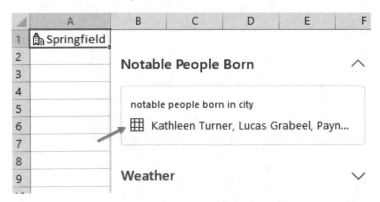

Click the Array icon and the card changes to show you all the notable people born in Springfield MO.

Each of those people have an icon. Click the icon to the left of Kathleen Turner. Go to her Notable Works. Click on the Movie icon for the War of the Roses. Click on Cast. Click on Danny DeVito. Click on Notable Works. Choose One Flew Over the Cuckoo's Nest. Choose Cast. Choose Scatman Carruthers. Choose Place of Death. Choose Los Angeles. Choose Notable People Born. Choose Marilyn Monroe. Choose Notable Works. Choose There's No Business Like Show Business. Choose Cast. Finally, choose to add this to the grid.

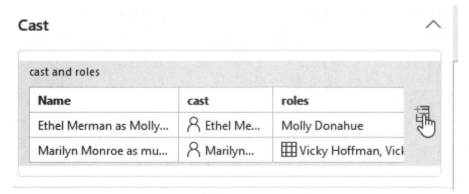

Excel MVP David Benaim calls the card the "Excel Encyclopedia". After adding it to the grid, Excel remembers the entire chain that got you from Springfield MO to Ethel Merman. The formula for the results is `=INDEX(INDEX(INDEX(INDEX(INDEX(INDEX(INDEX(A1.[notable people born in city],1,1).[notable film appearances],7,1).[cast and roles],3,1). cast.[notable film appearances],1,1).[cast and roles],4,1).cast.[place of death].[notable people born in city],4,1).[notable film appearances],13,1).[cast and roles]`.

#67 Getting Historical Weather For a City

The new Wolfram Alpha data type for Location includes Weather History. It takes several clicks to drill down to the weather data and even more manipulation to change from metric to Fahrenheit.

1. Start with a city name in A1. In my example, I am using Columbus, Indiana.

2. Convert that to a Location data type by using the Data Types gallery on the Data tab.

3. Click the icon to the left of the city. Scroll down to the Weather section. Click the icon for "Weather for Columbus".

4. In the next panel, the only option is another weather icon called "Weather History for Columbus". Click the icon.

4

5. You now have three tables offering daily, weekly, or monthly weather history. Choose a table and click the Extract icon to the right of the table.

6. Say that you had chosen monthly weather history. You now have 12 cells that say "January weather (monthly)." Each cell has an icon to the left of the word.

7. Click the icon for January and you will have choices for average temperature, average high, average low, record high, record low, and average precipitation.

8. Choose to add Mean Maximimum Temperature to the grid. You will get one cell with the average high temperature for January in Celsius.

C1	▼	⋮	✕ ✓ *fx*	=B1.[mean maximum temperature]	

◢	A	B	C
1	🏢 Columbus	◈ January weather (monthly)	15.22
2		◈ February weather (monthly)	
3		◈ March weather (monthly)	

9. Edit the formula in C1. Wrap it in =CONVERT(<formula>,"C","F") to convert from Celsius to Fahrenheit.

10. While editing the formula in C1, type a Hash (#) character after B1. This tells Excel to return the answers for the entire array starting in B1.

⋮	✕ ✓ *fx*	=CONVERT(B1#.[mean maximum temperature],"C","F")

B	↗	C
◈ January weather (monthly)		59.4
◈ February weather (monthly)		58.6
◈ March weather (monthly)		70.3
◈ April weather (monthly)		81.5
◈ May weather (monthly)		86.7
◈ June weather (monthly)		91.0
◈ July weather (monthly)		91.5
◈ August weather (monthly)		91.1
◈ September weather (monthly)		90.1
◈ October weather (monthly)		83.0
◈ November weather (monthly)		68.9
◈ December weather (monthly)		62.4

In the download files for this book, I have an example returning daily precipitation in inches for a city. The data type returns the dates as text, so a formula of =DATEVALUE(B2#.day&", 2020") is needed to create a date that can be charted. The data type is returning rainfall in centimeters, so a formula of =CONVERT(B2#.[mean precipitation],"cm","in").

The following chart shows average daily rainfall for Quibdo, Colombia, often cited as the rainiest city on Earth.

If you type Las Vegas, NV in cell A2 and wait for 30 seconds, the data and chart will update and show rainfail for the driest city in the United States.

Caution: The formulas will briefly show as #FIELD! as Excel tries to resolve Las Vegas as a location and then everything will show as #BUSY! while the new data is downloaded from the Internet.

#68 Create Your Own Data Types Using Power Query

Data types sound great, but wouldn't you like to have your own company data as a data type? Imagine if you had your company product list in a data type. You could store the SKU in a column and then extract item information using XLOOKUP or dot formulas such as =A2.Country.

In late 2020, Microsoft added the first custom data types to Microsoft 365. This feature will certainly be evolving over the course of 2021, but here is where it stands in February of 2021.

First - find a table of information that you want to appear in a data type. Create a workbook with a single worksheet. Store the table starting in cell A1. Declare it to be a table with Ctrl+T and change the name from Table1 to something meaningful. In this example, I have a list of all my friends who make Excel videos on YouTube. I've named the table YTChannels.

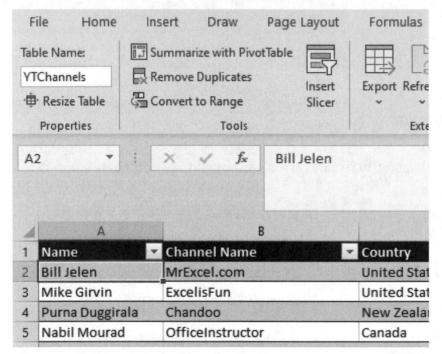

From any workbook, go to Data, Get Data, From File, From Workbook. Browse to the workbook created above.

In the Navigator that appears, they offer a list of tables and a list of worksheets. Choose your table. In the lower right, click Transform Data.

In the Power Query Editor, the first column will be selected. Shift-click on the last column heading in order to select all of your data.

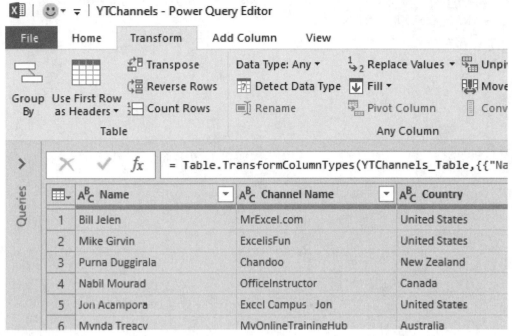

In the Power Query ribbon, choose the Transform tab. The right-most icon is Create Data Type.

In the Create Data Type dialog, give a good name to the Data Type. Choose which column should be displayed in Excel as the default column.

4

In Power Query, all of your data excel for the first column will appear to disappear. But notice the Data Type icon to the left of the heading. That means the data type was successfully created.

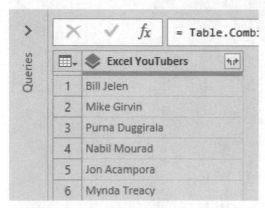

In Power Query, click Home, Close & Load. The data will load to a single column in Excel.

Click on any icon in column A to display the card for that person.

	A	B	C	D	E
1	Excel YouTubers ▼				
2	◈ Bill Jelen				
3	◈ Mike Girvin				
4	◈ Purna Duggirala				
5	◈ Nabil Mourad				
6	◈ Jon Acampora				
7	◈ Mynda Treacy				
8	◈ Alan Murray				
9	◈ Ajay Anand				
10	◈ Oz du Soleil				
11	◈ Frédéric LE GUEN				
12	◈ Abiola David				
13	◈ Faraz Shaikh				
14	◈ David Benaim				
15	◈ Jordan Goldmeier				
16	◈ Paula Guilfoyle				
17	◈ Wyn Hopkins				
18	◈ Sumit Bansal				
19	◈ John Michaloudis				
20	◈ Leila Gharani				
21	◈ Cristiano Galvão				
22	◈ John MacDougall				
23	◈ Randy Austin				

Mike Girvin

Name
Mike Girvin

Channel Name
ExcelisFun

Country
United States

Channel URL
https://www.youtube.com/user/ExcelIsF
un

Date Joined
2/15/2008

Top Video
Excel for Accounting: Formulas,
VLOOKUP & INDEX, PivotTables,
Recorded Macros, Charts, Keyboards

Use the Add Field icon to extract information from the data type to the grid.

You can extract any columns that you need from the Data Type.

You can also use data stored in the data type without extracting it to the grid. Here the SORTBY uses the Lifetime Videos field to sort descending.

4

Below, a Data Validation list uses the range containing the Data Types. You can extract information from the selected item.

G3	▼	:	✕	✓	*fx*	Oz du Soleil			

	G	H	I	J	K
2	Using Data Validation				
3	◈ Oz du Soleil				
4					
5	Excel on Fire	=G3.[Channel Name]			
6	12/14/2010	=G3.[Date Joined]			
7	Excel 2013: Slicers & Tables	=G3.[Top Video]			
8	https://www.youtube.com/c/OzduSoleilDATA	=HYPERLINK(G3.[Channel URL])			
9					
10					

Caution: Hyperlinks stored in data types do not automatically show up as live links. For custom data types created from Power Query, wrap them in the =HYPERLINK() function as shown in row 8 above. For built-in data types, add .link to the end of the formula.

Below, you can use XLOOKUP to retrieve the channel name from a plain text name.

fx	=XLOOKUP(N5, YTChannels[Excel YouTubers].Name, YTChannels[Excel YouTubers].[Channel Name])

	N	P	Q	R
	Using XLOOKUP			
	Name	Channel Name		
	Bill Jelen	MrExcel.com		
	John MacDougall	How to Excel		
	Ajay Anand	Ajay Anand		
	Nabil Mourad	OfficeInstructor		
	David Benaim	David Benaim		

This example is one that I hope gets improved in 2021. If I have a range of names elsewhere in my data, it would be great to select those names and use the Data Type gallery to convert the names to data types. Instead, for now, you have to use this XLOOKUP to add a column with data types.

fx	=XLOOKUP(N5, YTChannels[Excel YouTubers].Name, YTChannels[Excel YouTubers])

	N	O
	Converting Plain Text to Data Type	
	Name	Data Type
	Bill Jelen	◈ Bill Jelen
	John MacDougall	◈ John MacDougall
	Ajay Anand	◈ Ajay Anand
	Nabil Mourad	◈ Nabil Mourad
	David Benaim	◈ David Benaim

Some notes:

- Excel MVP Alan Murray (ComputerGaga on YouTube) provided the idea of storing the source data in a separate workbook. You could also store it inside your report workbook, but then the data is being stored twice.

- If you add new data to the first workbook, you can update the data in the second workbook using Data, Refresh All.

- Excel MVP John MacDougall pointed out that the column with data types can be uploaded to Excel Online and it continues to work, even though Excel Online does not yet support Power Query.

- If you need to widely distribute your workbook and you don't want people without access to the original list trying to refresh, you can break the link to the query. Show the Queries & Connections panel using Data, Queries & Connections. Right-click the query and choose Delete. The data types will remain. But they can't be refreshed, so do this on a copy of the workbook.

- Real data types support images and arrays. These custom data types from Power Query do not yet support that.

  Tip: Download the workbook for this chapter and check out the YouTube channels from the people in this list.

Thanks to Excel MVP John MacDougall for the idea of using Excel YouTubers as a custom data type.

#69 IF Based on Installed Language in a Bilingual Worksheet

If you have a workbook that is used in a bilingual company, how will you know if the person using the workbook has English or Portuguese installed? =LEFT(TRUE) will return T for English or V for Portuguese. You can use =IF(LEFT(True)="T","Welcome to the Budget","Bem-vindo ao Orçamento").

Thanks to Cristiano Galvão from the Excel Turbo channel on YouTube for this technique.

#70 Dynamic Arrays Can Spill

Introduced in 2019, the new Dynamic Arrays represent a major change to the Excel calculation engine. While the old Ctrl+Shift+Enter array formulas could return several results into a pre-selected range, these new formulas do not require Ctrl+Shift+Enter and you don't have to pre-select the range.

For example, let's say you type =B2:B8*C1 into cell C2. In the past, this formula would have required dollar signs around $C$1. You would copy the formula to all 7 cells and something called implicit intersection would make sure the numbers were correct.

▲	A	B	C	D
1	Product	Amount	10%	
2	Apple	5460	=B2:B8*C1	
3	Banana	4370		
4	Cherry	1520		
5	Date	1410		
6	Elderberry	5470		
7	Fig	1620		
8	Guava	2330		
9				

4

But now, with Dynamic Arrays, one formula in cell C2 will spill over and return results into many cells.

C2		fx	=B2:B8*C1

	A	B	C	D
1	Product	Amount	10%	
2	Apple	2060	206	
3	Banana	1530	153	
4	Cherry	2560	256	
5	Date	2760	276	
6	Elderberry	4450	445	
7	Fig	4790	479	
8	Guava	3940	394	
9				

When you select any cell from C2:C8, a blue outline appears around the cells to let you know that the values are the result of a single formula. That single formula only exists in C2. If you select any other cell in the range, the formula appears in the formula bar, but it is greyed out.

If the range B2:B8 grows (by someone inserting rows in the middle), the spilled results will grow as well. However, simply typing new values in A9:B9 will not cause the formula to extend, unless you format the whole range with Ctrl+T before adding values.

	fx	=B2:B8*C1

B	C	D
Amount	10%	
2060	206	
1530	153	
2560	256	

What if a formula can not spill? What if there are non-empty cells in the way? Rather than return partial results, the formula will return the new #SPILL! error.

B	C	
Amount	10%	
1 0	#SPILL!	
2420		
2060	stuff	
4030	in	
4740	the	
1490	way	

Open the yellow dropdown to the left of the error and you can select the obstructing cells.

B	C	D
nount	10%	
1 ! ▾	#SPILL!	
2	Spill range isn't blank	
2	Help on this Error	
4	Select Obstructing Cells	
4	Show Calculation Steps...	
1	Ignore Error	
3	Edit in Formula Bar	
	Error Checking Options...	

Once you clear the obstructing cells, the answers will appear again.

#71 Sorting with a Formula

Sorting data in Excel is easy. Unless, you are building a dashboard for your manager's manager. You can't ask that person to select C3, go to the Data tab and click the AZ button every time they want an updated report. The new SORT and SORTBY functions allow you to easily sort with a formula.

You can pass three arguments to the SORT function. The first is the range to be sorted. Leave the headings out of this argument. Next, which column do you want to sort by. If your data is in B:D and you want to sort by column D, you would specify column 3 as the sort column. The third argument is a 1 for ascending or -1 for descending.

In this figure, the data is sorted by Amount descending:

| F3 | | : | × | ✓ | f_x | =SORT(B3:D9,3,-1) | | |

◢	A	B	C	D	E	F	G	H
1		**Sort by Amount (column 3), descending (-1)**						
2		Product	Team	Amount				
3		Apple	Red	1220		Elderberry	Red	4740
4		Banana	Blue	2420		Lime	Blue	4030
5		Cherry	Red	2060		Guava	Red	3890
6		Elderberry	Red	4740		Banana	Blue	2420
7		Fig	Blue	1490		Cherry	Red	2060
8		Guava	Red	3890		Fig	Blue	1490
9		Lime	Blue	4030		Apple	Red	1220

What if you want to do a two-level sort? You can specify an array constant for both the second and third argument. In this case, the data is sorted by Team ascending and Amount descending. For the sort column, specify {2;3}. For the sort order, specify {1;-1}.

| F3 | | : | × | ✓ | f_x | =SORT(B3:D9,{2;3},{1;-1}) | | |

◢	A	B	C	D	E	F	G	H
1		**Sort by Team ascending and Amount descending**						
2		Product	Team	Amount				
3		Apple	Red	1220		Lime	Blue	4030
4		Banana	Blue	2420		Banana	Blue	2420
5		Cherry	Red	2060		Fig	Blue	1490
6		Elderberry	Red	4740		Elderberry	Red	4740
7		Fig	Blue	1490		Guava	Red	3890
8		Guava	Red	3890		Cherry	Red	2060
9		Lime	Blue	4030		Apple	Red	1220

4

The Excel Calc team also gave you the SORTBY function. Say you want to return a list of products but not the associated amounts. You want the products to be sorted by the amount. The formula below says to return the products from B3:B9 sorted descending by the amounts in D3:D9.

F3			✕	✓	fx	=SORTBY(B3:B9,D3:D9,-1)

▲	A	B	C	D	E	F	G	H
1	**Sort products by amount, but only show products**							
2		Product	Team	Amount				
3		Apple	Red	1220		Elderberry		
4		Banana	Blue	2420		Lime		
5		Cherry	Red	2060		Guava		
6		Elderberry	Red	4740		Banana		
7		Fig	Blue	1490		Cherry		
8		Guava	Red	3890		Fig		
9		Lime	Blue	4030		Apple		

#72 Filter with a Formula

The FILTER function is new as part of the dynamic arrays feature. There are three arguments: array, include, and an optional [if empty].

```
=filter(
    FILTER(array, include, [if_empty])
```

Say you want to be able to enter a team name in G1 and extract all of the records for that team. Use a formula of =FILTER(B3:E9,C3:C9=G1).

G3			✕	✓	fx	=FILTER(B3:E9,C3:C9=G1)

▲	A	B	C	D	E	F	G	H	I	J
1		**Filter to Red Team**					Red			
2		Product	Team	Status	Amount					
3		Apple	Red	O	1220		Apple	Red	O	1220
4		Banana	Blue	C	2420		Cherry	Red	C	2060
5		Cherry	Red	C	2060		Elderberry	Red	O	4740
6		Date	Blue	O	4030		Guava	Red	C	3890
7		Elderberry	Red	O	4740					
8		Fig	Blue	C	1490					
9		Guava	Red	C	3890					
10										

If cell G1 changes from Red to Blue, the results change to show you the blue team records.

F	G	H	I	J
	Blue			
	Banana	Blue	C	2420
	Date	Blue	O	4030
	Fig	Blue	C	1490

In the above examples, the optional [If Empty] argument is missing. If someone is allowed to enter the wrong team name in G1, then you will get a #CALC! error.

=FILTER(B3:E9,C3:C9=G1)

	E	F	G	H	I
			Yellow		
	Amount				
	1220	!	#CALC!		
	2420		Empty Array		
	3060		Help on this Error		

To avoid the #CALC! error, add a third argument.

=FILTER(B3:E9,C3:C9=G1,"None Found")

	E	F	G	H	I
			Yellow		
	Amount				
	1220		None Found		
	2420				

You can specify an array constant for the third argument if you want to fill each column of the answer array.

=FILTER(B3:E9,C3:C9=G1,{"No","Team","O",0})

	E	F	G	H	I	J
			Green			
	Amount		Product		Team	Statu Amount
	1220		No		Team	O	0
	2420					

4

To filter to records where multiple conditions are met, multiply the conditions together.

| G3 | | | × ✓ fx | =FILTER(B3:E9,(C3:C9=G1)*(D3:D9="O"),"None |

	A	B	C	D	E	F	G	H	I	J
1	**Filter to Red Team & Status=O**						Red			
2		Product	Team	Status	Amount					
3		Apple	Red	O	1220		Apple	Red	O	122(
4		Banana	Blue	C	2420		Elderberry	Red	O	474(
5		Cherry	Red	C	2060					
6		Date	Blue	O	4030					
7		Elderberry	Red	O	4740					
8		Fig	Blue	C	1490					
9		Guava	Red	C	3890					

Bonus Tip: Understanding Array Constants

You've just seen a few examples that included an array constant. Here is a simple way to understand them. A comma inside an array constant means to move to the next column. A semi-colon means to move to the next row. How do you remember which is which? The semi-colon on your keyboard is located near the Enter or Return key which also goes to the next row.

| A4 | | | × ✓ fx | ={1;2 |

	A	B	C
1	Separators in an Array Co		
2			
3	Semi-colons (located near Ente		
4	1		
5	2		

When you see an array constant with a mix of commas and semi-colons, remember that each semi-colon moves to a new row.

| ✓ fx | ={1,2,3;4,5,6} |

	G	H	I	J
	Separators in an Array Constant			
	Columns and rows:			
	1	2	3	
	4	5	6	

#73 Formula for Unique or Distinct

The UNIQUE function will provide either a list of unique or distinct values.

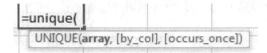

If you ask me for the list of unique values from this list: Apple, Apple, Banana, Cherry, Cherry, I would tell you that the list of unique values is Apple, Banana, Cherry. If you ask 100 accountants, about 92 of them would agree with me. But there is a segment of the population who disagrees and says that the only unique thing in the list is Banana because it is the only item that appears once.

This unusual definition of "unique" comes from the SQL Server world, where database pros would say that "Apple, Banana, Cherry" is a list of distinct values and Banana is the only unique value.

The new UNIQUE function will return either list. If you simply ask for =UNIQUE(R5:R9), you get my definition of all values that occur one or more times. But, if you are a database pro or Casey Kasem, then you can put a True as the third argument.

	R	S	T	U	V	W
3	**Unique or Distinct?**					
4						
5	Apple		Apple		Banana	
6	Apple		Banana			
7	Banana		Cherry			
8	Cherry					
9	Cherry					
10			=UNIQUE(R5:R9)			
11					=UNIQUE(R5:R9,,TRUE)	

Here is a list of all the Billboard Top 10 Hits from 1979 - 1993.

	A	B	C	D
1	**Top 10 Hits 1979-1993**			
3	ID	Artist	Track	Genre
4	1979_001	Knack, The	My Sharona	Rock
5	1979_002	Donna Summer	Bad Girls	Rock
6	1979_003	Rod Stewart	Do Ya Think I'm Sexy?	Rock
7	1979_004	Peaches & Herb	Reunited	Rock

To get a list of genres, use =UNIQUE()

=UNIQUE(D4:D6132)

E	F	G
	List of all Genres	
	Rock	
	Easy	
	Vocal	
	Pop	

4

Bonus Tip: Use # "The Spiller" to Refer to All Array Results

In the previous screenshot, the UNIQUE function is in cell F5. You never really know how many results that formula will return. To refer to "the entire array returned by the formula in F5", you would write F5#. There is no official name for this notation, so I am using an idiom coined by Excel MVP Ingeborg Hawighorst: The Spiller.

#74 Other Functions Can Now Accept Arrays as Arguments

Once you see the list of genres, you might want to know how frequently each genre appears. That would normally require a series of COUNTIF or COUNTIFS formulas. For example, =COUNTIF(D$4:D$6132,"Rock") would count how many songs were in the Rock genre. But rather than entering a bunch of COUNTIF functions, you could enter a single COUNTIF function and pass an array as the second argument. The formula below uses The Spiller syntax to ask Excel to repeat the COUNTIF for each answer in the UNIQUE function in F5.

	=COUNTIF(D4:D6132,F5#)	
E	F	G
	List of all Genres	
	Rock	4608
	Easy	18
	Vocal	69
	Pop	25

#75 One Hit Wonders with UNIQUE

For me, I can't imagine why I would ever need a list of items that have been sold exactly once. My only example is the One-Hit Wonders segment on Casey Kasem's American Top 40 radio show.

To get a list of artists who had exactly one hit, use =UNIQUE(B4:B6132..True). In the figure below, the UNIQUE function is wrapped in a SORT function so the resulting list is alphabetical.

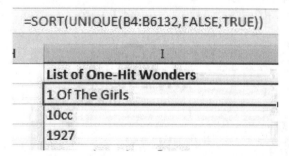

=SORT(UNIQUE(B4:B6132,FALSE,TRUE))

I
List of One-Hit Wonders
1 Of The Girls
10cc
1927

To get the titles in column J, a VLOOKUP uses an array as the first argument. This is pretty wild - one VLOOKUP formula is actually doing over 1000 lookups and returning all 1000 results.

fx	=VLOOKUP(I5#,B4:C6132,2,FALSE)	
	I	J
	List of One-Hit Wonders	Title
	Peaches & Herb	Reunited
	M	Pop Muzik

Another approach is to use a FILTER function combined with IFERROR and MATCH.

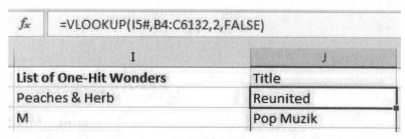

=FILTER(A4:D6132,
IFERROR(MATCH(B4:B6132,
UNIQUE(B4:B6132,FALSE,TRUE),0),FALSE))

L	M	N	O	P
	1979_004	Peaches & Herb	Reunited	Rock

#76 SEQUENCE inside of other Functions such as IPMT

After SORT, SORTBY, FILTER, and UNIQUE, the SEQUENCE and RANDARRAY functions seem pretty tame. SEQUENCE will generate a sequence of numbers.

	A	B	C	D
1	=SEQUENCE(			
2	SEQUENCE(**rows**, [columns], [start], [step])			

It does not seem like this is very interesting. Who needs to generate a list of numbers?

	A	B	C	D
1	=SEQUENCE(5)		=SEQUENCE(5,2,3,9)	
2				
3	1		3	12
4	2		21	30
5	3		39	48
6	4		57	66
7	5		75	84

Try putting SEQUENCE inside other functions. Here, IPMT calculates the interest in the 7th month of a loan:

	G	H	I
1	How much interest will be paid		
2	during month 7 of this loan?		
3	Principal	250000	
4	Term	60	
5	Rate	5%	
6			
7	($948.80)	=IPMT(H5/12,7,H4,H3)	

Thanks to SEQUENCE, this formula calculates the interest paid during 12 months starting in month 7:

	G	H	I	J	K	L
1	How much interest will be paid					
2	during months 7-18 of this loan?					
3	Principal	250000				
4	Term	60				
5	Rate	5%				
7	($10,334.60)	=SUM(IPMT(H5/12,SEQUENCE(12,1,7),H4,H3))				
8						
9		**12 numbers starting with 7**				

Two formulas create a forward-looking calendar:

	A	B	C	D	E	F	G
1	**Tue**	**Wed**	**Thu**	**Fri**	**Sat**	**Sun**	**Mon**
2	Jan-29	Jan-30	Jan-31	Feb-1	Feb-2	Feb-3	Feb-4
3	Feb-5	Feb-6	Feb-7	Feb-8	Feb-9	Feb-10	Feb-11
4	Feb-12	Feb-13	Feb-14	Feb-15	Feb-16	Feb-17	Feb-18
5	Feb-19	Feb-20	Feb-21	Feb-22	Feb-23	Feb-24	Feb-25
6	Feb-26	Feb-27	Feb-28	Mar-1	Mar-2	Mar-3	Mar-4
7	A1: =TEXT(A2:G2,"DDD") B1: =SEQUENCE(5,7,TODAY())						

=SEQUENCE(52,1,TODAY(),-7) would produce a list of the past 52 weeks.

#77 Replace a Pivot Table with 3 Dynamic Arrays

As the co-author of *Pivot Table Data Crunching*, I love a good pivot table. But Excel Project Manager Joe McDaid and Excel MVP Roger Govier both pointed out that the three formulas shown here simulate a pivot table and do not have to be refreshed.

To build the report, **=SORT(UNIQUE(C2:C392))** provides a vertical list of customers starting in **F6**. Then, **=TRANSPOSE(SORT(UNIQUE(A2:A392)))** provides a horizontal list of products starting in **G5**.

When you specify **F6#** and **G5#** in arguments of **SUMIFS**, Excel returns a two-dimensional result: **=SUMIFS(D2:D392,C2:C392,F6#,A2:A392,G5#)**.

G6				*fx*	=SUMIFS(D2:D392,C2:C392,F6#,A2:A392,G5#)				

	A	B	C	D	E	F	G	H	I
1	Product	Date	Customer	Revenue	F6:	=SORT(UNIQUE(C2:C392))			
2	DEF	2/8/2017	ABC Stores	20610	G5:	=TRANSPOSE(SORT(UNIQUE(A2:A392)))			
3	DEF	2/23/2017	ABC Stores	8116	G6:	=SUMIFS(D2:D392,C2:C392,F6#,A2:A392,G5#)			
4	DEF	8/16/2017	ABC Stores	7032					
5	DEF	5/2/2018	ABC Stores	18290			ABC	DEF	XYZ
6	XYZ	1/6/2017	AT&T	2401		ABC Stores	0	54,048	0
7	XYZ	3/2/2017	AT&T	6765		AT&T	0	271,339	227,598
8	DEF	3/9/2017	AT&T	21357		BankUnited	406,326	0	0

Bonus Tip: Replace Ctrl+Shift+Enter with Dynamic Arrays.

Before dynamic arrays, people would use these crazy Ctrl+Shift+Enter formulas.

Say that you have a friend who is superstitious about Friday the 13th. You want to illustrate how many Friday the 13ths your friend has lived through. Before Dynamic Arrays, you would have to use the formula below.

	A	B	C	D	E
1	Birth Date	2/17/1965			
2	Today	6/12/2018			
3					
4	Number of Friday the 13th's				
5	that you've survived:				
6		91			
7					
8		=SUMPRODUCT(			
9		--(DAY(ROW(INDIRECT(B1&":"&B2)))=13),			
10		--(WEEKDAY(ROW(INDIRECT(B1&":"&B2)),2)=5))			
11					

The same formula after dynamic arrays is still complicated, but less intimidating:

B5				*fx*	=SUMPRODUCT(
					(DAY(SEQUENCE(B4,,B3))=13)*
					(WEEKDAY(SEQUENCE(B4,,B3),2)=5))

	A	B	C	D	E	F	G
1	Start	2/17/1965					
2	End	6/12/2018					
3	Start as a number	23790					
4	# of Days	19474	=B2-B1+1				
5	# Friday the 13ths	91					
6							

Another example from Mike Girvin's Ctrl+Shift+Enter book is to get a unique list.

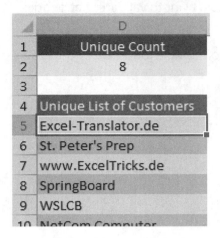

Here is the formula. I won't try to explain it to you.

```
{=IF(ROWS(D$5:D5)>$D$2,"",
INDEX($B$2:$B$146,
SMALL(IF(FREQUENCY(IF($B$2:$B$146<>"",
MATCH($B$2:$B$146,$B$2:$B$146,0)),
ROW($B$2:$B$146)-1),
ROW($B$2:$B$146)-1),
ROWS(D$5:D5)))))}
```

The replacement formula with dynamic arrays is =UNIQUE(B2:B146).

#78 Dependent Validation using Dynamic Arrays

The Data Validation feature lets you choose from a dropdown list in Excel. It works great until someone wants to have two lists. The items in the second list are dependent on what is chosen in the first list. This is called dependent validation.

In the figure below, the items for the first dropdown list appear in **D4#**, thanks to **=SORT(UNIQUE(B4:B23))**. The validation in **H3** points to **=D4#**. The list for the second validation appears in **E4#** because of the formula **=SORT(FILTER(A4:A23,B4:B23=H3,"Choose Class First"))**. The validation in **H5** uses **=E4#**.

	A	B	C	D	E	F	G	H	I	J
1	Product Database									Data Validation
2										
3	**Product**	**Classification**		**Classification**	Product		Class	Tree Fruit		Settings / Input
4	Apple	Tree Fruit		Berry	Apple					Validation criteria
5	Banana	Berry		Citrus	Cherry		Product			Allow: List
6	Cherry	Tree Fruit		Melon	Date			Apple		
7	Date	Tree Fruit		Tree Fruit	Fig			Cherry Date		Data: between
8	Elderberry	Berry		Vegetable	Guava			Fig Guava		
9	Fig	Tree Fruit			Kiwi			Kiwi		Source:
10	Guava	Tree Fruit			Mango			Mango Nectarine		=D4#
11	Honeydew	Melon			Nectarine					
12	Iceberg	Vegetable			Plum	D4	=SORT(UNIQUE(B4:B23))			
13	Kiwi	Tree Fruit			Star fruit	E4	=FILTER(A4:A23,B4:B23=H3,"Choose Class First")			
14	Lime	Citrus								
15	Mango	Tree Fruit								
16	Nectarine	Tree Fruit								
17	Orange	Citrus								

#79 Complex Validation Using a Formula

The method above is fine if you have Dynamic Arrays. But a lot of people running perpetual versions of Excel won't have Dynamic Arrays for years. Other published methods for Dependent Validation require a new named range for every possible choice in the first and second drop-down.

I was doing a seminar in Mobile, Alabama and several people there wanted to set up a three-level validation, but they did not care about having drop-downs to choose from. "I just want to validate that people are typing the correct values."

Rather than use the option to allow a list, you can set up custom validation using a formula. Say that you have a table with hundreds of valid selections.

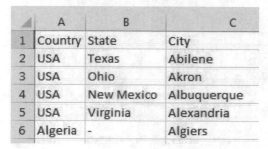

⊿	A	B	C
1	Country	State	City
2	USA	Texas	Abilene
3	USA	Ohio	Akron
4	USA	New Mexico	Albuquerque
5	USA	Virginia	Alexandria
6	Algeria	-	Algiers

If you think that your list will grow over time, format it as a Table using Ctrl+T.

Set up a named range for each of the three columns. This step is necessary so you can refer to each column and the names will grow as the table grows.

Select A2:A551. In the Name Box, type cCountry and press enter.

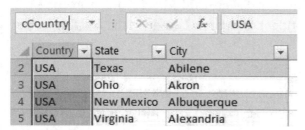

Name B2:B551 as cState. Name C2:C551 as cCity.

Here is the area where you want people to type a Country, State, and City.

It is always easier to build and test your formulas for conditional formatting and validation in a cell first. Take a look at the formulas shown below to test each of the entries.

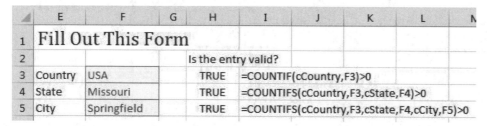

⊿	E	F	G	H	I	J	K	L	N
1	**Fill Out This Form**								
2				Is the entry valid?					
3	Country	USA		TRUE	=COUNTIF(cCountry,F3)>0				
4	State	Missouri		TRUE	=COUNTIFS(cCountry,F3,cState,F4)>0				
5	City	Springfield		TRUE	=COUNTIFS(cCountry,F3,cState,F4,cCity,F5)>0				

Once those formulas are working, edit cell H3. Using the mouse, select the characters in the formula bar and press Ctrl+C to copy. Select F3 and press Alt+D L to open the Data Validation drop-down. In the Allow box, choose Custom. This will reveal a Formula box. Paste your formula in that box.

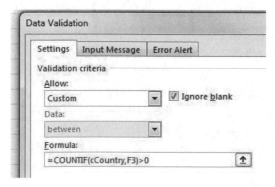

Optionally, fill out an Input Message and Error Alert. Repeat to put the H4 formula as the validation for F4 and the H5 formula for validation for F5. The result: it will prevent a wrong entry.

#80 Use A2:INDEX() as a Non-Volatile OFFSET

There is a flexible function called OFFSET. It can point to a different-sized range that is calculated on-the-fly. In the image below, if someone changes the # Qtrs dropdown in H1 from 3 to 4, the fourth argument of OFFSET will make sure that the range expands to include four columns.

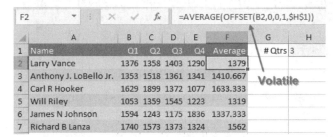

Spreadsheet gurus hate OFFSET because it is a volatile function. If you go to a completely unrelated cell and enter a number, all of the OFFSET functions will calculate—even if that cell has nothing to do with H1 or B2. Most of the time, Excel is very careful to only spend time calculating the cells that need to calculate. But once you introduce OFFSET, all of the OFFSET cells, plus everything downline from the OFFSET, starts calculating after every change in the worksheet.

In the formula below, there is a colon before the INDEX function. Normally, the INDEX function shown below would return the 1403 from cell D2. But when you put a colon on either side of the INDEX function, it starts returning the cell address D2 instead of the contents of D2. It is wild that this works.

Why does this matter? INDEX is not volatile. You get all of the flexible goodness of OFFSET without the time-sucking recalculations over and over.

I first learned this tip from Dan Mayoh at Fintega. Thanks to Access Analytic for suggesting this feature.

#81 Subscribe to Microsoft 365 for Monthly Features

From 1997 to 2013, there was a predictable release cycle for Microsoft Office. A new version would come out every three years. Your IT department would wait one year for the Service Pack to come out and then would consider upgrading.

All of the Office apps had to ship on the same day. This created pressure on each individual team to have their features ready in time. No one wanted to be the person who caused the Office release date to slip. Some great Excel features got ripped out of the product because the team wasn't sure they could complete those features in time. If a feature did not make it into an Excel version, there would not be another opportunity for three years for that feature to make it into the product.

Today, the paradigm has changed. The Excel team has an opportunity to release a new feature to Microsoft 365 on any given Tuesday. If a feature is not quite done this Tuesday, it only slips seven days, until the next Tuesday. There is no pressure to have 15 new features all ready on a certain day.

The net result is that Microsoft 365 subscribers are getting access to many more features. While it can be annoying that this book is obsolete the Tuesday after it prints, I appreciate getting great new features every month instead of every three years.

Your IT department still has a measure of control over when you get the features. There are several channels for distributing features:

- People who are not doing mission-critical work and want to test the latest bits can sign up for the Insider (Beta) channel. You run the risk of having bugs arrive on any given Tuesday.

- People who like to see new features but who don't want less bugs can sign up for the Monthly Channel (Targeted) channel.

- Your IT department is likely going to have you on the semi-annual channel. These people get features every 26 weeks. The features have been tested by millions of other customers and are safe to use.

So a feature can be used by all Microsoft 365 customers about 6 months after it is released. This beats the 3-year wait for a new version of Office and then the 12-month wait for your IT department to see the Service Pack and know it is safe to install.

> **Caution**: Microsoft still sells a perpetual version of Office 2019 or Office 2021. You pay once and never pay a monthly fee. But you will not get the new features. I feel bad for the people who paid $400 for Office 2019 but are not getting all of the new features such as Dynamic Arrays, Geography Data Types or Ask a Question About Your Data.

> **Note**: Microsoft 365 does not mean you are running Office in the cloud. When you subscribe to Microsoft 365, you agree to pay a monthly or annual fee, and you are using the real version of Office for Windows. As part of the bundle, you can also run Office on an iPad, a Mac, Android, or in a web browser. For most people, those are not where most work gets done.

Here are some of the features that debuted for Microsoft 365 subscribers:

- Co-authoring: Your whole team can now be editing the same Excel workbook at the same time.

- Excel will not nag you twice when you want to save as CSV.

- XLOOKUP with 12 benefits over VLOOKUP or INDEX/MATCH.

- A new Superscript and Subscript icon have been added.

- Improved function autocomplete: If you start to type =LOOKUP, the tooltip will offer VLOOKUP, XLOOKUP, HLOOKUP, and LOOKUP.

- Power Query has new features, including the ability for Split to Rows. This will split every delimiter to a new row. It also adds Column by Example, similar to Flash Fill. And a new Fuzzy Match merge feature.

- Dynamic Arrays and new functions like SORT, SORTBY, UNIQUE, and FILTER.

- You can now store formula logic in LAMBDA functions or re-use formula logic in LET.

- Picture transparency is now controlled with a slider on the Picture Tools tab.

- Artificial Intelligence with Data Ideas.

- Ask Me a Question About Your Data.

- Unhide Multiple Sheets

By the time you read this book, several more new features will have been added.

#82 Performance Improvements in 2020 for Microsoft 365

Subscribers to Microsoft 365 should be noticing faster calculation times with updates that began rolling out in fall 2020.

SUMIFS improvements:

Say you're using SUMIFS to get department and region totals for 150 departments. Each of the 450 formulas are looking at data stored in cells A2:G90001. With the new update, as Excel is calculating the total for the first department, it's efficiently building an index in memory of where each department is located. The first SUMIFS in cell J2 might take slightly longer as the indices are built, but the remaining 449 SUMIFS will calculate in a fraction of the time. With a large set of formulas, the calculation times should fall to about one-third the original calculation time.

Other improvements introduced during 2020:

- Similar improvements are implemented for SUMIF, COUNTIF, AVERAGEIF, SUMIFS, COUNTIFS, AVERAGEIFS, MAXIFS, and MINIFS. Note that you'll only notice the improvement if you have multiple formulas pointing to the same database of values.

- **Real-Time Data**: Some people use Excel to connect to the RealTimeData (RTD) function for getting real-time data from the stock market. In the past, support for RTD was only able to use a single core of your computer's processor. The Excel team improved the underlying memory structures, removed bottlenecks, and made the process able to run on multiple cores. In an example in their demo, speed increased from 2,000 cells retrieved per minute to 23,000 cells retrieved per minute.

- **Alt-Key Shortcuts**: If you press and release the Alt key, there was a slight delay while Excel displayed the tooltips. Expert Excel users aren't looking at the ribbon—they already know the keys to press. Excel now evaluates the shortcut key presses even before the tooltips appear.

- **Convert to Number**: If you had a large range of text numbers and used the Convert to Number command, Excel would sometimes appear to hang as it recalculated all formulas after each number. This has been eliminated.

- **Macro speed tip**: If you have the VBA Editor open and run a macro, the title bar in VBA will update to show the word "Running." Imagine that a function is operating on 1,000 cells. For each cell, Excel is changing the VBA title bar to display—and then not display—"Running." Closing the VBA Editor when running UDFs ensures Excel doesn't have the overhead of updating the VBA title bar.

- **Paste from Clipboard**: If you're pasting large sections of HTML or images from outside Excel, there were bottlenecks in getting that data into Excel. Microsoft made improvements to the underlying streaming data structure to make that happen faster.

4

- **Inserting Columns in Filtered Data**: This was a problem particularly when the hidden rows contained thick borders. Calculating border thickness is a time-consuming process, and there's no need to do it for the hidden rows in the data.

- **Deleting Ranges that Contain Merged Cells**: Excel was iterating through the rows multiple times before performing the delete. This has been improved.

- **Check for Errors**: In the past, using Check for Errors on 10,000 rows of data with some empty cells would take minutes or hours. Most people assumed that Excel had frozen and would kill the task. The command now builds an efficient data structure and should return the results in seconds instead of minutes.

- **Faster International Text Comparisons**: The code to perform comparisons of text that contain international characters has been improved.

#83 Unhide Multiple Worksheets

This is a great improvement introduced near the end of 2020 for Microsoft 365 subscribers. In the past, you could hide multiple worksheets at once, but you had to unhide them one at a time. With the change, you right-click any sheet tab and choose Unhide….

Excel now lets you multi-select which worksheets to unhide. The first time you use the feature, a guide appears telling you how to multi-select.

#84 Write Your Data with the Action Pen

The new Action Pen on the Draw tab of the Ribbon lets you hand-write data in a cell. After a moment, Excel converts the drawing to text or numbers as if you had typed the characters.

#85 Many Task Panes Now Collapse into a Tab Strip

There are several features in Excel that open a task pane on the right side of Excel. Sometimes, you would end up with 2, 3, or even 4 task panes open and it would cover your entire screen.

In February 2020, Microsoft 365 started collapsing task panes when more than 1 is open. A tab strip on the right side holds all the open task panes.

In the figure above, five task panes are available. The fourth is highlighted in grey and is the currently open PivotTable Fields task pane. Click the icon to collapse the currently open task pane.

Note: It is possible to collapse and open the task panes using the right arrow key to collapse and the left arrow key to open. In this state, you can move up and down the task panes using the arrow keys. However, it is also possible for focus to get stuck in the task pane strip and you can't use your arrows to navigate around the grid. In this case, press the F6 key three times to return focus to the grid.

Tip: What if you like having two task panes open at the same time? Grab the title of a task pane and drop it on the grid. Or grab the title of a task pane and drag it off the left side of the worksheet. This will dock the task pane on the left. Anything docked on the left will never collapse. You could even dock four task panes on the left if you needed to.

4

#86 How to Provide Usable Feedback to the Excel Team

If you encounter a bug in Excel, here is the best way to get it fixed quickly. On the Help tab in the Ribbon, choose the Feedback icon. This opens a Feedback pane on the right side. Follow all of these steps:

1. Choose "I Don't Like Something". No one reads the "I Like Something" submissions.

2. Type a description of the problem.

3. Choose "Attach Logs to Help Troubleshoot"

4. Choose "Include Screenshot"

5. Choose "You can contact me about this feedback" and provide an e-mail address.

If you don't do all five of these, no one reads your feedback. But if you complete all five steps, a live person from the Excel team reads it and often a fix is sent out in a week.

How can you report a crash? Re-open Excel. Immediately send Feedback. In step 2, type "Excel crashed on the last session". The logs from step 3 will help pinpoint the problem.

#87 Date Tricks in Excel

Column C in the figure below shows several cool date formulas. Given a date in B1, you can use EOMONTH to get to the end or start of the month. You can break out the YEAR, MONTH, DAY and then put it back together using the DATE function.

You can use the TEXT function to isolate the weekday name or month name. The WORKDAY and NETWORKDAYS in row 9 and 13 are similar to "#52 Calculate Nonstandard Work Weeks" on page 131.

	A	B	C
1	Date	4/15/2024	Formula to achieve result
2	End of this month	4/30/2024	=EOMONTH(B1,0)
3	Start of this month	4/1/2024	=EOMONTH(B1,-1)+1
4	Year	2024	=YEAR(B1)
5	Month	4	=MONTH(B1)
6	Day	15	=DAY(B1)
7	3 Months Later	7/15/2024	=DATE(YEAR(B1),MONTH(B1)+3,DAY(B1))
8	18 Months Later	10/15/2025	=DATE(YEAR(B1),MONTH(B1)+18,DAY(B1))
9	30 Workdays Later	5/27/2024	=WORKDAY(B1,30)
10	Weekday Name	Monday	=TEXT(B1,"DDDD")
11	Weekday Abbrev.	Mon	=TEXT(B1,"DDD")
12	Month Name	April	=TEXT(B1,"MMMM")
13	Fridays between B1 & B8	78	=NETWORKDAYS.INTL(B1,B8,"1111011")

#88 Use the LET Function to Re-Use Variables in a Formula

The LET function debuted during 2020 for Microsoft 365 Subscribers. There are all sorts of calculations in Excel that can benefit from re-using an intermediate calculation.

Note: The actual problem presented in this topic is not important. This is just a problem that is representative of the kind of problem that LET will make easier.

Someone e-mailed me and needed a formula to find the next-to-last word in a series of phrases stored in column A. Each cell might have anywhere from 5 to 10 words. I know that I can solve this type of problem, but I know the solution will have a lot of parts. So – my strategy is to insert a bunch of columns and work it out, piece by piece.

The solution requires me to count the words by taking the LEN of the phrase and then the LEN of the phrase with the spaces removed. Once you know the number of words, you can change the correct space to a ^ and then use FIND to isolate the location of the caret. Once you use MID to get the text after the caret, you find the space between the last and next-to-last word and use LEFT. While each step is simple, knowing how to put all of those together is tricky.

In the figure below, I have built the solution using five formulas. It is working and I could likely explain it to anyone who uses Excel 10 hours a week.

▲	A	B	C	D	E	F
1	Find the Second-to-Last Word					
3	**Phrase**	**TRIM**	**Which Word?**	**Add Caret**	**After Caret**	**Answer**
4	hi you airport id	hi you airp	2	hi you^airport id	airport id	airport
5	web do thousands museur	web do th	2	web do^thousands museu	thousands m	thousands
6	second house a do ball	second ho	3	second house a^do ball	do ball	do
7	allowed tax do yesterday s	allowed ta	5	allowed tax do yesterday s	classroom lo	classroom
8		B4:	=TRIM(A4)			
9		C4:	=LEN(B4)-LEN(SUBSTITUTE(B4," ",""))-1		E4 is used twice in F4	
10		D4:	=SUBSTITUTE(B4," ","^",C4)		D4 is used four times	
11		E4:	=MID(D4,FIND("^",D4)+1,30)		C4 is used four times	
12		F4:	=LEFT(E4,FIND(" ",E4)-1)		B4 is used 12 times!	

However, I've also learned that some people just want the formula to solve this, and they don't want to know how it works. Those people want the whole formula to be in a single cell.

At this point, I often try to merge everything into a single formula. The formula in cell F4 refers to the formula in E4 twice. Select E4. Using the mouse in the Formula Bar, carefully select everything after the equals sign and then copy it. Edit the original formula in F4. Select the characters "E4" in the formula and use CTRL+V to paste to replace "E4" with the actual formula from E4. Continue in this fashion until you have a single formula.

The formula keeps growing, and eventually the B4 formula of TRIM(A4) appears a total of 12 tImes In the final formula. Excel has to perform the TRIM operation 12 times for each cell. Explaining this formula to someone else will be difficult, if not impossible.

```
=LEFT(MID(SUBSTITUTE(TRIM(A4)," ","^",LEN(TRIM(A4))-LEN(SUBSTITUTE(TRIM(A4)," ","")))-1),
FIND("^",SUBSTITUTE(TRIM(A4)," ","^",LEN(TRIM(A4))-LEN(SUBSTITUTE(TRIM(A4)," ","")))-
1))+1,30),FIND(" ",MID(SUBSTITUTE(TRIM(A4)," ","^",LEN(TRIM(A4))-LEN(SUBSTITUTE(TRIM(A4),
" ","")))-1),FIND("^",SUBSTITUTE(TRIM(A4)," ","^",LEN(TRIM(A4))-LEN(SUBSTITUTE(TRIM(A4),
" ","")))-1))+1,30))-1)
```

This is where the LET function helps. The LET function starts out with pairs of arguments where you give a variable name and the definition for that variable. The calculation for the second variable can re-use the logic assigned to the first variable. The final argument in the function is the calculation returned to the cell.

4

You can plan out your LET function as shown here:

Variable	Stands For	Calculation		
T	Trimmed phrase	TRIM(A4)		
WW	Which word	LEN(T)-LEN(SUBSTITUTE(T," ",""))-1		
CT	Careted Text	SUBSTITUTE(T," ","^",WW)		
LastTwo	After Caret	MID(CT,FIND("^",CT)+1,30)		
Word	LastTwo up to first space	LEFT(LastTwo,FIND(" ",LastTwo)-1)		

And then wrap that logic in the LET function:

The best practice for LET is to use Alt+Enter to go to a new line in the formula bar after each pair of arguments. This makes the formula easier to read.

The LET function will simplify an entire class of problems where you need to repeatedly refer to an earlier component later in the formula.

#89 Store Complex Formula Logic in LAMBDA function

Excel has a great formula language with hundreds of built-in calculations, but it doesn't have functions for every possible calculation. A new research project from Microsoft's Calc Intelligence team in England will allow you to create your own functions and store them in Excel's Name Manager.

The new function, LAMBDA, is available for any Microsoft 365 subscribers who opt into the Office Insiders program's Beta Channel. It's named in honor of Princeton University mathematician Alonzo Church, who invented lambda calculus in 1936. Church was the doctoral advisor of Alan Turing, the famous mathematician who proposed the Turing machine to perform calculations long before modern computers were invented.

Imagine performing a complex calculation and passing variables to it. The variable names and logic are stored in the LAMBDA function and – after testing in the worksheet – you create a Name and insert the logic into name manager.

Let's start with a simple example. In a right triangle, the length of the hypotenuse is the square root of A squared plus B squared. To calculate the hypotenuse, you would use a formula such as =LAMBDA(A,B,SQRT(A^2+B^2)).

In this formula, the first two arguments are variables to hold values that will be passed to the function. The final argument is the logic to perform the calculation. You aren't limited to just two input variables. Everything up to the last argument is considered to be a variable. The final argument always holds the calculation logic.

While you're making sure the logic works, you can test the formula in the grid by adding the values for A and B in parentheses at the end of the formula. The formula =LAMBDA(A,B,SQRT(A^2+B^2))(3,4) would return the answer of 5.

But the real power of the LAMBDA function is when you store the LAMBDA in a Name. On the Formulas tab, choose Name Manager. In the New Name dialog, create an easy-to-remember name for your function. You might call it HYPOTENUSE or, to make it even easier, shorten the name to HYP. Then paste the formula =LAMBDA(A,B,SQRT(A^2+B^2) into the "Refers to" box. Click OK to create the name.

Now that the name is defined, you can enter a formula of =HYP(A2,B2) in the workbook, and Excel will calculate the result. The logic is stored once and can be reused in thousands of cells. If you need to change the logic in the future, edit the formula in the Name Manager.

In the past, people might have used VBA to write their own user-defined functions. These were fine when everyone was using a PC or a Mac. But slowly, the small percentage of people using Excel on an iPad or Android or Excel Online is growing, and those versions of Excel can't support VBA. LAMBDA functions, however, can be used with Excel online or a mobile device.

The team that developed LAMBDA is the same one that created data types and the LET function. That means LAMBDA was designed to work perfectly with Data Types. This enables more complex uses of LAMBDA.

Say that you have city pairs in column A and B. You convert these to Geography data types using the Data Type gallery on the Data tab of the ribbon. The Map icons mean that each cell contains many fields about the city. Two of those fields are Latitude and Longitude.

	A	B	C	
C2		=MILES(A2,B2)		
1	From	To	Distance in Miles	
2	Cleveland	Orlando	894.54	
3	Pago Pago	Timbuktu	11600.38	
4	Montvale	Springfield	1063.37	
5	Bangor	San Diego	2694.10	

```
=LAMBDA(From,To,(3959*2)*
ASIN(SQRT(0.5-COS((To.Latitude-
From.Latitude)*PI()/180)/2+
COS(From.Latitude*PI()/180)*
COS(To.Latitude*PI()/180)*
(1-COS((To.Longitude-From.Longitude)*PI()
/180))/2)))
```

There's a complicated formula for calculating the distance between two cities using their respective latitude and longitude. You start out assuming the radius of the Earth is 3,959 miles. The formula uses functions for arcsine and cosine and is generally one that most people would never remember:

```
=(3959*2)*ASIN(SQRT(0.5-COS((B2.Latitude-A2.Latitude)*PI()/180)/2+COS(A2.
Latitude*PI()/180)*COS(B2.Latitude*PI()/180)*(1-COS((B2.Longitude-A2.
Longitude)*PI()/180))/2)).
```

If you wrap that formula in the LAMBDA function as =LAMBDA(From,To,(3959*2)*ASIN(SQRT(0.5-COS((To.Latitude-From.Latitude)*PI()/180)/2+COS(From.Latitude*PI()/180)*COS(To.Latitude*PI()/180)*(1-COS((To.Longitude-From.Longitude)*PI()/180))/2))) and then store it in the Name Manager with an easy name like MILES, then you can calculate the distance between two cities using a formula as simple as =MILES(A2,B2).

To move that formula from one workbook to another, you simply copy any worksheet from the original workbook to a new workbook, and the names will travel along. With this portability, it's possible to envision a company's accounting department that has a library of custom LAMBDA functions that move from workbook to workbook.

> **Note**: Mathematicians are celebrating that the LAMBDA function makes Excel "Turing Complete" and can solve any mathematical problem.

Bonus Tip: Perform a Loop with a Recursive LAMBDA

A LAMBDA function can also call other LAMBDA functions, and it can recursively call itself. This lets you create a LAMBDA function that keeps calling itself until the task is complete.

These are likely the most complicated topic in the whole book. Let me demonstrate how one LAMBDA can solve a problem that would be pretty difficult with regular Excel functions.

I frequently write articles for MrExcel.com. My full stack developer is Suat Ozgur. When Suat is converting my article to a web page, he puts the title in the URL to help with Search Engine Optimization. Converting a title from "Why I say 'Bazinga!' - my #1 Reason for Using =INDEX(MATCH())!!", to a URL requires certain rules. The only characters that are used in our URLs are the lower case letters a through z and the digits 0

through 9 and a dash. As you scan through any article title, there are 37 characters that can be left alone. Another 26 upper case characters need to be converted to lower case. That leaves 192 other characters that have to be replaced with an dash. (Technically, Suat thinks he only has to check the 31 illegal characters that are on a U.S. keyboard. Because he thinks I am too lazy to type a =CHAR(149) to get a bullet point. But Suat doesn't realize that I can press the Alt key and 7 on the number keypad to get bullet points. ••••••
So he better check all 192 potential bad characters because he never knows when I might surprise him.)

Getting rid of bad characters with SUBSTITUTE would take a long time. To be really safe, you would have to use one SUBSTITUTE function for each of the 192 characters. Since you can not nest more than 64 functions, you would have to break the formula into four columns. Even if you tried to only handle the 31 illegal characters that are on a U.S. keyboard, the problem would be overwhelming.

The process of converting the above phrase to "why-i-say-bazinga-my-1-reason-for-using-index-match-" is called turning the title into a slug. The people who deal with web pages have made word this into a verb, saying that you have to "slugify" next month's article titles.

If you were going to build this in regular Excel formulas, the logic might go like this:

1. Start with character position 1. Store this in a cell column that we will call Index.

2. Convert that character to lowercase using LOWER()

3. See what ASCII code that letter is.

4. If the code for that letter between 48-57 or between 97 to 122? If it is, then use that character. If it is not, then use a hyphen.

5. Take the characters to the left of index, the new character from step 4, and the characters to the right of index. This is the new phrase.

6. Add 1 to the Index.

7. Check to see if the new Index is greater than the number of characters in the title. If it is, then do a final SUBSTITUTE to replace any instances of a double -- with a single hypen. You are done. Stop calculating.

8. But if the Index is not greater than the LEN, go to step 2, this time processing the 2nd character.

It is a crazy worksheet. I managed to convert my article title using just 630 formulas in A3:J65. Here is a tiny fraction of the worksheet.

A3   =MID(LOWER(G2),H2,1)

	A	B	C	D	E	F	G	H	I	J
1	Character	Char Code	Code OK	Left Part	This Part	Right Part	Phrase	Index	Are We Done?	Answer
2							Why I say 'Bazinga!" - my #1 Reason f	1	FALSE	
3	w	119	TRUE		w	hy I say 'Bazinga!" - my #1 Reas‹	why I say 'Bazinga!" - my #1 Reas‹	2	FALSE	
4	h	104	TRUE	w	h	y I say 'Bazinga!" - my #1 Reaso‹	why I say 'Bazinga!" - my #1 Reas‹	3	FALSE	
5	y	121	TRUE	wh	y	I say 'Bazinga!" - my #1 Reason	why I say 'Bazinga!" - my #1 Reas‹	4	FALSE	
6		32	FALSE	why	-	I say 'Bazinga!" - my #1 Reason	why-I say 'Bazinga!" - my #1 Reas‹	5	FALSE	
7	i	105	TRUE	why-	i	say 'Bazinga!" - my #1 Reason f	why-i say 'Bazinga!" - my #1 Reas‹	6	FALSE	

At the end of the worksheet, the index is finally greater than the LEN, and you finally get an answer in cell J65.

=IF(I65,SUBSTITUTE(SUBSTITUTE(SUBSTITUTE(G65,"--","-"),"--","-"),"--","-"),"")

H	I	J	K	L	M	N	O
Index	Are We Done?	Answer					
61	FALSE						
62	FALSE						
63	FALSE						
64	TRUE	why-i-say-bazinga-my-1-reason-for-using-index-match-					

I want us to agree that the above method is pretty ugly and not really reasonable. I don't want to have to explain the formulas that I used above, since we are abandoning that method. However, in case you really want to see the formulas, here they are:

A3	Character	=MID(LOWER(G2),H2,1)	Get "this" character
B3	Char Code	=CODE(A3)	
C3	Code OK	=OR(AND(B3>96,B3<123),AND(B3>47,B3<58))	Check if it is okay
D3	Left Part	=LEFT(G2,H2-1)	
E3	This Part	=IF(C3,A3,"-")	If it is not okay, use a dash
F3	Right Part	=RIGHT(G2,LEN(G2)-H2)	
G3	Phrase	=CONCAT(D3:F3)	Put left, this, right back together
H3	Index	=1+H2	Add 1 to the index
I3	Are We Done?	=H3>LEN(G3)	Are we done?
J3	Answer	=IF(I3,SUBSTITUTE(SUBSTITUTE(SUBSTITUTE(G3,"--","-"),"--","-"),"--","-"),"")	

All of the above is ugly. 630 formulas. If the phrase gets longer, you will need more formulas.

It can all be replaced with one LAMBDA function stored in a name called SLUGIFY.

As the author of this book, I am hoping you ignored everything above this. **But I really hope you try and understand everything that follows.** This is the part that shows you how recursive LAMBDAs work.

Start the function with =LAMBDA and name the two arguments that will be passed to it. The first argument is a phrase. The second argument will always be a 1 and will be stored in a variable called "ndx" because this sounds like "index" but is 40% shorter.

> **Tip**: For the VBA programmers reading this, "ndx" is our loop counter. Unlike VBA where you could just create a variable on the fly, for LAMBDA, we have to send a 1 in as an argument. Trust me - it is a small compromise.

Call Slugify by passing a phrase and index of 1

```
=LAMBDA(phrase,ndx, ←
  IF(ndx <= LEN(phrase),
    Slugify(
      LET(
        char, LOWER(MID(phrase, ndx, 1)),
        charcode, CODE(char),
        LEFT(phrase, ndx - 1) &
        IF(OR(AND(charcode > 96, charcode < 123), AND(charcode > 47, charcode < 58)), char, "-")
        & RIGHT(phrase, LEN(phrase) - ndx) ),
        ndx + 1),
    SUBSTITUTE(TRIM(SUBSTITUTE(phrase, "-", " "))," ","-")
  )
)
```

Start off with an IF function that checks to see if we are done. Is the ndx beyond the end of the phrase?.

Have we processed all characters?

```
=LAMBDA(phrase,ndx,
  IF(ndx <= LEN(phrase),
    Slugify(
      LET(
        char, LOWER(MID(phrase, ndx, 1)),
        charcode, CODE(char),
        LEFT(phrase, ndx - 1) &
        IF(OR(AND(charcode > 96, charcode < 123), AND(charcode > 47, charcode < 58)), char, "-")
        & RIGHT(phrase, LEN(phrase) - ndx) ),
        ndx + 1),
    SUBSTITUTE(TRIM(SUBSTITUTE(phrase, "-", " ")),"  ","-")
  )
)
```

The part in the box below is the Value_if_True part of the IF statement. If we aren't done with Slugify, then call Slugify again, but make the Index be 1 more than the last time. The inner logic is described after the figure.

This is the "not done yet" clause of IF

```
=LAMBDA(phrase,ndx,
  IF(ndx <= LEN(phrase),
    Slugify(      Call Slugify again(!)
      LET(
        char, LOWER(MID(phrase, ndx, 1)),  These 6 lines calculate the
        charcode, CODE(char),               phrase for the next call to Slugify
        LEFT(phrase, ndx - 1) &
        IF(OR(AND(charcode > 96, charcode < 123), AND(charcode > 47, charcode < 58)), char, "-")
        & RIGHT(phrase, LEN(phrase) - ndx) ),
        ndx + 1),      & the index will be 1 more than last time
    SUBSTITUTE(TRIM(SUBSTITUTE(phrase, "-", " ")),"  ","-")
  )
)
```

These six lines are the part of the formula that build the PHRASE for the next call to Slugify. If you use Excel frequently, all of the functions in this part should feel familiar. Use LOWER and MID to isolate this character. Get the CODE of that character. If the CODE is a letter or digit, then use it, otherwise use a hyphen. The phrase for the next time is going to be the left part, the newly fixed character, and the right part.

Isolate *this* character

```
LET(
  char, LOWER(MID(phrase, ndx, 1)),    get the character code
  charcode, CODE(char),
  LEFT(phrase, ndx - 1) &         text to the left of this character
  IF(OR(AND(charcode > 96, charcode < 123), AND(charcode > 47, charcode < 58)), char, "-")
  & RIGHT(phrase, LEN(phrase) - ndx) ),       text to the right
```

4

Deep inside the LAMBDA is the one line that really does the work. If we have a letter or a digit, keep it. If it is one of the other 192 bad characters, then use a hyphen.

```
LET(    if char is lower-case letter
   char, LOWER(MID(phrase, ndx, 1)),      or a digit        then use char
   charcode, CODE(char),
   LEFT(phrase, ndx - 1) &
 | IF(OR(AND(charcode > 96, charcode < 123), AND(charcode > 47, charcode < 58)), char, "-")
   & RIGHT(phrase, LEN(phrase) - ndx) ),
                                                  otherwise use -
```

The first time you call Slugify, it will be fixing the first character. The Excel calculation engine will then call Slugify to fix the 2nd character. This keeps going. Eventually, Excel calls Slugify to fix the 64th character, but that's bad because there are only 63 characters in this phrase. So, when ndx is greater than the LEN of the phrase, it is time to finally return the result.

The SUBSTITUTE / TRIM / SUBSTITUTE logic replaces any multiple hyphens with a single hyphen.

```
         Are we done?
=LAMBDA(phrase,ndx,
   IF(ndx <= LEN(phrase),      when ndx is beyond end of phrase
     Slugify(
       LET(
         char, LOWER(MID(phrase, ndx, 1)),
         charcode, CODE(char),
         LEFT(phrase, ndx - 1) &
         IF(OR(AND(charcode > 96, charcode < 123), AND(charcode > 47, charcode < 58)), char, "-")
         & RIGHT(phrase, LEN(phrase) - ndx) ),
         ndx + 1),
     SUBSTITUTE(TRIM(SUBSTITUTE(phrase, "-", " ")),"  ","-")
   )
)         then return the phrase, replacing -- with -
```

Note that up to this point, I've been building the LAMBDA in notepad or in a textbox in Excel.

> **Minor Rant**: Building a LAMBDA in a textbox is not fun. Building it in the Add Name dialog is much worse. At least with the textbox above, I could space things out. There is no good way to test a LAMBDA that calls itself other than putting it in the Name Box. In my case, I had misspelled one of the SUBSTITUTE functions and the Name Box simply refuses to take the formula without telling you why. This will get better later. Microsoft will have to give us a new formula editing experience and that will happen well before 2026.

So, you've written your LAMBDA. You have to give it a name so you can call it. On the Formulas tab, click New Name. Name it Slugify. Paste the formula from the textbox, spaces and all into the Refers To box.

Here is the payoff... you now have a function called SLUGIFY that you can use repeatedly.

	A	B
	B2 ▾ : ✕ ✓ *fx* =Slugify(A2,1)	
1	Article Title	URL Slug
2	Why I say 'Bazinga!" - my #1 Reason for Using =INDEX(MATCH())!!	why-i-say-bazinga-my-1-reason-for-using-index-match
3	PowerPivot? PowerPoint?	powerpivot-powerpoint
4	Return Zero instead of #N/A	return-zero-instead-of-n-a
5	Bug with Rand() in Excel 2003	bug-with-rand-in-excel-2003
6	Prevent #N/A! in Excel VLOOKUP	prevent-n-a-in-excel-vlookup
7	Convert 11.5 to 11 Minutes and 30 Seconds	convert-11-5-to-11-minutes-and-30-seconds

The rebel in me (and perhaps in you) wonders what would happen if I changed the 1 in the second argument to 5. What do I get with =Slugify(A2,5)? I tried it. It sort of works. It just does not fix any of the first 4 characters.

Before LAMBDA, I would have created this as a VBA user-defined function. That requires you to understand VBA. And it won't ever work in Excel Online. Now, with LAMBDA, you can simply use familiar Excel logic to build a function that loops through all of the characters in a cell.

Bonus Tip: Branching in a LAMBDA

On an earlier version of the previous LAMBDA, I was getting multiple hyphens in the result. I wondered if you could have a second loop to clean those. Could you do the first task - replacing illegal characters with dash, and then have a second task of looping to look for consecutive hyphens.

Later, I realized that replacing - with space, using TRIM, and then replacing space with hyphen solved the problem without the need for a second loop. However, this formula assigned to the name Slugify.Plus is an example of branching, so I am leaving it in.

The following formula offers two routines. The Branch parameter controls which part of the code is used.

original slugify logic

```
=LAMBDA(phrase,ndx,branch,
   IF(branch=1,

     IF(ndx > LEN(phrase),          ← Are we done?
       SLUGIFY.PLUS(phrase, 0,2),   ← Call Slugify branch 2
       SLUGIFY.PLUS(
         LET(
           character, LOWER(MID(phrase, ndx, 1)),
           charcode, CODE(character),
           LEFT(phrase, ndx - 1) &
           IF(OR(AND(charcode > 96, charcode < 123), AND(charcode > 47, charcode < 58)), character, "-") &
           RIGHT(phrase, LEN(phrase) - ndx) ),
         ndx + 1, 1 ) ),
   IF(LEN(phrase)-LEN(SUBSTITUTE(phrase, "--", "")) = 0,
     LET( clearleft, IF(LEFT(phrase, 1)="-", RIGHT(phrase, LEN(phrase)-1), phrase),
       clearright, IF(RIGHT(clearleft, 1)="-", LEFT(clearleft, LEN(clearleft)-1), clearleft),
       clearright),
     SLUGIFY.PLUS(
       SUBSTITUTE(phrase, "--", "-"), 0, 2 ) )))
```

These six lines are Branch 2 - a recursive routine to clean multiple hyphens

Note that the ndx argument is not used in Branch 2. But since LAMBDA arguments are not optional, you have to put something - I chose 0 - when calling branch 2.

Thanks to Suat Ozgur and Richard Simpson for help with Recursion and Branching.

4

Bonus Tip: Using LAMBDA to return a Picture

The Microsoft Research team in Cambridge and their Calc Intelligence project had a hand in dynamic arrays, data types, LET and LAMBDA. All of these work with LAMBDA, which means that LAMBDA can return arrays, query data types, and even return pictures.

In this figure, B2 & B3 allow you to choose movies. Note the icon to the left of the movie name indicating that the cells contain data types.

```
=LAMBDA(MovieOne,MovieTwo,
  LET(
    CastOne,MovieOne.[cast and roles].cast,
    CastTwo,MovieTwo.[cast and roles].cast,
    InMovieTwo,IFNA(XMATCH(CastOne,CastTwo),0),
    MatchingCast,FILTER(CastOne,InMovieTwo>0),
    Photos,MatchingCast.Image,
    Names,MatchingCast.Name,
    IFERROR(Photos,Names)))
```

The InBothCasts function gets a list of a people in the cast of the first movie and stores it in an array variable called CastOne. The people from the second movie are stored in a second array variable called CastTwo. You then do a lookup of everyone in CastOne to see if they are in CastTwo. This happens with an XMATCH and an IFNA. At this point, you have an array in memory with a list of people in the first movie and a second array with 1's or 0's to indicate if they are in second movie. To isolate just the people in both movies, use a FILTER function. The results for these two movies are four actors. But it is not just the name of the actor - it is a data type about the actor. You can get the .Image or .Name for each actor.

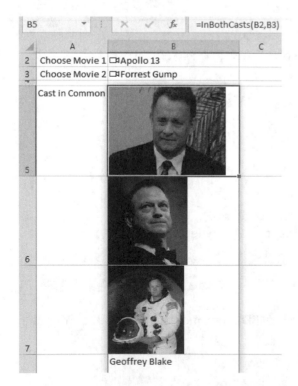

Notice that one formula is returning an array of four cells. The picture of Geoffrey Blake is not available and returns a #FIELD! error.

The last few lines of the LAMBDA check for the error and insert the name of the actor when the photo is not available.

Geoffrey Blake has been in thirty film projects. For whatever reason, Wikipedia does not have a photo of him, and subsequently, Wolfram Alpha doesn't have a photo either.

It actually is a good example of how you can work around the #FIELD! error and show another field from the Data Type.

#90 Find Largest Value That Meets One or More Criteria

One of the new Microsoft 365 functions added in February 2016 is the MAXIFS function. This function, which is similar to SUMIFS, finds the largest value that meets one or more criteria: You can either hard-code the criterion as in row 7 below or point to cells as in row 9. A similar MINIFS function finds the smallest value that meets one or more criteria.

	A	B	C	D	E	F	G	H
1	Largest	$99,876.41	=MAX($D$12:$D$125)					
2	2nd Largest	$99,588.23	=LARGE($D$12:$D$125,2)					
3	3rd Largest	$98,469.33	=LARGE($D$12:$D$125,3)					
4	3rd Smallest	$14,691.12	=SMALL($D$12:$D$125,3)					
5	2nd Smallest	$14,469.75	=SMALL($D$12:$D$125,2)					
6	Smallest	$13,593.04	=MIN($D$12:$D$125)					
7	Smallest Widget	$13,593.04	=MINIFS($D$12:$D$125,$B$12:$B$125,"Widget")					
8	Choose Criteria:	Widget	Central ▼					
9	Largest with Criteria	$90,861.70	=MAXIFS($D$12:$D$125,$B$12:$B$125,B8,$C$12:$C$125,C8)					
10								
11	Name		Item	Region	Amount			
12	Peter Albert		Gadget	East	$40,292.39			
13	Amy Andrae		Whatzit	Central	$28,872.16			
14	Frank Arendt-Theilen		Gadget	West	$88,640.58			
15	Fr Tony Azzarto		Gadget	East	$49,898.29			
16	Lorna Banuilos		Widget	Central	$90,861.70			

While most people have probably heard of MAX and MIN, but how do you find the second largest value? Use LARGE (rows 2 and 3) or SMALL (rows 4 and 5).

What if you need to sum the top seven values that meet criteria? The orange box below shows how to solve with the new Dynamic Arrays. The green box is the Ctrl+Shift+Enter formula required previously.

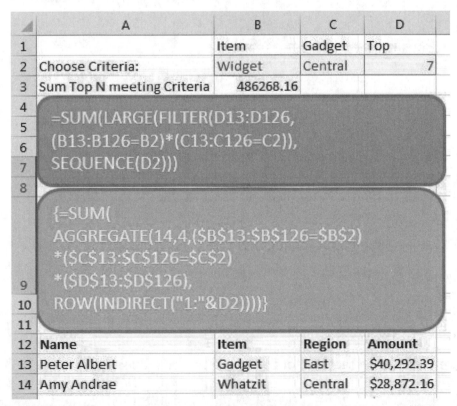

	A	B	C	D
1		Item	Gadget	Top
2	Choose Criteria:	Widget	Central	7
3	Sum Top N meeting Criteria	486268.16		
4				

```
=SUM(LARGE(FILTER(D13:D126,
(B13:B126=B2)*(C13:C126=C2)),
SEQUENCE(D2)))
```

```
{=SUM(
AGGREGATE(14,4,($B$13:$B$126=$B$2)
*($C$13:$C$126=$C$2)
*($D$13:$D$126),
ROW(INDIRECT("1:"&D2))))}
```

	A	B	C	D
12	Name	Item	Region	Amount
13	Peter Albert	Gadget	East	$40,292.39
14	Amy Andrae	Whatzit	Central	$28,872.16

4

Bonus Tip: Concatenate a Range by Using TEXTJOIN

My favorite new calculation function in Microsoft 365 is TEXTJOIN. What if you needed to concatenate all of the names in A1:A10? The formula =A1&A2&A3&A4&A5&A6&A7&A8&A9&A10 would jam everyone together like AndyBobCaroleDaleEdFloGloriaHelenIkeJill. By using TEXTJOIN, you can specify a delimiter such as ", ". The second argument lets you specify if blank cells should be ignored. =TEXTJOIN(", ",True,A1:A10) would produce Andy, Bob, Carole, and so on.

> **Tip**: TEXTJOIN works with arrays. The array formula shown in A7 uses a criterion to find only the people who answered Yes. Make sure to hold down Ctrl + Shift while pressing Enter to accept this formula. The alternate formula shown in A8 uses the Dynamic Array FILTER function and does not require Ctrl+Shift+Enter.

	A	B
1	List of invitees:	
2	Zack Barresse, Jeremy Bartz, Simon Benninga, Caroline Bonner, Melanie Breden, Derek Brown, Brian Canes, John Cockerill, Rob Collie	
3	=TEXTJOIN(", ",TRUE,$A$10:$A$18)	
5	List where RSVP is Yes:	
6	Zack Barresse, Melanie Breden, John Cockerill, Rob Collie	
7	{=TEXTJOIN(", ",TRUE,IF(B10:B18="Yes",A10:A18,""))}	
8	=TEXTJOIN(", ",TRUE,FILTER(A10:A18,B10:B18="Yes"))	
9	Name	RSVP
10	Zack Barresse	Yes
11	Jeremy Bartz	No
12	Simon Benninga	No
13	Caroline Bonner	No
14	Melanie Breden	Yes
15	Derek Brown	No
16	Brian Canes	No
17	John Cockerill	Yes
18	Rob Collie	Yes

#91 Less CSV Nagging and Better AutoComplete

Some people have to create CSV files hundreds of times per day. Excel used to hassle you when you saved a CSV file: "Some features in your workbook might be lost if you save as CSV." People who have to export as CSV understand this and wanted Excel to stop hassling them. Starting in 2017, people with Microsoft 365 are no longer hassled for choosing to save as CSV.

Another small change in Microsoft 365: If you type an equals sign and start to type a function name, the tooltip offers partial matching. Type LOOK, and you will see all three functions that contain the text LOOK.

#92 Speed Up VLOOKUP

VLOOKUP is a relatively expensive function. When you are looking for an exact match, Excel has to look through the lookup table one row at a time. Previous editions of this book demonstrated a Charles Williams formula to make VLOOKUP faster. Starting in 2018, Microsoft 365 includes a re-engineered VLOOKUP that is as fast as the Charles Williams trick.

=IF(VLOOKUP(A2,Table,1)=A2,VLOOKUP(A2,Table,1),"Not Found")

#93 Protect All Formula Cells

The use of worksheet protection in Excel is a little strange. Using the steps below, you can quickly protect just the formula cells in your worksheet.

It seems unusual, but all 16 billion cells on a worksheet start out with their Locked property set to True. You need to unlock all of the cells first:

1. Select all cells by using the icon above and to the left of cell A1.

2. Press Ctrl+1 (that is the number 1) to open the Format Cells dialog.

3. In the Format Cells dialog, go to the Protection tab. Uncheck Locked. Click OK.

While all cells are still selected, select Home, Find & Select, Formulas.

At this point, only the formula cells are selected. Press Ctrl+1 again to display the Format Cells dialog. On the Protection tab, choose Locked to lock all of the formula cells.

Locking cells does nothing until you protect the worksheet. On the Review tab, choose Protect Sheet. In the Protect Sheet dialog, choose if you want people to be able to select your formula cells or not.

> **Note**: Scroll down a few rows in the Protect Sheet dialog box to reveal popular choices: Use AutoFilter and Use PivotTable & PivotChart. If you want allow people to interact with these features, scroll down and select them.

> **Caution**: Don't bother putting in a password. Passwords are easily broken and easily lost. You will find yourself paying $39 to the Estonians who sell the Office password-cracking software.

#94 Back into an Answer by Using Goal Seek

Do you remember from ""#50 Discover New Functions by Using fx" on page 127, that I showed you how to calculate a loan payment by using the Insert Function dialog? Back in that example, the monthly loan payment was going to be $493.54. I did not mention it at the time, but my monthly budget for car payments is $425.

If you are about the same age as me and spent your summers watching TV, you might remember a crazy game show called *The Price Is Right*. Long before Drew Carey, the venerable Bob Barker would give away prizes using a variety of games. One that I recall is the Hi Lo game. Bob would give you the car if you could state the price of the car. You would guess. Bob would shout "Higher" or "Lower." I think you had 20 seconds to narrow your guesses to the exact price.

5

A lot of times, I feel like those summers watching Bob Barker trained me to find answers in Excel. Have you ever found yourself plugging in successively higher and lower values into an input cell, hoping to arrive at a certain answer?

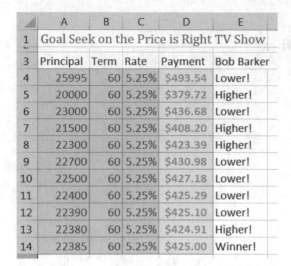

	A	B	C	D	E
1	Goal Seek on the Price is Right TV Show				
3	Principal	Term	Rate	Payment	Bob Barker
4	25995	60	5.25%	$493.54	Lower!
5	20000	60	5.25%	$379.72	Higher!
6	23000	60	5.25%	$436.68	Lower!
7	21500	60	5.25%	$408.20	Higher!
8	22300	60	5.25%	$423.39	Higher!
9	22700	60	5.25%	$430.98	Lower!
10	22500	60	5.25%	$427.18	Lower!
11	22400	60	5.25%	$425.29	Lower!
12	22390	60	5.25%	$425.10	Lower!
13	22380	60	5.25%	$424.91	Higher!
14	22385	60	5.25%	$425.00	Winner!

Illustration: Chad Thomas

A tool that is built in to Excel does exactly this set of steps. Select the cell with the Payment formula. On the Data tab, in the Data Tools group, look for the What-If Analysis dropdown and choose Goal Seek….

The figure below shows how you can try to set the payment in B5 to $425 by changing cell B1

Goal Seek finds the correct answer within a second.

Note that the formula in B5 stays intact. The only thing that changes is the input value typed in B1.

Also, with Goal Seek, you are free to experiment with changing other input cells. You can still get the $425 loan payment and the $25,995 car if your banker will offer you a 71.3379-month loan!

	A	B
1	Principal	25995
2	Term	71.3379
3	Rate	5.25%
4		
5	Payment	$425.00

Thanks to Jon Wittwer of Vertex42.com and to @BizNetSoftware for suggesting this Goal Seek trick.

#95 Do 60 What-If Analyses with a Sensitivity Analysis

Goal Seek lets you find the set of inputs that lead to a particular result. Sometimes, you want to see many different results from various combinations of inputs. Provided that you have only two input cells to change, the Data Table feature will do a sensitivity analysis.

Using the loan payment example, say that you want to calculate the price for a variety of principal balances and for a variety of terms.

	A	B	C	D	E	F
1	Principal	25995	Test from $20,995 to $29,995			
2	Term	60	Test from 36 to 72			
3	Rate	5.25%				
4						
5	Payment	$494				

Make sure that the formula you want to model is in the top-left corner of a range. Put various values for one variable down the left column and various values for another variable across the top.

B5   ▼   :   ✕   ✓ f_x =PMT(B3/12,B2,-B1)

	A	B	C	D	E	F	G	H
5	Payment	$494	36	48	54	60	66	72
6		20,995						
7		21,995						
8		22,995						

From the Data tab, select What-If Analysis, Data Table….

What-If Analysis ▾

    Scenario Manager...

    Goal Seek...

    Data Table...

5

You have values along the top row of the input table. You want Excel to plug those values into a certain input cell. Specify that input cell for Row Input Cell.

You have values along the left column. You want those plugged into another input cell. Specify that cell for the Column Input Cell.

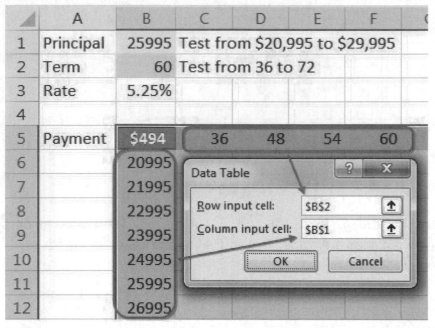

When you click OK, Excel repeats the formula in the top-left column for all combinations of the top row and left column. In the image below, you see 60 different loan payments, based on various inputs.

$494	36	48	54	60	66	72
20,995	632	486	437	399	367	341
21,995	662	509	458	418	384	357
22,995	692	532	479	437	402	373
23,995	722	555	500	456	419	389
24,995	752	578	521	475	437	405
25,995	782	602	542	494	454	422
26,995	812	625	562	513	472	438
27,995	842	648	583	532	489	454
28,995	872	671	604	550	507	470
29,995	902	694	625	569	524	487

> **Note**: I formatted the table results to have no decimals and used Home, Conditional Formatting, Color Scale to add the red/yellow/green shading.

Here is the great part: This table is "live." If you change the input cells along the left column or top row, the values in the table recalculate. Below, the values along the left are focused on the $23K to $24K range.

$494	48	51	54	57	60	63
22,995	532	504	479	457	437	418
23,095	534	506	481	459	438	420
23,195	537	508	483	461	440	422

Tip: You can build far more complex models and still use a data table. In my podcast 2141 "Will Asteroid Bennu Strike the Earth" on YouTube, I had a model with 100K NORM.INV and 100K VLOOKUP. Those 200,000 formulas were sent to a SUM function that summarized them. I used a Data Table to run those 200,001 formulas 100 times. The whole thing recalcs in about 11 seconds.

Thanks to Owen W. Green for suggesting this tables technique.

Bonus Tip: Create a Data Table from a Blank Cell

Note: If you took a class on financial modeling in college, you likely used a textbook written by Professor Simon Benninga. He showed me this cool Excel trick.

Simon Benninga tells a story of a game called Penny Pitching. You and another student would each flip a penny. If you get one head and one tail, you win the penny. If the coins match (heads/heads or tails/tails), the other student gets the penny.

It is simple to model this game in Excel. If RAND()>.5, you win a penny. Otherwise, you lose a penny. Do that for 25 rows and chart the result. Press F9 to play 25 more rounds.

This is known as a Random Walk Down Wall Street. Simon would point out a result like the one below, where a hot young stock analyst is on fire with a series of wins, but then a series of losses wipe out the gain. This is why they say that past results are not a guarantee of future returns.

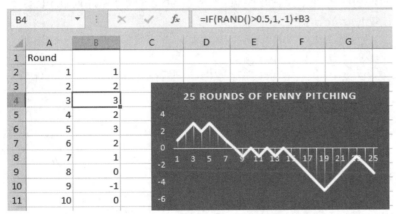

Instead of 25 trials, extend your table in columns A and B to run 250 trials. This would be like playing one round of penny pitching every work day for a year. Build a row of statistics about that year, as shown below.

	G	H	I	J	K	L
	Max	Min	Average	Win Streak	Lose Streak	Final
	3	-30	-14.7	6	8	-30

=MAX(B2:B251)

Create an odd data table where the blank cell in column F is the corner cell. Leave Row Input Cell blank. Specify any blank cell for Column Input Cell.

When you create the table, Excel runs the 250 coin flips, once per row. This 30-row table models the entire career of a stock analyst. Every time you press F9, Excel runs the 250-row model for each of 30 years. You can watch an entire 30-year career be modeled with the simple press of F9.

	G	H	I	J	K	L
13	Max	Min	Average	Win Streak	Lose Streak	Final
14	2	-16	-5.412	6	9 ▼	-12
15	3	-26	-14.028	5	6 ▼	-22
16	21	-5	6.772	12	7 ▲	+14
44	19	-3	9.78	12	7 ▬	0

Note: The download file for this chapter shows a few different ways to calculate the Win Streak and Loss Streak.

Thanks to Professor Simon Benninga for showing me this technique.

#96 Find Optimal Solutions with Solver

Excel was not the first spreadsheet program. Lotus 1-2-3 was not the first spreadsheet program. The first spreadsheet program was VisiCalc in 1979. Developed by Dan Bricklin and Bob Frankston, VisiCalc was published by Dan Fylstra. Today, Dan runs Frontline Systems. His company wrote the Solver used in Excel. Frontline Systems has also developed a whole suite of analytics software that works with Excel.

If you have Excel, you have Solver. It may not be enabled, but you have it. To enable Solver in Excel, press Alt+T followed by I. Add a checkmark next to Solver Add-in.

To successfully use Solver, you have to build a worksheet model that has three elements:

- There has to be a single Goal cell. This is a cell that you either want to minimize, maximize, or set to a particular value.

- There can be many input cells. This is one fundamental improvement over Goal Seek, which can deal with only one input cell.

- There can be constraints.

Your goal is to build the scheduling requirements for an amusement park. Each employee will work five straight days and then have two days off. There are seven different possible ways to schedule someone for five straight days and two off days. These are shown as text in A4:A10 in the figure below. The blue cells in B4:B10 are the input cells. This is where you specify how many people you have working each schedule.

The Goal cell is total Payroll/Week, shown in B17. This is straight math: Total People from B11 times $68 salary per person per day. You will ask Solver to find a way to minimize the weekly payroll.

The red box shows values that will not change. This is how many people you need working the park on each day of the week. You need at least 30 people on the busy weekend days—but as few as 12 on Monday and Tuesday. The orange cells use SUMPRODUCT to calculate how many people will be scheduled each day, based on the inputs in the blue cells.

The icons in row 15 indicate whether you need more people or fewer people or whether you have exactly the right number of people.

First, I tried to solve this problem without Solver. I went with 4 employees each day. That was great, but I did not have enough people on Sunday. So, I started increasing schedules to get more Sunday employees. I ended up with something that works: 38 employees and $2,584 of weekly payroll.

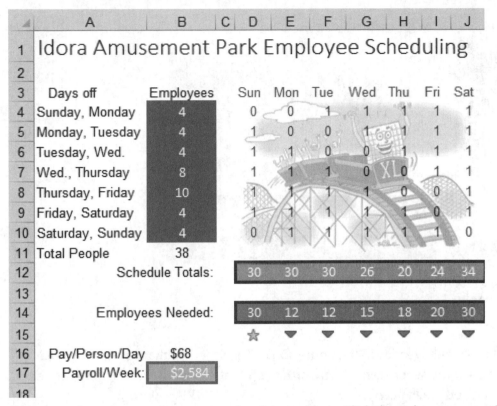

	A	B	C/D	E	F	G	H	I/J
1	Idora Amusement Park Employee Scheduling							
3	Days off	Employees	Sun	Mon	Tue	Wed	Thu	Fri	Sat
4	Sunday, Monday	4	0	0	1	1	1	1	1
5	Monday, Tuesday	4	1	0	0	1	1	1	1
6	Tuesday, Wed.	4	1	1	0	0	1	1	1
7	Wed., Thursday	8	1	1	1	0	0	1	1
8	Thursday, Friday	10	1	1	1	1	0	0	1
9	Friday, Saturday	4	1	1	1	1	1	0	1
10	Saturday, Sunday	4	0	1	1	1	1	1	0
11	Total People	38							
12	Schedule Totals:		30	30	30	26	20	24	34
14	Employees Needed:		30	12	12	15	18	20	30
15			☆	▼	▼	▼	▼	▼	▼
16	Pay/Person/Day	$68							
17	Payroll/Week:	$2,584							

Of course, there is an easier way to solve this problem. Click the Solver icon on the Data tab. Tell Solver that you are trying to set the payroll in B17 to the minimum. The input cells are B4:B10.

Constraints fall into obvious and not-so-obvious categories.

The first obvious constraint is that D12:J12 has to be >= D14:J14.

But, if you tried to run Solver now, you would get bizarre results with fractional numbers of people and possibly a negative number of people working certain schedules.

While it seems obvious to you that you can't hire 0.39 people, you need to add constraints to tell Solver that B4:B10 are >= 0 and that B4:B10 are integers.

Solver Parameters

Set Objective: $B$17

To: ○ Max ● Min ○ Value Of:

By Changing Variable Cells:

$B$4:$B$10

Subject to the Constraints:

$D$12:$J$12 >= $D$14:$J$14
$B$4:$B$10 = integer
$B$4:$B$10 >= 0

Choose Simplex LP as the solving method and click Solve. In a few moments, Solver presents one optimal solution.

5

Solver finds a way to cover the amusement park staffing by using 30 employees instead of 38. The savings per week is $544—or more than $7000 over the course of the summer.

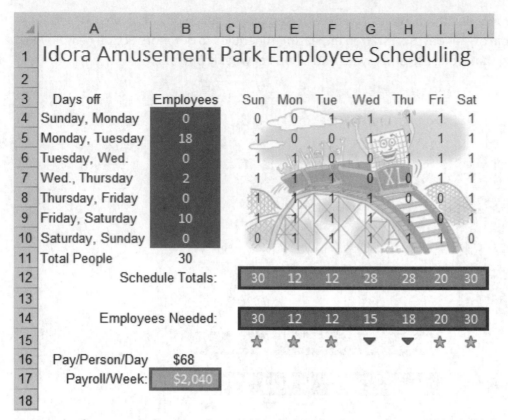

Notice the five stars below Employees Needed in the figure above. The schedule that Solver proposed meets your exact needs for five of the seven days. The by-product is that you will have more employees on Wednesday and Thursday than you really need.

I can understand how Solver came up with this solution. You need a lot of people on Saturday, Sunday, and Friday. One way to get people there on those day is to give them Monday and Tuesday off. That is why Solver gave 18 people Monday and Tuesday off.

But just because Solver came up with an optimal solution does not mean that there are not other equally optimal solutions.

When I was just guessing at the staffing, I didn't really have a good strategy.

Now that Solver has given me one of the optimal solutions, I can put on my logic hat. Having 28 college-age employees on Wednesday and Thursday when you only need 15 or 18 employees is going to lead to trouble. There won't be enough to do. Plus, with exactly the right head count on five days, you will have to call in someone for overtime if someone else calls in sick.

I trust Solver that I need to have 30 people to make this work. But I bet that I can rearrange those people to even out the schedule and provide a small buffer on other days.

For example, giving someone Wednesday and Thursday off also ensures that the person is at work Friday, Saturday, and Sunday. So, I manually move some workers from the Monday, Tuesday row to the Wednesday, Thursday row. I keep manually plugging in different combinations and come up with the solution shown below which has the same payroll expense as Solver but better intangibles. The overstaff situation now exists on four days instead of two. That means you can handle absences on Monday through Thursday without having to call in someone from their weekend.

	Days off	Employees	Sun	Mon	Tue	Wed	Thu	Fri	Sat
3	Days off	Employees	Sun	Mon	Tue	Wed	Thu	Fri	Sat
4	Sunday, Monday	0	0	0	1	1	1	1	1
5	Monday, Tuesday	10	1	0	0	1	1	1	1
6	Tuesday, Wed.	0	1	1	0	0	1	1	1
7	Wed., Thursday	10	1	1	1	0	0	1	1
8	Thursday, Friday	0	1	1	1	1	0	0	1
9	Friday, Saturday	10	1	1	1	1	1	0	1
10	Saturday, Sunday	0	0	1	1	1	1	1	0
11	Total People	30							
12	Schedule Totals:		30	20	20	20	20	20	30
14	Employees Needed:		30	12	12	15	18	20	30
16	Pay/Person/Day	$68							
17	Payroll/Week	$2,040							

Is it bad that I was able to come up with a better solution than Solver? No. The fact is that I would not have been able to get to this solution without using Solver. Once Solver gave me a model that minimized costs, I was able to use logic about intangibles to keep the same payroll.

If you need to solve problems that are more complex than Solver can handle, check out the premium Excel solvers available from Frontline Systems: mrx.cl/solver77.

Thanks to Dan Fylstra and Frontline Systems for this example. Walter Moore illustrated the XL roller coaster.

#97 Improve Your Macro Recording

I loved the 1985 version of the Macro Recorder in Lotus 1-2-3. The code was hard to understand, but it worked. There are some defaults in the Excel Macro Recorder that cause misery for anyone trying to record macros. Here are three tips to make the macro experience possibly better.

Tip 1: Turn on Relative Reference for Every Macro.

Say that you start in A2 and record a simple macro that moves to A4. I would call that macro MoveDownTwoCells. But if you run this macro while the cell pointer is in J10, the macro will move to cell A4. This is rarely what you want to have happen. But you can change the behavior of the macro recorder by selecting View, Macros, Use Relative References before you record the macro.

5

If you record the MoveDownTwoCells macro with this setting turned on, the macro will work from any cell.

> **Caution**: The setting stays turned on only until you close Excel. Tomorrow, you will have to turn it back on again.

> **Tip**: What if you actually need to record a macro that always jumps to cell A4? Even with Relative References enabled, you could press F5 for Go To and use the Go To dialog to go to A4. The macro recorder will record code that will always jump to A4.

Tip 2: Use Ctrl+Shift+Arrow to move to the end of a data set.

Say that you want to add a total at the bottom of yesterday's invoice register. You want the total to appear in row 9 today, but tomorrow, it might need to be in row 17 or row 5, depending on how many rows of data you have.

Find a column that is reliably 100% filled. From the top of that column, record the action of pressing Ctrl+Shift+Down Arrow. Press the Down Arrow key one more time, and you will know you are in the row where the totals should be.

	A	B	C	D	E
1	InvoiceDate	InvoiceNun	SalesRepN	CustomerN	ProductRe
2	5/8/2021	123829	S21	C8754	21000
3	5/8/2021	123830	S45	C3390	188100
4	5/8/2021	123831	S54	C2523	510600
5	5/8/2021	123832	S21	C5519	86200
6	5/8/2021	123833	S45	C3245	800100
7	5/8/2021	123834	S54	C7796	339000
8	5/8/2021	123835	S21	C1654	161000
9			**Ctrl+Shift+↓**		
10					

Tip 3: Type =SUM(E$2:E8) instead of pressing the AutoSum button

The macro recorder will not record the intent of AutoSum. When you press AutoSum, you will get a sum function that starts in the cell above and extends up to the first non-numeric cell. It does not matter if you have Relative References on or off; the macro recorder will hard-code that you want to sum the seven cells above the active cell.

Instead of using the AutoSum icon, type a SUM function with a single dollar sign before the first row number: =SUM(E$2:E8). Use that formula while recording the macro, and the macro will reliably sum from the cell above the active cell all the way up to row 2, as shown below.

=SUM(E$2:E8)

	E	
۱erN	ProductRe	Servi
	21000	
	188100	
	510600	
	86200	
	800100	
	339000	
	161000	
	2106000	

Bonus Tip: Use TypeScript to Write Macros for Excel Online

VBA has been the macro language in Excel for decades. This was fine when "Excel" meant Excel running on a PC with Windows or a Mac. But today, there are versions of "Excel" running on an iPhone, on Android, or in an browser. Microsoft is never going to support VBA in those endpoints.

In 2020, they debuted a new macro language called TypeScript. It was designed for those people running Excel in a browser. TypeScript will let you run macros on a PC or Excel Online. As the usage of Excel Online picks up, there will be more scenarios where you want your macros developed in TypeScript.

The new language is hard to find. You need to opt into a preview. This video will get you started: https://www.youtube.com/watch?v=bNbu5ANUeAw

#98 Clean Data with Power Query

Power Query is built in to Windows versions of Microsoft 365, Excel 2016, Excel 2019 and is available as a free download in Windows versions of Excel 2010 and Excel 2013. The tool is designed to extract, transform, and load data into Excel from a variety of sources. The best part: Power Query remembers your steps and will play them back when you want to refresh the data. This means you can clean data on Day 1 in 80% of the normal time, and you can clean data on Days 2 through 400 by simply clicking Refresh.

I say this about a lot of new Excel features, but this really is the best feature to hit Excel in 20 years.

I tell a story in my live seminars about how Power Query was invented as a crutch for SQL Server Analysis Services customers who were forced to use Excel in order to access Power Pivot. But Power Query kept getting better, and every person using Excel should be taking the time to learn Power Query.

Get Power Query

You may already have Power Query. It is in the Get & Transform group on the Data tab.

But if you are in Excel 2010 or Excel 2013, go to the Internet and search for Download Power Query. Your Power Query commands will appear on a dedicated Power Query tab in the Ribbon.

Clean Data the First Time in Power Query

To give you an example of some of the awesomeness of Power Query, say that you get the file shown below every day. Column A is not filled in. Quarters are going across instead of down the page.

To start, save that workbook to your hard drive. Put it in a predictable place with a name that you will use for that file every day.

5

	A	B	C	D	E	F
1	Product	Customer	Q1	Q2	Q3	Q4
2	Apple	SkyWire, Inc.	225	151	126	183
3		Tennessee Moo	156	185	150	273
4		SlinkyRN Excel I	284	111	130	281
5		University of No	185	230	259	123
6		Spain Enterprise	223	281	242	159
7		SkyWire, Inc.	267	174	213	204
8	Banana	Steve Comer	176	252	143	214
9		The Lab with Le	295	198	134	172
10		Steve Comer	132	234	193	255

In Excel, select Get Data, From File, From Workbook.

Browse to the workbook. In the Preview pane, click on Sheet1. Instead of clicking Load, click Transform Data. You now see the workbook in a slightly different grid—the Power Query grid.

Now you need to fix all the blank cells in column A. If you were to do this in the Excel user interface, the unwieldy command sequence is Home, Find & Select, Go To Special, Blanks, Equals, Up Arrow, Ctrl+Enter.

In Power Query, select Transform, Fill, Down.

All of the null values are replaced with the value from above. With Power Query, it takes three clicks instead of seven.

Next problem: The quarters are going across instead of down. In Excel, you can fix this with a Multiple Consolidation Range pivot table. This requires 12 steps and 23+ clicks.

In Power Query select the two columns that are not quarters. Open the Unpivot Columns dropdown on the Transform tab and choose Unpivot Other Columns, as shown below.

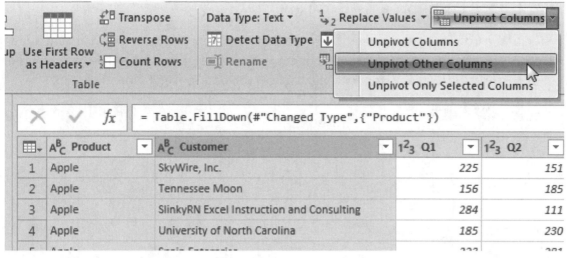

= Table.FillDown(#"Changed Type",{"Product"})

	A^B_C Product	A^B_C Customer	1²₃ Q1	1²₃ Q2
1	Apple	SkyWire, Inc.	225	151
2	Apple	Tennessee Moon	156	185
3	Apple	SlinkyRN Excel Instruction and Consulting	284	111
4	Apple	University of North Carolina	185	230

Right-click on the newly created Attribute column and rename it Quarter instead of Attribute. Twenty-plus clicks in Excel becomes five clicks in Power Query.

	A^B_C Product	A^B_C Customer	A^B_C Quarter	1.2 Value
1	Apple	SkyWire, Inc.	Q1	225
2	Apple	SkyWire, Inc.	Q2	151
3	Apple	SkyWire, Inc.	Q3	126
4	Apple	SkyWire, Inc.	Q4	183
5	Apple	Tennessee Moon	Q1	156
6	Apple	Tennessee Moon	Q2	185

Now, to be fair, not every cleaning step is shorter in Power Query than in Excel. Removing a column still means right-clicking a column and choosing Remove Column. But to be honest, the story here is not about the time savings on Day 1.

When you are done cleaning the data, click Close & Load as shown below.

Tip: If your data is more than 1,048,576 rows, you can use the Close & Load dropdown to load the data directly to the Power Pivot Data Model, which can accommodate 995 million rows if you have enough memory installed on the machine.

In a few seconds, your transformed data appears in Excel. Awesome.

	Product	Customer	Quarter	Value
7	Apple	Tennessee Moon	Q2	185
8	Apple	Tennessee Moon	Q3	150
9	Apple	Tennessee Moon	Q4	273
10	Apple	SlinkyRN Excel Instruction and Consulting	Q1	284
11	Apple	SlinkyRN Excel Instruction and Consulting	Q2	111
12	Apple	SlinkyRN Excel Instruction and Consulting	Q3	130
13	Apple	SlinkyRN Excel Instruction and Consulting	Q4	281
14	Apple	University of North Carolina	Q1	185
15	Apple	University of North Carolina	Q2	230

5

But Wait: Power Query Remembers All of Your Steps

Look on the right side of the Power Query window. There is a list called Applied Steps. It is an instant audit trail of all of your steps. Click any gear icon to change your choices in that step and have the changes cascade through the future steps. Click on any step for a view of how the data looked before that step.

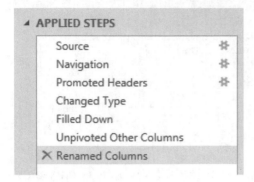

The Payoff: Clean Data Tomorrow With One Click

But again, the Power Query story is not about the time savings on Day 1. When you select the data returned by Power Query, a Queries & Connections panel appears on the right side of Excel, and on it is a Refresh button. (We need an Edit button here, but because there isn't one, you have to right-click the original query to view or make changes to the original query).

It is fun to clean data on Day 1. I love doing something new. But when my manager sees the resulting report and says "Beautiful. Can you do this every day?" I quickly grow to hate the tedium of cleaning the same data set every day.

So, to demonstrate Day 400 of cleaning the data, I have completely changed the original file. New products, new customers, smaller numbers, more rows, as shown here. I save this new version of the file in the same path and with the same filename as the original file.

	A	B	C	D	E	F
1	Product	Customer	Q1	Q2	Q3	Q4
17		leanexcelbooks.	12	95	42	62
18		Mary Maids	65	80	15	52
19	Guava	MAU Workforce	26	34	91	69
20		MN Excel Consu	89	61	44	37
21		MrExcel.com	57	54	55	42
22		myexcelonline.c	83	51	80	76
23		MyOnlineTrainii	55	21	20	73
24		MySpreadsheet	78	49	50	73
25	**More rows**					
26	**New Customers**					
27	**Different Numbers**					

If I open the query workbook and click Refresh, in a few seconds, Power Query reports 92 rows instead of 68 rows.

Cleaning the data on Day 2, Day 3, Day, 4,...Day 400,...Day Infinity now takes two clicks.

89	Guava	MyOnlineTrainingHub.com	Q4	73
90	Guava	MySpreadsheetLab	Q1	78
91	Guava	MySpreadsheetLab	Q2	49
92	Guava	MySpreadsheetLab	Q3	50
93	Guava	MySpreadsheetLab	Q4	73
94				

This one example only scratches the surface of Power Query. I have several more YouTube videos in a playlist at http://mrx.cl/pqplaylist. You will learn about other features, such as these:

- Combining all Excel or CSV files from a folder into a single Excel grid

- Converting a cell with Apple;Banana;Cherry;Dill;Eggplant to five rows in Excel

- Doing a VLOOKUP to a lookup workbook as you are bringing data into Power Query

- Making a single query into a function that can be applied to every row in Excel

Bonus Tip: Tame the Sequence of Refresh All

Say that you have a Power Query and then build a pivot table on the results. When you go to the Data Tab and click Refresh All, you need the Power Query refresh to complete before the pivot table refreshes. Excel MVP Celia Alves from SolveAndExcel.ca offers this important tip: Right-click the query in the Queries & Connections pane and choose Properties. Make sure to uncheck the Enable Background Refresh setting. This forces the Power Query to finish refreshing before the pivot table is updated. Otherwise, you will have to click Refresh All twice in order to get the pivot table to update.

Bonus Tip: Data Profiling in Power Query

Some excellent data profiling options appeared in late 2019. They are not obvious to find, as they are on the View tab in Power Query. Use the Column Quality, Column Distribution, and Column Profile boxes.

5

My favorite is the Column Profile. As you would expect, Weekday has 7 distinct values.

Choose one column and then Column Profile. You will see a window at the bottom with statistics and a frequency distribution.

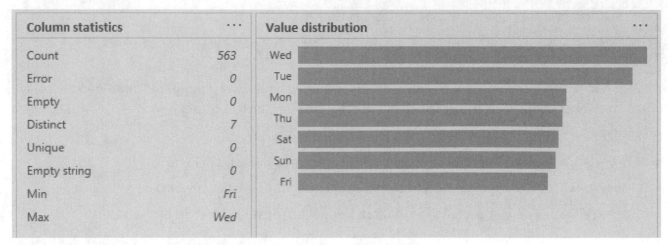

Column Quality shows if you have any empty or error cells in each column:

For a complete description of Power Query, check out *M Is for (Data) Monkey* by Ken Puls and Miguel Escobar. By the end of 2021, the retitled second edition, *Master Your Data*, might be available.

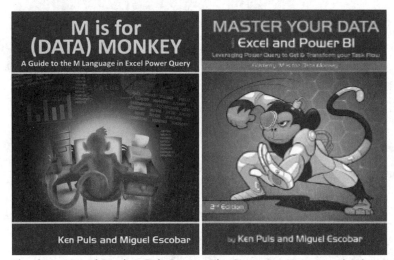

Thanks to Miguel Escobar, Rob Garcia, Mike Girvin, Ray Hauser, and Colin Michael for nominating Power Query.

#99 Use Fuzzy Match in Power Query

There's a research and development team at Microsoft known as Microsoft Labs. Almost 10 years ago, it invented a free Fuzzy Match add-in for Excel. A fuzzy matching algorithm looks for words that share a percentage of characters in common.

The figure below shows two data sets that need to be matched. Columns A and B contain the list of employees. Columns D and E contain the names of the employees who filled out a required form. You need to identify the people who haven't yet returned the form. Unfortunately, a VLOOKUP or XLOOKUP won't work since column A uses a "last name, first name" format while column D contains a nickname and last name. These two data sets can be matched using the Fuzzy Match tool that's now built into Windows versions of Microsoft 365.

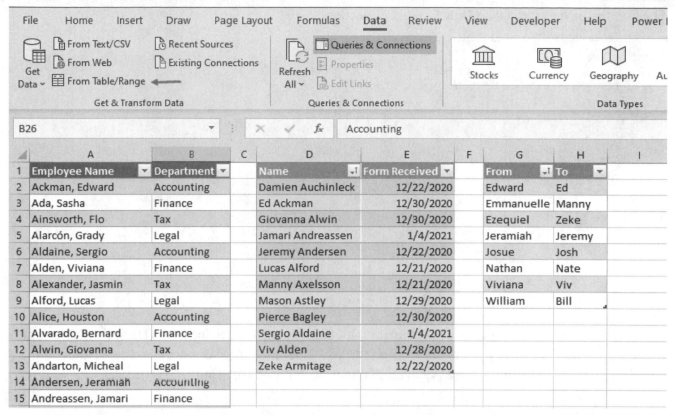

Columns G and H show a translation table that will be used by the fuzzy match to help match full first names with their nicknames. The translation table requires two columns, labeled "From" and "To." The fuzzy match will likely match Kris and Kristy because they share many letters. But it will need an entry in the translation table for Bill and William or Bob and Robert.

Before you can perform the match, all three ranges of data have to be converted to a table by selecting each individual range and pressing Ctrl+T. Then Rrname each table: Select one cell in a table. Go to the Table Tools tab in the Ribbon and type a meaningful name such as "Census," "Forms," and "Nicknames."

You need to convert each of the three tables to a connection in Excel. From cell A1, select, Data, From Table/Range (as shown at the red arrow in Figure 1). Excel will open the Power Query Editor. The first icon on the Home tab says "Close and Load." Click the drop-down menu below it and choose "Close and Load To…" to open the Import Data dialog box.

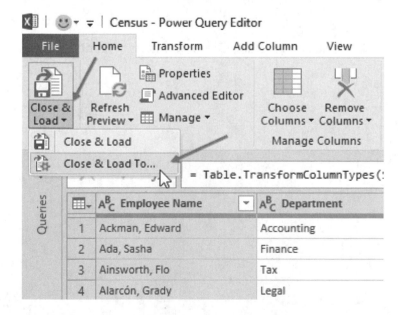

5

Choose the fourth item, called Only Create Connection.

Repeat the process of creating a connection for the other two tables, starting in cell D1 and cell G1, respectively. If you created all three connections correctly, you should see three queries listed as "Connection Only" in the Queries & Connections panel on the right side of the Excel window.

Select a blank cell in your worksheet. From the Data tab, select Get Data, Combine Queries, Merge to open the Merge dialog.

There are many subtle settings in this dialog that aren't intuitive. The figure at right shows the 8 steps:

1. From the top drop-down menu, select the Census table.

2. In the small data preview, click on the heading(s) of the fields to be used for the matching. In this case, it's the Employee Name heading.

3. From the second drop-down menu, choose the name of the lookup table. In this case, Forms.

4. In the data preview, click on the heading(s) of the fields to be used for matching, such as Name.

5. Choose a Join Kind of Left Outer. Choose the box for "Use Fuzzy Matching to Perform the Merge."

6. Several special settings are hidden behind the Fuzzy Matching Options drop-down menu. Click the triangle to reveal this section.

7. Scroll to the bottom of the section and set Nicknames as the Transformation Table.

8. Verify that the number of matches found is the same as the number of records in the Forms table.

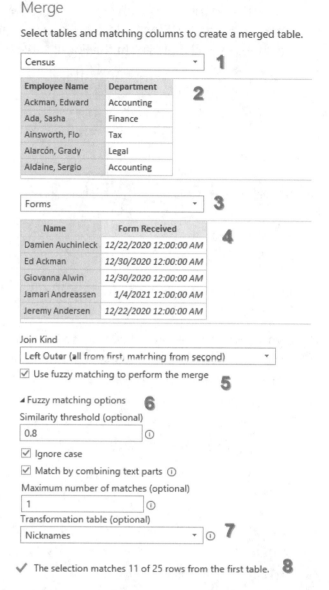

Tip: If you become comfortable with fuzzy matching, you might change the Join Kind from Left Outer to Left Anti in order to return only the list of people in the first table who do not have a match in the second table.

If there are fewer records than you expect, you might experiment with the "similarity threshhold." By default, the similarity threshold requires an 80% match. You could try changing this to 0.7 or 0.6 to see if it improves the number of matches. But be careful. If you set this too low, you risk the chance of false matches happening. For example, at 0.4 similarity, both Mason Astley and Lucy Astley would be seen as a match.

Click OK to perform the Merge. The grid in the Power Query editor will show columns for Employee Name, Department, and then a column called Forms. The value in each row for Forms simply says "Table" in each row. To the right of the "Forms" heading is an Expand icon with two arrows pointing left and right. Click this icon to choose which fields from the Forms table to return.

	ABC Employee Name	ABC Department	Forms
1	Ackman, Edward	Accounting	Table
2	Ada, Sasha	Finance	Table
3	Ainsworth, Flo	Tax	Table
4	Alarcón, Grady	Legal	Table
5	Aldaine, Sergio	Accounting	Table
6	Alden, Viviana	Finance	Table
7	Alexander, Jasmin	Tax	Table
8	Alford, Lucas	Legal	Table

By default, the new fields will have the table name followed by a period and then the field name (such as "Forms.Form Received"). To prevent this, uncheck the box for "Use Original Column Name As Prefix."

Once you have the preview shown in the Power Query Editor, go to Home, Close & Load to deliver the results to a new table on a new worksheet. You could optionally use Close & Load To… and specify a location on an existing worksheet for the table.

	A	B	C	D	E
1	Employee Name	Department	Name	Form Received	
2	Ackman, Edward	Accounting	Ed Ackman	12/30/2020 0:00	
3	Ada, Sasha	Finance			
4	Ainsworth, Flo	Tax			
5	Alarcón, Grady	Legal			
6	Aldaine, Sergio	Accounting	Sergio Aldaine	1/4/2021 0:00	
7	Alden, Viviana	Finance	Viv Alden	12/28/2020 0:00	
8	Alexander, Jasmin	Tax			
9	Alford, Lucas	Legal	Lucas Alford	12/21/2020 0:00	
10	Alice, Houston	Accounting			
11	Alvarado, Bernard	Finance			
12	Alwin, Giovanna	Tax	Giovanna Alwin	12/30/2020 0:00	
13	Andarton, Micheal	Legal			
14	Andersen, Jeramiah	Accounting	Jeremy Andersen	12/22/2020 0:00	
15	Andreassen, Jamari	Finance	Jamari Andreassen	1/4/2021 0:00	
16	Annan, Aliza	Tax			
17	Annesley, Carissa	Legal			
18	Appleby, Celeste	Accounting			
19	Appleby, Lizbeth	Finance			
20	Armitage, Ezequiel	Tax	Zeke Armitage	12/22/2020 0:00	
21	Astley, Mason	Legal	Mason Astley	12/29/2020 0:00	
22	Astley, Lucy	Accounting			
23	Auchinleck, Damien	Finance	Damien Auchinleck	12/22/2020 0:00	
24	Audley, Theodora	Tax			
25	Axelsson, Emmanuelle	Legal	Manny Axelsson	12/21/2020 0:00	
26	Ayres, Nyasia	Accounting			
27					

At this point, review the results to make sure no false matches were found. If everything looks good, you can sort or filter to remove the records that show a match, leaving the people who haven't turned in a form.

There's an easy audit method to look for people in the Forms table who did not show up in the Merge query. Use Data, Get Data, Combine Queries, Merge. Specify Forms as the first table, using Name as the key field. Specify Merge1 as the second table, using Name as the key field. For the Join Kind, specify Left Anti (Rows Only In the First Table}.

Ever since my Accounting 101 class, I was taught that "close" is never acceptable in accounting. This leads to a reluctance to trust the fuzzy matching algorithm. Yet there are cases where the fuzzy match tool is the only solution short of manually matching records.

As more people turn in their forms, choosing Data, Refresh All will automatically perform the fuzzy match again.

#100 Render Excel Data on an iPad Dashboard Using Power BI

Power BI provides a new way of creating interactive modern dashboards using data from Excel.

To get started, sign up for a free account at http://powerbi.microsoft.com. You need to sign up with a work e-mail address; you can't use Gmail, Yahoo mail, or other third-party e-mail providers.

Then download the free app called Power BI Desktop.

In Power BI Desktop, start with the Get Data button.

The experience will be exactly like with Power Query, as discussed in ""#98 Clean Data with Power Query"." You can also define relationships between tables, as in ""#43 Eliminate VLOOKUP or XLOOKUP with the Data Model" on page 107, and define new calculations, as discussed in "Bonus Tip: Portable Formulas" on page 112.

Once you have your data loaded into Power Query, choose a visualization from the top right and drag fields to the various drop zones.

After you design several dashboard tiles, you can publish your dashboard. Anyone that you invite will be able to view the dashboard in a browser or on an iPhone, iPad, or Android device.

#101 Build a Pivot Table on a Map Using 3D Maps

3D Maps (formerly Power Map) is available in the Microsoft 365 versions of Excel 2013 and all versions of Excel 2016. Using 3D Maps, you can build a pivot table on a map. You can fly through your data and animate the data over time.

3D Maps lets you see five dimensions: latitude, longitude, color, height, and time. Using it is a fascinating way to visualize large data sets.

3D Maps can work with simple one-sheet data sets or with multiple tables added to the Data Model. Select the data. On the Insert tab, choose 3D Map. (The icon is located to the right of the Charts group.) If you have Excel 2013 you might have to download Power Map Preview from Microsoft to use the feature.

Next, you need to choose which fields are your geography fields. This could be Country, State, County, Zip Code, or even individual street addresses.

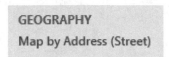

You are given a list of the fields in your data set and drop zones named Height, Category, and Time.

Hover over any point on the map to get details such as last sale date and amount.

In the default state of 3D Maps, each data point occupies about one city block. To be able to plot many houses on a street, select the Gear Wheel, Layer Options and change the thickness of the point to 10%.

To get the satellite imagery, open the Themes dropdown and use the second theme.

3D Maps provides a completely new way to look at your data. It is hard to believe that this is Excel.

Here is a map of Merritt Island, Florida. The various colors are different housing allotments. Each colored dot on the map is a house with a dock, either on a river or one of many canals dredged out in the 1960s and 1970s.

Using the time slider, you can go back in time to any point. Here is the same area at the time when NASA landed the first man on the Moon. The NASA engineers had just started building waterfront homes here, a few miles south of Kennedy Space Center.

Use the wheel mouse to scroll in. You can actually see individual streets, canals, and driveways.

Hold down the Alt key and drag sideways to rotate the map. Hold down the Alt key and drag up to tip the map so your view is closer to the ground.

Thanks to Igor Peev and Scott Ruble at Microsoft for this cool new feature.

5

#102 The Forecast Sheet Can Handle Some Seasonality

Before Excel 2016, Excel offered a few forecasting tools that did not fit in every situation. If your sales data included some seasonality, the old forecasting tools would do a bad job. Consider a movie theatre where sales peak on the weekend and plummet on Monday. Using the old linear trendline, Excel shows an R-Squared of 0.02, meaning that the trendline is doing a horrible job of predicting the future.

Excel 2016 introduced a new set of forecasting functions and an icon on the Data tab of the Ribbon to create a Forecast Sheet. If you have data with Date in column A and Sales in column B, select the data and choose Data, Forecast Sheet.

In the Create Forecast Worksheet dialog, click Options and review the Seasonality and ask for stats. Click Create and Excel inserts a new worksheet with FORECAST.ETS functions to create a forecast. The 3% error shown means that this forecast is explaining most of the variability.

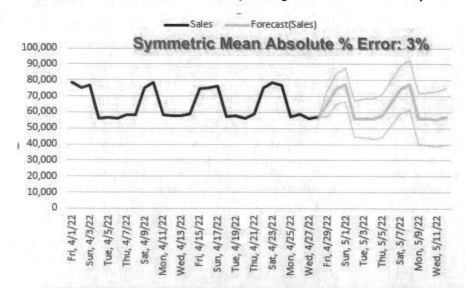

Caution: The Forecast Sheet works fine if you have one level of seasonality: More movie-goers on Friday or more gift buyers in November and December. But if your real-life data calls for <u>both</u> a December boom and a Saturday/Sunday peak, the FORECAST.ETS won't handle it.

#103 Perform Sentiment Analysis in Excel

It is easy to quantify survey data when it is multiple choice: You use a pivot table to figure out the percentage for each answer. But what about free-form text answers? These are hard to process if you have hundreds or thousands of them.

Sentiment analysis is a machine-based method for predicting if an answer is positive or negative. Microsoft offers a tool that does sentiment analysis in Excel. It is called Azure Machine Learning.

Traditional sentiment analysis requires a human to analyze and categorize 5% of the statements. Excel uses MPQA Subjectivity Lexicon. This generic dictionary includes 5,097 negative and 2,533 positive words. Each word is assigned a strong or weak polarity. This works great for short sentences, such as tweets or Facebook posts.

Look in the Add-ins group of the Insert tab. The first icon used to be called Store and now is called My Apps. Click that icon and search for Azure Machine Learning.

Specify an input range and two blank columns for the output range.

The heading for the input range has to match the schema tweet_text.

The results show positive, negative, or neutral and a percentage score. Items near 99% are very likely positive. Items near 0% are very likely negative.

	A	B	C
1	tweet_text	Sentiment	Score
2	Hello, I'm having trouble working this one. In col	positive	98.800%
3	OK, so it's Monday morning and I obviously cann	neutral	51.651%
4	Hi all, There has been a post previous to this reg	negative	0.000%
5	hi, would like to have a formula or vb code for th	positive	97.175%
6	Hi, I need to collect data (selected range) from	positive	95.626%

#104 Build Org Charts with the Visio Data Visualizer in Excel

Most people with Microsoft 365 will have a new Visio Data Visualizer tool in Excel. It is found on the Insert tab, in the Add-Ins group.

The easiest way to get started is to go to File, New and search the templates for "flowcharts". There should be five results, but these three are for the Visio tool.

| Basic Flowchart from Data | Cross-Functional Flowchart... | Organization Chart from D... |

Choose Org Chart and then click Create. There are five styles to choose from. Choose one style. Excel will open with some sample data, the chart from that data, and three more worksheets explaining how it works.

	A	B	C	D	E
1	Employee ID	Name	Title	Manager ID	Role Type
2	ID1	scano	Director		Executive
3	ID2	ejev	Manager, Marketing	ID1	Manager
4	ID3	nus	Manager, Products	ID1	Manager
5	ID4	inese	PR Coordinator	ID2	Staff
6	ID5	Mattia Sabbatini	Content Strategist	ID2	Consultant
7	ID6	Mai Aare	Engineering Lead	ID3	Staff
8	ID7	Aet Kangro	Design Lead	ID3	Staff

(Tooltip overlay: **Employee ID** — Enter a unique ID for each employee.)

After you replace the sample data with your data, you click Refresh on the org chart.

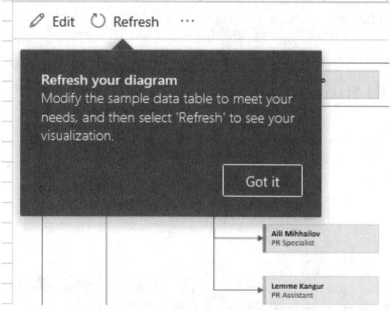

Caution: There are resize handles on the diagram, but you have to first click on the edge of the frame around the diagram. This drove me crazy at first.

Note: The same tool can create flowcharts, swim-lane charts, process charts, and cross-functional org charts.

Tip: Same the workbook to OneDrive or SharePoint Online. Then when you View in Web, you have some additional functionality from Visio online.

#105 Fill in a Flash

Excel 2013 added a data-cleansing tool called Flash Fill.

In the figure below, you see full names in column A. You want to get the person's first initial and last name in column B. Rather than try to puzzle out =PROPER(LEFT(A2,1)&" "&MID(A2,FIND(" ",A2)+1,50)), you simply type a sample of what you want in B2.

Type the first initial in B3. Excel sees what you are doing and "grays in" a suggested result.

Press Enter to accept the suggestion. Bam! All of the data is filled in.

Look carefully through your data for exceptions to the rule. Two people here have middle initials listed. Do you want the middle initials to appear? If so, correct the suggestion for Dennis P. Jancsy in cell B4. Flash Fill will jump into action and fix Martha K. Wendel in B9 and any others that match the new pattern. The status bar will indicate how many changes were made.

In the above case, Excel gurus could figure out the formula. But Flash Fill is easier. In the example shown below, it would be harder to write a formula to get the last word from a phrase that has a different number of words and more than one hyphen.

	A	B
1	Customer	Type
2	900 bradedgar.com - consulting	Consulting
3	1164 Frontline Systems - applications	
4	1156 California Blazing Chile Farms - retail	
5	1175 Safety Elements Ltd. - services	
6	918 Hybrid Software - applications	
7	947 IMA Houston Chapter - associations	
8	1048 Fintega Financial Modelling - consulting	
9	1001 Roto-Rooter - services	
10	1103 MN Excel Consulting - consulting	
11	1145 Open Sky Martial Arts - training	

Flash Fill makes this easy. Go to cell B3 and press Ctrl+E to invoke Flash Fill.

	A	B
1	Customer	Type
2	900 bradedgar.com - consulting	Consulting
3	1164 Frontline Systems - applications	Applications
4	1156 California Blazing Chile Farms - retail	Retail
5	1175 Safety Elements Ltd. - services	Services
6	918 Hybrid Software - applications	Applications
7	947 IMA Houston Chapter - associations	Associations
8	1048 Fintega Financial Modelling - consulting	Consulting

Note: Flash Fill will not automatically fill in numbers. If you have numbers, you might see Flash Fill temporarily "gray in" a suggestion but then withdraw it. This is your signal to press Ctrl+E to give Flash Fill permission to fill in numbers.

Thanks to Chad Rothschiller at Microsoft for building this feature. Thanks also to Olga Kryuchkova.

#106 Format as a Façade

Excel is amazing at storing one number and presenting another number. Choose any cell and select Currency format. Excel adds a dollar sign and a comma and presents the number, rounded to two decimal places. In the figure below, cell D2 actually contains 6.42452514. Thankfully, the built-in custom number format presents the results in an easy-to-read format.

	A	B	C	D
1	Rep	Qty	Revenue	Avg Price
2	Andrew Spain	26,850	172,498.50	$6.42
3	Geoffrey G Lilley	24,458	157,921.10	$6.46
4	Kevin J Sullivan	24,754	160,180.30	$6.47
5	Peter Polakovic	24,090	143,880.50	$5.97

The custom number format code in D2 is $#,##0.00. In this code, 0s are required digits. Any #s are optional digits.

However, formatting codes can be far more complex. The code above has one format. That format is applied to every value in the cell. If you provide a code with two formats, the first format is for non-negative numbers, and the second format is for negative numbers. You separate the formats with semicolons. If you provide a code with three formats, the first is for positive, then negative, then zero. If you provide a code with four formats, they are used for positive, negative, zero, and text.

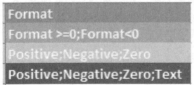

```
Format
Format >=0;Format<0
Positive;Negative;Zero
Positive;Negative;Zero;Text
```

Even if you are using a built-in format, you can go to Format Cells, Number, Custom and see the code used to generate that format. The figure below shows the code for the accounting format.

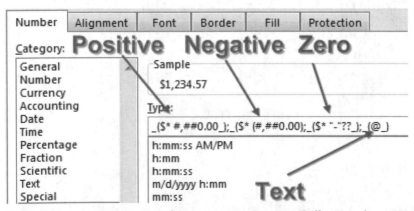

To build your own custom format, go to Format Cells, Number, Custom and enter the code in the Type box. Check out the example in the Sample box to make sure everything looks correct.

In the following example, three zones are used. Text in quotes is added to the number format to customize the message.

1	Format in C: "Please Remit "$0.00;"Credit Balance of "$0.00" (Do not pay)";"No Balance"		
3	Customer	Balance	Formatted
4	Wag More Dog Store, San Antonio	-18.03	Credit Balance of $18.03 (Do not pay)
5	How To Excel At Excel.Com	192.28	Please Remit $192.28
6	SurtenExcel.com	27.72	Please Remit $27.72
7	University of North Carolina	-187.38	Credit Balance of $187.38 (Do not pay)
8	Yesenita	120.15	Please Remit $120.15

If you create a zone for zero but put nothing there, you will hide all zero values. The following code uses color codes for positive and negative. The code ends in a semicolon, creating a zone for zero values. But since the zone is empty, zero values are not shown.

Illustration: Walter Moore

You can extend this by making all zones blank. A custom format code ;;; will hide values in the display and printout. However, you'll still be able to see the values in the formula bar. If you hide values by making the font white, the ;;; will stay hidden even if people change the fill color. The following figure includes some interesting formatting tricks.

	A	B	C
1	Value	Display	Format Code
2	123.45	********** 123.45	**0.00
3	123.45	!!!!!!!!!!!!!! 123.45	*!0.00
4	123456	123K	0,K
5	4565789	4.6M	0.0,,"M"
6	One	Enter a number!	0;-0;0;"Enter a number!"
7	62	62	[Red][<70]0;[Blue][>90]0;0
8	85	85	[Red][<70]0;[Blue][>90]0;0
9	99	99	[Red][<70]0;[Blue][>90]0;0
10	1234	1 2 3 4	0_W_W0_N0_i0

In B2 and B3, if you put ** before the number code, Excel will fill to the left of the number with asterisks, like the old check writer machines would do. But there is nothing that says you have to use asterisks. Whatever you put after the first asterisk is repeated to fill the space. Row 3 uses *! to repeat exclamation points.

In B4 and B5, each comma that you put after the final zero will divide the number by 1000. The code 0,K shows numbers in thousands, with a K afterward. If you want to show millions, use two commas. The "M" code must include quotation marks, since M already means months.

In B6, add a stern message in the fourth zone to alert anyone entering data that you want a number in the cell. If they accidentally enter text, the message will appear.

5

In B7 to B9, the normal zones Positives, Negatives, and Zero are overwritten by conditions that you put in square brackets. Numbers under 70 are red. Numbers over 90 are blue. Everything else is black.

In B10, those odd _(symbols in the accounting format are telling Excel to leave as much space as a left parenthesis would take. It turns out that an underscore followed by any character will leave as much white space as that character. In B10, the code contains 4 zeros. But there are different amounts of space between them. The space between the 1 and 2 is the width of 2 W characters. The space between 2 and 3 is the width of an N. The space between 3 and 4 is the width of a lowercase letter i.

The following figure shows various date formatting codes.

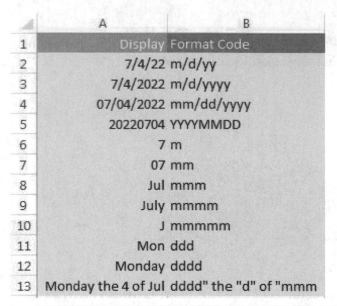

	A	B
1	Display	Format Code
2	7/4/22	m/d/yy
3	7/4/2022	m/d/yyyy
4	07/04/2022	mm/dd/yyyy
5	20220704	YYYYMMDD
6	7	m
7	07	mm
8	Jul	mmm
9	July	mmmm
10	J	mmmmm
11	Mon	ddd
12	Monday	dddd
13	Monday the 4 of Jul	dddd" the "d" of "mmm

Note: The mmmmm format in row 10 is useful for producing J F M A M J J A S O N D chart labels.

Thanks to Dave Baylis, Brad Edgar, Mike Girvin, and @best_excel for suggesting this feature.

#107 Show All Open Workbooks in the Windows Taskbar

Here is a great trick from Marlette Toole of the FL Space Coast chapter of the Institute of Internal Auditors. Since you are spending most of your work life in Excel, wouldn't it be nice to see all open workbooks in the Windows taskbar instead of just one tile with the Excel logo?

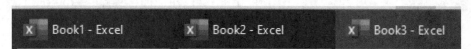

Right-click in an empty area of the Taskbar and choose Taskbar Settings. In the Combine Taskbar Settings drop-down menu, choose Never.

Combine taskbar buttons

Never ⌄

#108 Surveys & Forms in Excel

I often start my live Excel seminars off by asking you to point your cell phone camera at a giant bar code I have projected on the screen. That QR code leads to a three-question survey. Answers automatically flow into my Excel worksheet and those answers get used in the afternoon demo of 3D Maps.

Start at Forms.Office.com.

A browser will open and you can build your form. Click New Question. Forms offers support for seven question types. Don't miss the useful Ranking or Likert types hidden behind the three dots.

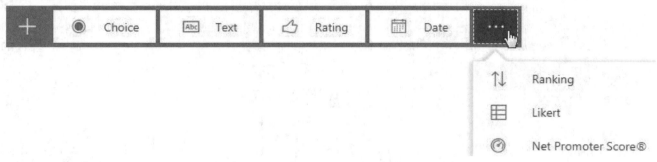

Type the question and possible answers.

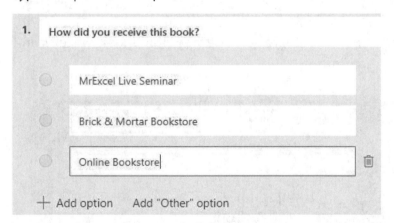

Branching is now supported: Click the 3 Dots icon in the top right corner of Forms.Office.Com.

When you are done with all questions, click Share in the top right corner. You can share via a link, or via e-mail, or using the QR Code. Try it: point your cell phone camera at the bar code on the right.

#109 Use the Windows Magnifier

If you received this book while attending one of my live Power Excel seminars, you likely saw me use the Windows Magnifier. Someone always asks how to use this, so I will write up the key steps.

First, there are three versions of the magnifier. To start the magnifier, press the Windows key and the Plus sign on the Numeric Keypad. To stop the magnifier, press the Windows key and Esc.

The first time that you use the magnifier, it opens in a view called Full Screen. Everything on the screen becomes bigger and you can use the mouse to move around. I don't like this version. Look for the floating Magnifier toolbar. Open Views and choose Lens.

A magnifier lens follows your mouse cursor around the screen. You can use the Settings (gear wheel) icon in the toolbar to change the size of the lens.

On some computers, the Magnifier toolbar starts out as an icon that looks like a magnifying glass. Click the icon to open the toolbar. More magnifier settings are in Windows, Settings, Ease of Access, Magnifier.

#110 Word for Excellers

Note: Katie Sullivan is a project manager on the Microsoft Word team. For this tip in the book, I turn the podium over to Katie.

While Excel fans sometimes tease that Word and PowerPoint are freeware apps that come with Excel, there are times when Microsoft Word offers a feature that Excel does not. In those cases, it makes sense to copy your data from Excel, paste to Word, do the command, then copy back to Excel. Here are some examples of techniques that are better handled in Word than in Excel.

Technique 1: Convert to Upper, Lower, Proper

If you have to convert from uppercase to lowercase or proper case, Word has a keystroke shortcut. Copy the data to Word and toggle the case using Shift+F3.

Technique 2: Add Bullets

If you want to add bullets to Excel cells, it is far easier in Word than in Excel. Copy the cells to Word and apply a bullet style. Copy from Word and paste back to Excel. You might have to use the Reduce Indent icon a few times.

Tip: Since the first edition of this book, I learned of an easier way to do bullets in Excel. If you have a range of cells that contain text, select the range and press Ctrl+1 to open the Format Cells dialog. Then, on the Number tab, choose Custom from the list on the left. Click in the Type box and clear out whatever is there. Hold down the Alt key while pressing the 7 on the numeric keypad. A bullet should appear. Type a space and then an @.

Technique 3: Visualize and Color Formulas

If you have a massively long formula, say one with 10 nested IF statements, you can paste to Word and use colors and Shift+Enter to space the formula to help make sense of it. (One rebuttal from the Excel team: You can expand the formula bar and use Alt+Enter to split a formula into many lines. Or, you can use the great RefTreeAnalyser add-in from Jan Karel Pieterse; see http://mrx.cl/jkpformula.)

Technique 4: Faster SmartArt

Word offers the Convert Text to SmartArt option. While Excel offers SmartArt, too, it is not very handy there because you have to copy the entries one at a time into the SmartArt pane.

5

Technique 5: Extract Data from a PDF

Say that someone has an Excel workbook and saves that workbook as a PDF. They send it to you. This is annoying, and clearly they don't want you to reuse the data. If you open the PDF in Acrobat Reader, copy the data, and paste to Excel, it will unwind into a single column. But here is the secret: Paste that data to Word first. The rows and columns will paste properly. You can then copy from Word and paste back into Excel. (If you are stuck in a pre-2013 version of Office, I recommend Able2Extract: mrx.cl/pdftoxl.)

The original data is shown on the left below, and you can see on the right and how it looks when you paste directly from PDF to Excel. You can see that the data "unwinds," with B1:C1 going to A2:A3 and so on.

	A	B	C
1	Trait	Dogs	Cats
2	Protective instinct	Yes	No
3	Always happy to see you when return	Yes	No
4	Spit up hairballs	No	Yes
5	Big or small	Yes	Only small
6	Chase tennis balls	Yes	No
7	Herd small children	Yes	No
8	Swim with you	Yes	No
9	Do tricks	Yes	No

	A	B
1	Trait	
2	Dogs	
3	Cats	
4	Protective instinct	
5	Yes	
6	No	
7	Always happy to see you	
8	Yes	
9	No	

Paste that same data to Word (below left), then copy from Word and paste to Excel (below right). The data stays in the original order. You can unapply Word Wrap and adjust the column widths to get back to the original data.

Trait	Dogs	Cats
Protective instinct	Yes	No
Always happy to see you when	Yes	No

Trait	Dogs	Cats
Protective e instinct	Yes	No
Always happy to see you	Yes	No

Technique 6: Change Formatting of Words Within Excel

If you have sentences of text in Excel, it is possible to select one word while in Edit mode and change the color of that word. But globally changing the color of all occurrences of the word in Excel is tedious. Instead, paste the data to Word and press Ctrl+H. Change dog to dog. Click More>> and then choose Format, Font. Choose Red. Click Replace All. Copy from Word and paste back to Excel. The figure below shows what you end up with.

	A	B	C	D	E	F	G	H
1	Original							
2	A dog is always happy to see you when you return home.							
3	If you have children, a dog will be protective of the children. If it is a herding dog, i							
4	Certain breeds of dog love to swim. You can not keep my dog Bella from diving in t							
5	A dog has no problems chasing a tennis ball all day.							
6								
7	After doing Replace in Word and pasting back to Excel							
8	A dog is always happy to see you when you return home.							
9	If you have children, a dog will be protective of the children. If it is a herding dog, i							
10	Certain breeds of dog love to swim. You can not keep my dog Bella from diving in t							
11	A dog has no problems chasing a tennis ball all day.							
12								

Technique 7: Replace While Keeping Character Formatting

Word also handles a similar problem: replacing text but leaving the text formatting as it is. Below is a survey about the best pet. Someone has highlighted certain words in the text.

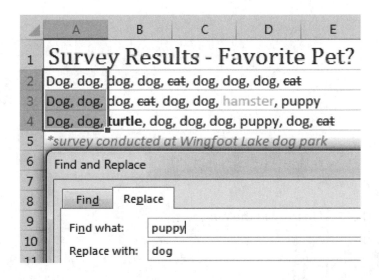

Use Ctrl+H to do a Find and Replace, as shown on the left. When you use Replace All, if a sentence was changed, your in-cell formats will be lost. In the figure below, the strikethrough remains in the first row because that row did not have an occurrence of the word *puppy* and thus was not changed.

Dog, dog, dog, dog, ~~cat~~, dog, dog, dog, ~~cat~~
Dog, dog, dog, cat, dog, dog, hamster, dog
Dog, dog, turtle, dog, dog, dog, dog, dog, cat

To keep the formatting in the original text, copy to Word. Do the replace in Word. Copy from Word and paste back to Excel.

Bonus Tip: Merge Shapes

Here's a brief plug for PowerPoint: If you need to create a shape in Excel that is a combination of other shapes, create the shapes in PowerPoint. Select all the shapes you want to include. On the Drawing Tools Format tab, choose Merge Shapes. You can then select Union, Combine, Fragment, Intersect, or Subtract to combine the shapes. (The Subtract feature lets you cut a hole in a shape.) Then copy that shape and paste to Excel (or Word).

Bonus Tip: Use the Eye Dropper

Another feature unique to PowerPoint is the eye dropper. If you want to use a particular color, you can just click the eye dropper on the color. When you open the Power Point color menu again, choose More Colors, and you can see the RGB colors. To use the eye dropper outside the PowerPoint frame, hold down the left mouse button and pick from any website or picture you have visible on your desktop.

Thanks to Katie Sullivan (a project manager on the Word team!) for contributing this tip. Katie clearly prefers dogs to cats. Thanks to Glenna Shaw and Oz du Soleil for contributing ideas to this tip. Zack Barresse and Echo Swinford pointed out the Merge Shapes option in PowerPoint. Sam Radakovitz added the eye dropper tip and noted the Subtract feature for shapes.

5

#111 Avoid Whiplash with Speak Cells

I hate having to hand-key data into Excel. Between the Internet and Power Query, there almost always is a way to find the data somewhere. I hate when people send a PDF where they scanned some numbers and are sending the numbers as a picture. A free trial of Able2Extract Pro (mrx.cl/ExtractPDF) will get the actual number into Excel. Even so, sometimes you end up keying data into Excel.

One of the painful parts about keying in data is that you have to proofread the numbers. So, you are looking at the sheet of paper, then the screen, then the paper, then the screen. You will end up with a sore neck. Wouldn't it be nice if you had someone to read you the screen so you can keep your eye on the paper? It's built in to Excel.

Right-click on the Quick Access Toolbar and choose Customize Quick Access Toolbar.

Change the top-left dropdown to Commands Not in the Ribbon. Scroll down to the S entries until you find Speak Cells. Add all five of these commands to the Quick Access Toolbar.

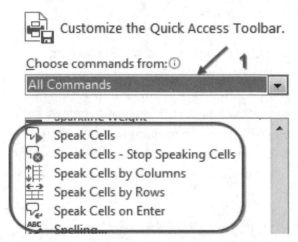

Select your range of numbers and click Speak Cells. Excel reads you the numbers.

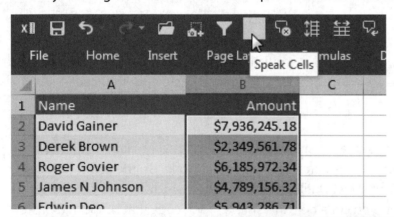

Tip: You can customize the voice in the Windows Control Panel. Search for Text to Speech. There is a setting for Voice Speed. Drag that slider to halfway between Normal and Fast to have the voice read your cells faster.

Bonus Tip: Provide Feedback with Sound

New in July 2017: Go to Excel Options. From the left category list, choose Ease of Access. Select the checkbox for Provide Feedback with Sound and choose Modern. (The other choice, Classic, should be called Annoying!)

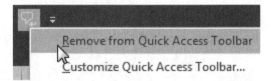

Excel now provides confirmation with gentle sounds when you do any of these tasks: Copy, Paste, Undo, Redo, AutoCorrect, Save, Insert Cells, Delete Cells.

Bonus Tip: A Great April Fool's Day Trick

Do you want a harmless prank to pull on a co-worker? When he leaves his desk to grab a cup of coffee, add the fifth icon to his Quick Access Toolbar: Speak Cells on Enter. Click the icon once, and the computer will say, "Cells will now be spoken on Enter."

Once you've turned on Speak Cells on Enter, right click the icon in the Quick Access Toolbar and choose Remove from Quick Access Toolbar to hide any sign that you were there.

Your co-worker comes back, sits down, and starts to build a worksheet. The computer repeats back everything the co-worker types.

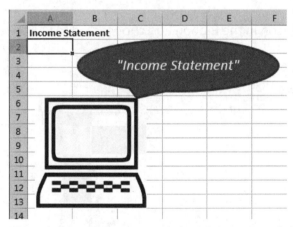

If you have a little more time and want Speak Cells on Enter with attitude, add the following macro to the code pane for the current worksheet..

```
Private Sub Worksheet_Change(ByVal Target As Range)
    Application.Speech.Speak "Damn Straight!  " & Target.Value
End Sub
```

#112 Customize the Quick Access Toolbar

As I mentioned in "#1 Ask Excel's A.I. a Question About Your Data" on page 1, the Excel team had not added any new features to the Home tab since January 30, 2007. Ideas is the first feature that was deemed worthy of being on the Home tab.

Even though the Excel team does not think many features are Home-tab-worthy, you can add your favorite features to the Quick Access Toolbar (hereafter called QAT).

I always like asking people what they have added to their QAT. In a Twitter poll in January 2019, I had over 70 suggestions of favorite features that could be added to the QAT.

To me, a "good" addition to the QAT is a command that you use frequently that is not already on the Home tab. Any of the features in the Commands Not In The Ribbon category are candidates if you ever have to use them.

Previously in this book, I've suggested the following icons on the QAT:

- The AutoFilter icon was used in "#5 Filter by Selection" on page 9
- Change Shape in "Bonus Tip: Old Style Comments Are Available as Notes" on page 35
- Speak Cells in "#111 Avoid Whiplash with Speak Cells" on page 238
- Speak Cells on Enter in "Bonus Tip: A Great April Fool's Day Trick" on page 239

Below are more icons that you might want to add to your QAT.

The Easy Way to Add to the QAT

The easiest way to add an icon to the QAT is to right-click the icon in the Ribbon and choose Add to Quick Access Toolbar.

Adding Formulas, Calculation Options, Manual to the QAT gives you a clear indication of when your workbook is in Manual calculation mode:

The Hard Way to Add to the QAT

Sometimes, the command you want can not be right-clicked. For example, in "Bonus Tip: Copy the Subtotal Rows" on page 69, I suggested using Alt+; as a shortcut for Visible Cells in the Go To Special dialog box.

Visible Cells Only is available to add to the QAT. But you can't add it by right-clicking in the dialog box. To make matters worse, when you follow these steps, you have to look for a command called "Select Visible Cells" instead of a command called "Visible Cells Only".

1. Right-click anywhere in the Ribbon and choose Customize Quick Access Toolbar. The Excel Options dialog box opens showing a list of Popular Commands. I reject many of these popular commands because they are already a single-click on the Home tab of the Ribbon.

2. Open the drop-down menu to the right of Popular Commands and choose either All Commands or Commands Not In the Ribbon.

3. Scroll through the left list box to find the command.

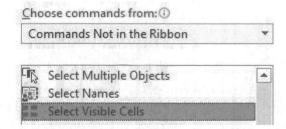

5

4. Click the Add>> button in the center of the screen.

5. Click OK to close Excel Options.

6. Hover over the newly added icon to see the tooltip and possibly learn of a keyboard shortcut.

Favorite QAT Icons From Twitter

If you are looking for something to make Twitter more interesting, consider following @MrExcel. You can then play along in fun surveys like this one:

Bill Jelen
@MrExcel

Following ∨

Friday #Excel poll: What are you favorite icons to add to the Quick Access Toolbar? Mine: AutoFilter and Insert Screen Clipping.

3:02 AM - 18 Jan 2019

6 Retweets **44** Likes

36   6   44

Presented below are several suggestions from people on Twitter.

Back in "#47 Quickly Convert Formulas to Values" on page 121 I had nine different ways to Paste Values. Here is a tenth way. The most popular suggestion on Twitter was the Paste Values icon.

Thanks to ExcelCity, Adam Warrington, Dan Lanning, Christopher Broas. Bonus point to AJ Willikers who suggested both Paste Values and Paste Values and Number Formatting shown to the right of Paste Values above.

Bonus Tip: Sometimes, You Don't Want the Gallery

The next most popular command to add to the QAT is Freeze Panes. Go to the View tab. Open the Freeze Panes drop-down menu. Right-click on Freeze Panes and Excel offers "Add Gallery to the Quick Access Toolbar".

Freeze panes is a tricky command. If you want to freeze row 1 and columns A:B, you have to put the cell pointer in C2 before you invoke Freeze Panes.

Some people don't understand this, and in Excel 2007, the Excel team made the Freeze Panes gallery with choices to freeze top row and freeze first column for people who did not know to select C2 before invoking Freeze Panes.

Since you understand how Freeze Panes works, you don't want the gallery on the QAT. You just want the icon that does Freeze Panes.

When you look for commands in the Excel Options, there are two choices for Freeze Panes. The one with the arrow is the gallery. The first one is the one you want.

Thanks to Debra Dalgleish, Colin Foster and @Excel_City for suggesting Freeze Panes

In other cases, the Gallery version is superior to the non-gallery version. Here is an example. Jen (who apparently is a @PFChangsAddict) suggested adding Save As to the QAT. Alex Waterton suggested adding Save As Other Formats. When I initially added the non-gallery version of Save As Other Formats, I realized that both icons open the Save As dialog box.

Instead, use the Gallery version of Save As

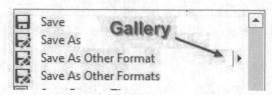

Here are those four icons in the QAT. The Save As Other Format gallery offers the most choices.

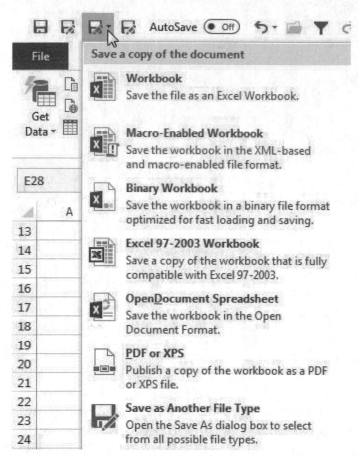

If you are planning on creating a lot of PDF files, Colin Foster suggests adding Publish as PDF or XPS to the QAT.

The First 9 Icons in QAT Have Easy Shortcut Keys

Most people who customize the QAT add new icons after the AutoSave, Save, Undo, Redo commands that are in the default QAT. But those first 9 QAT spots have super-easy keyboard shortcuts. AJ Willikers pointed out that the first 9 icons have easy short cut keys.

Press and release the Alt key. Key tips appear on each ribbon tab. So, Alt, H, S, O would sort descending. If you sort descending a lot, add the icon as one of the first 9 icons on the QAT. Press and release Alt, Then press 1 to invoke the first icon on the QAT. Note that the key tips for items 10 and beyond require you to press Alt, 0, 1 so they aren't quite as easy as the first 9 icons.

Thanks to AJ Willikers for pointing out the Alt 1-9 keyboard shortcuts.

The Camera Tool versus Paste as Linked Picture

Another popular QAT command on Twitter was the Camera. This awesome hack dates back to Excel 97. It is great because it allows you to paste a live picture of cells from Sheet17 on the Dashboard worksheet. It was hard to use and Microsoft re-worked the tool in Excel 2007, rebranding it as Paste As Linked Picture. But the operation of the tool changed and some people like the old way better.

For background on the tool, see "Bonus Tip: Line Up Dashboard Sections with Different Column Widths" on page 99. Say that you wanted to paste a picture of these cells in your dashboard:

Old way: You could select the cells. Click the Camera icon. The mouse pointer changes to a cross hair. Click anywhere that you want to paste the picture of the cells.

New way: Copy the cells. Click in the new location. Choose Paste As Linked Picture. If you don't want the picture lined up with the top-left corner of the cell, drag to nudge the picture into position.

Thanks to Manoel Costa, Brad Edgar, and Duncan Williamson for suggesting the Camera.

Screen Clipping to Capture a Static Image From Another Application

One of my favorite commands for the QAT is Insert Screen Clipping. Say that you want to grab a picture of a website and put it in your Excel worksheet. To effectively use the tool, you need to make sure that the web page is the most-recent window behind the Excel workbook. So - visit the web page. Then switch directly to your Excel Workbook. Choose Insert Screen Clipping and wait a few moments. The Excel screen disappears, revealing the web page. Wait for the web page to grey out, then use the mouse pointer to drag a rectangle around the portion of the web page. When you release the mouse button, a static picture of the web page (or any application) will paste in Excel. The Screen Clipping is also great for putting Excel charts in Power Point. Until you add this command to the QAT, it is hidden at the bottom of Insert, Screenshot. I don't like the Screenshot options because they put the entire full screen in Excel. Screen Clipping lets you choose just a part of the screen.

Two Icons Might Lead to the Same Place: Open Recent and Open

One of the popular QAT commands in Excel 2010 and Excel 2013 was the folder with a star - Open Recent File…. This command disappeared from Excel in Excel 2016. But people discovered that if you exported your settings from 2013 and then imported to 2016 or 2019, the icon would appear!

As I considered the prospect of dragging my Excel 2013 .tlb file around for the rest of my life, I inadvertently realized that the Open icon leads to the exact same place as the Open Recent File icon.

Thanks to Colin Foster and Ed Hansberry for suggesting Open Recent File.

5

Clear Filter and Reapply Filter

You hopefully already have the AutoFilter on your QAT after reading "#5 Filter by Selection" on page 9. Debra Dalgleish, Excel_City, and AJ Willikers suggests Clear Filters. This is a great way to reset your filters without visiting the Data tab.

Bathazar Lawson suggests adding Reapply Filter to the QAT. Here is how this becomes handy. Let's say you have a list of projects. You don't need to see anything where the status code is Complete. You set up a filter for this.

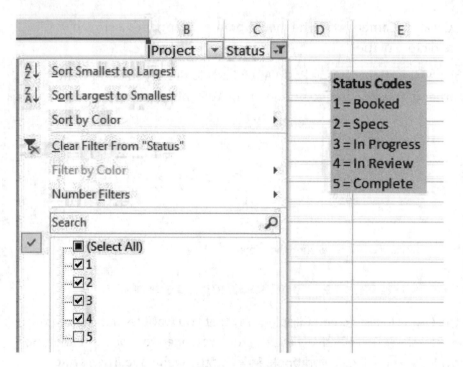

		Status Codes
		1 = Booked
		2 = Specs
		3 = In Progress
		4 = In Review
		5 = Complete

You change the status code on some projects. Some of the projects that used to be In Review are now Complete.

Project	Status
Project 115	3
Project 132	5
Project 38	2
Project 94	5
Project 106	5
Project 22	3
Project 17	5

Instead of re-opening the Filter drop-down, click Reapply Filter.

Excel will re-evaluate the data and hide the items which now have a 5.

Project	Status
Project 115	3
Project 38	2
Project 22	3
Project 21	4

Some Future Features Debut on the QAT and then Become Real Features

I was at a seminar in Topeka when Candace and Robert taught me that you could add an icon called Document Location to the QAT.

If you need to copy the document location to the clipboard, you can select the text from the QAT, right-click and choose Copy.

The Document Location has been available since at least Excel 2010. In early 2019, Microsoft 365 subscribers will notice that the File, Info screen now has new equivalents of Copy Path and Open File Location.

Easier Superscript and Subscripts

Add the new Superscript and Subscript icons to the QAT. As you are typing, click either icon to continue typing in subscript or superscript. This might be handy for a single character (such as the 2 in H_2O) or for several characters.

New Features from the Data Tab

The Data tab is like the Boardwalk and Park Place of the Excel ribbon. Every project manager wants to be on the Home tab, but most of the great features end up on the data tab. Excel 2016 introduced Get Data (Power Query), Relationships, and Refresh All. Add those to the QAT.

5

Build Formulas Without Ever Leaving the Mouse

Ha-ha! This advice flies in the face of what every Excel tipster teaches. Most people want you to build formulas without ever leaving the keyboard. But what if you hate the keyboard and want to use the mouse? You can add these operators to your QAT:

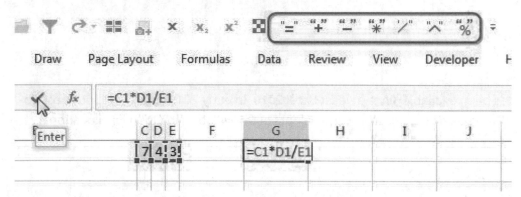

Using the mouse, you can click the Equals sign, then click on C1, then Multiply, then D1, then Divide, then E1. To complete the formula, click the green checkmark next to the formula bar to Enter. Surprisingly, Enter is not available for the QAT. But the formula bar is usually always visible, so this would work.

Those seven icons shown above are not located in one section of the Customize dialog. You have to hunt for them in the E, P, M, M, D, E, and P section of the list.

Bonus Tip: Show QAT Below the Ribbon

Right-click the Ribbon and choose Show Quick Access Toolbar Below The Ribbon. There are several advantages. First, it is a shorter mouse move to reach the icons. Second, when the QAT is above the Ribbon, you have less space until the icons run into the file name.

#113 Create Your Own QAT Routines Using VBA Macros

There are several short macros you can add to your Personal Macro Workbook and then add to the QAT. In this tip, you will see how to create the Personal Macro Workbook, type some macros, and then assign them to icons on the QAT.

Create a Personal Macro Workbook

Start from any workbook. Go to View, Macros, Record Macro. In the Record Macro dialog, type a one-word name such as HelloWorld. Choose Personal Macro Workbook. Click OK.

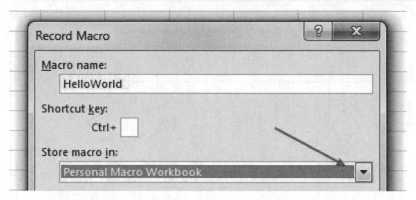

Type Hello in the active cell and press Enter. Then, select View, Macros, Stop Recording. These steps will create a Personal.xlsb on your computer where you can store new macros.

Open the VBA Editor and Find Module1 in Personal.xlsb

From Excel, press Alt+F11. (If you don't have Alt+F11, you can add the Visual Basic command to the QAT and click that.

Your first time in the VBA editor, it might be a vast expanse of grey. From the VBA menu, select View, Project Explorer.

Look for an entry called VBAProject (PERSONAL.XLSB). Click the + icon to expand it.

Look for and expand Modules. Right-click Module1 and choose View Code.

You will see your HelloWorld code. After the End Sub, type any of these procedures.

```
Sub VeryHideActiveSheet()
    ActiveSheet.Visible = xlVeryHidden
End Sub
Sub ShowAllSheets()
    For Each sh In ActiveWorkbook.Worksheets
        sh.Visible = True
    Next sh
End Sub
```

5

```
Sub UpperSelection()
    For Each cell In Selection.SpecialCells(2, 2)
        ' 2, 2 means xlCellTypeConstants, Text
        cell.Value = UCase(cell.Value)
    Next
End Sub
Sub LowerSelection()
    For Each cell In Selection.SpecialCells(2, 2)
        cell.Value = LCase(cell.Value)
    Next
End Sub
Sub ProperSelection()
    For Each cell In Selection.SpecialCells(2, 2)
        cell.Value = Application.WorksheetFunction.Proper(cell.Value)
    Next
End Sub
```

When you customize the QAT, choose Macros from the top left drop-down menu.

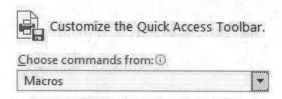

When you choose a macro and click Add>> the icon will default to a flow chart. Click Modify at the bottom right. Choose a new icon. Type a good tooltip.

Here is an explanation of how to use these five macros:

- **Very Hide**: Worksheets can be visible, hidden or very hidden. Few people know about Very Hidden sheets because you have to use VBA to create them. A worksheet that is Very Hidden will not show up in Home, Format, Hide and Unhide, Worksheets. (Thanks to -Sagar Malik)

- **Show All Sheets**: It is easy to select 12 sheets and hide them in a single command. But then unhiding the sheets is a one-at-a-time proposition. This macro will unhide all sheets (including very hidden sheets).

- **Upper Selection**: Converts all text in the selection to upper case.

- **Lower Selection**: Converts all text in the selection to lower case.

- **Proper Selection**: Converts all text in the selection to proper case.

Thanks to MF Wong for suggesting some of these macros.

Bonus Tip: Settings in the Excel Options Menu

Consider a few of these settings after you choose File, Options:

General, Start Up Options, Unselect Show The Start Screen When This Application Starts to skip the Home screen. Excel will open directly to a blank workbook. (Thanks to Dave Marriott)

Advanced, Editing Options, Unselect After Pressing Enter, Move Selection. When you type a value in a cell, Excel will stay in the same cell. (Thanks to Ed Hansberry)

Advanced, Editing Options, Automatically Insert a Decimal Point. You type 12345. Excel gets 123.45.

#114 Favorite Keyboard Shortcuts

As I started polling readers about their favorite Excel tips, a large number of them were keyboard shortcuts. Some readers, such as Matt Kellett, Olga Kryuchkova, Mike Dolan Fliss, and @model_citizen, suggested that the book has to include a section on favorite keyboard shortcuts.

These are presented in order of popularity. If a lot of readers suggested a tip, it is at the top. After the first eight or so, they are then sorted by my subjective sequence.

1. Ctrl+1 to Format a Selection

Ctrl+1 (the number one) works to format whatever is selected. Whether it is a cell, SmartArt, a picture, a

shape, or the March data point in a column chart, press Ctrl+1.

Thanks to Mitja Bezenšek, Alexa Gardner, Andrej Lapajne, Schmuel Oluwa, Jon Peltier, @ExcelNewss, and @JulianExcelTips.

2. Ctrl[+Shift]+Arrow to Navigate or Select

Your cell pointer is sitting at the top of 50K rows of data, and you need to get to the bottom. If you have a column with no blanks, press Ctrl+Down Arrow to jump to the end of the data set.

In the following figure, Ctrl+Down Arrow will jump to K545. Ctrl+Left Arrow will jump to A1. Ctrl+Right Arrow will jump the gap of empty cells and land on N1.

Add the Shift key in order to select from the active cell to the landing cell. Starting from A1 in the above figure, press Ctrl+Shift+Down Arrow to select A1:A545. While still holding down Ctrl+Shift, press the Right Arrow Key to select A1:K545. If it seems awkward at first, try it for a few days until you get the hang of it.

Thanks to Captain Excel, @Cintellis, José de Diego, Mike Girvin, Elchin Khalilov, Crystal Long, Paul Sasur, and @XLStudioWorks.

3. Ctrl+. to Jump to Next Corner

While you have a large range selected, press Ctrl+Period to move to the next corner of the selection. If the selection is rectangular, you move in a clockwise fashion. From the bottom-right corner, press Ctrl+. twice to move to the top left.

Thanks to Crystal Long, and Steve McCready.

4. Ctrl+5 for Strikethrough

This is great for crossing things off your to-do list. Why 5? If you are making hash marks, the fifth hash mark crosses out the first four.

5

5. Ctrl+* to Select Current Region

This one is easier if you have a number keypad so you don't have to press Shift to get to an asterisk. If I could slow down enough to stop pressing Ctrl+Shift+Down Arrow followed by Ctrl+Shift+Right arrow, I would realize that Ctrl+* is much shorter and does not get tripped up by blank cells. It is really superior in every way to keyboard tip #2. But my muscle memory still prefers tip #2. Thanks to @Excelforo.

6. Ctrl+Enter to Copy Formula into Entire Selection

Ken Puls, who is the king of Power Query, says, "You would think my favorite Excel tip would be Unpivot with Power Query, but my favorite all-time is Ctrl+Enter." Say that you want to enter a formula into 400 cells. Select the 400 cells. Type the formula in the first cell. Press Ctrl+Enter, and Excel enters a similar formula in all cells of the selection.

Gavin White points out another use. You enter a formula in G2. You need to copy the formula down but not the formatting. Select G2:G20. Press the F2 key to put the cell in Edit mode. When you press Ctrl+Enter, the formula is copied, but no formatting is copied. Thanks to Crystal Long, Schmuel Oluwa, Ken Puls, Peter Raiff, Sven Simon, and Gavin Whyte.

7. Ctrl(+Shift)+; to Time or Date Stamp

Press Ctrl+Shift+: to enter the current time. Press Ctrl+; for the current date. Note the shortcut enters the *current* time, not a formula. To put both the Date & time in one cell, type either keystroke, a space, then the other keystroke. Excel will interpret it as the proper Date & time.

Thanks to Olga Kryuchkova, Roger Govier and Tim O'Mara.

8. Ctrl+Backspace to Bring the Active Cell into View

This is a great trick that I never knew. Say that C1 is the active cell. You've used the scrollbars, and now you are looking at ZZ999. To bring the window back to encompass the active cell, press Ctrl+Backspace.

Thanks to Olga Kryuchkova and Schmuel Oluwa.

9. Alt+= for AutoSum

Press Alt+= to invoke the AutoSum function. Thanks to Dawn Bjork Buzbee and Olga Kryuchkova.

10. Ctrl+Page Down and Ctrl+Page Up to Jump to Next Worksheet

If you need to move from Sheet1 to Sheet5, press Ctrl+Page Down four times. If you are at Sheet9 and need to move to Sheet3, press Ctrl+Page Up six times. Thanks to Jeneta Hot.

11. Ctrl+Click to Select Noncontiguous Cells

If you have to select two regions, select the first one, then hold down Ctrl while clicking on other cells or regions. – Thanks toThomas Fries

12. Tab to AutoComplete

This one is maddening. You type =VL to start VLOOKUP. The AutoComplete shows that there is only one function that starts with VL. But if you press Enter, you get a #NAME? error.

The correct way to choose VLOOKUP is to press Tab! Thanks to Ashish Agarwal.

13. Shift+F8 to Add to Selection

Select the first range. Press Shift+F8, and you are in Add to Selection mode. Scroll anywhere. Select the next range. Then select another range. And so on, without ever touching Ctrl. To return to normal, press Esc. Thanks to Neil Charles. A bonus tip from Bill Hazlett: if you select A1, press F8, then click in S20, you will select from A1:S20. Press Esc to exit the Extend Selection mode. Watch for the indicator in the status bar:

14. Ctrl+Spacebar and Shift+Spacebar to Select an Entire Column or Row

Ctrl+Spacebar selects a whole column. Shift+Spacebar selects a whole row. How can you remember which is which? The "C" in Ctrl stands for the "C" in column. Also, the "S" in Shift is adjacent in the alphabet to the "R" in row. Another way to remember which is which: The Shift key is much longer (like a row!) than Ctrl.

Thanks to Michael Byrne, Jeneta Hot, and Bob Umlas.

15. Ctrl+` to See All Formulas

Many folks in the United States think this is Ctrl+~, but it is actually the grave accent to toggle into and out of Show Formulas mode.

16. F3 to Paste a Name into a Formula

I am not a huge fan of this, since you can start typing the name and then choose from AutoComplete. But I know the trick has its fans, including Mike Girvin and Johan van den Brink.

17. Ctrl+Shift+1 to apply Number Formatting

I had never memorized these, but I am going to start using some of them. Ctrl+Shift+1 (also known as Ctrl+!), will apply a number format, 2 decimals, thousands separator, and negatives shown with a minus sign. The other five make some reasonable sense, as described below.

Key	AKA	Formats as	Example
Ctrl+Shift+1	!	Number	-1,234.56
Ctrl+Shift+2	@	Time	2:50 PM
Ctrl+Shift+3	#	Date	29-Jun-15
Ctrl+Shift+4	$	Currency	($1,234.56)
Ctrl+Shift+5	%	Percent	100%
Ctrl+Shift+6	^	Exponential	1.23E+08

Thanks to Matthew Bernath.

18. Ctrl+Shift+2 to Apply Time Formatting

Ctrl+Shift+2 or Ctrl+@ applies a time formatting. Say that you want to meet for dinner @ 5 o'click. Long before it became associated with e-mail addresses, the @ inferred time.

19. Ctrl+Shift+3 to Apply Date Formatting

Ctrl+Shift+3 or Ctrl+# applies a date formatting. The # symbol looks a bit like a calendar, if you lived in an alternate universe with three weeks per month and three days per week.

20. Ctrl+Shift+4 to Apply Currency Formatting

Ctrl+Shift+4 or Ctrl+$ applies a currency format with two decimal places.

21. Ctrl+Shift+5 for Percent Format

Ctrl+Shift+5 or Ctrl+% applies a percentage format with 0 decimal places.

22. Ctrl+Shift+6 for Scientific Format

Ctrl+Shift+6 or Ctrl+Shift+^ applies scientific notation. 1.23E+07 infers an exponent. A caret(^) is used to enter exponents in Excel.

23. Ctrl+[to Jump to Linked Cell

You are in a cell that points to Sheet99!Z1000. Press Ctrl+[to jump to that cell. This works if you have links between workbooks, even if the other workbook is closed! Thanks to @Heffa100 and Bob Umlas.

24. Ctrl+F1 to hide or show the Ribbon

To toggle the Ribbon between Pinned and Hidden, use Ctrl+F1.

25. Alt+F1 to Chart the Selected Data

Select some data. Press Alt+F1. You get a chart of the data. You might remember F11 doing the same thing. But F11 creates the chart as a chart sheet. Alt+F1 embeds the chart in the current sheet.

26. Shift+F11 to Insert a Worksheet

I never knew this one, but it makes sense as a corollary to F11. If F11 inserts a chart sheet, then Shift+F11 inserts a new worksheet. You can also use Alt+I, W to insert a worksheet, Alt+I, R to insert a row, or Alt+I, C to insert a column. Thanks to Olga Kryuchkova.

27. Alt+E, S, V to Paste Values

I can do Alt+E, S, V, Enter with my eyes closed. Alt+E opened the Excel 2003 Edit menu. S chose Paste Special. V chose Values. Enter selected OK. Thanks to Matthew Bernath and Laura Lewis.

28. Alt+E, S, T to Paste Formats

Alt+E, S, T, Enter pastes formats. Why t instead of f? Because Alt+E, S, F already was in use to paste formulas.

29. Alt+E, S, F to Paste Formulas

Alt+E, S, F, Enter pastes formulas without copying the cell formatting. This is handy to prevent cell borders from copying along with the formula.

30. Alt+E, S, W to Paste Column Widths

Alt+E, S, W pastes column widths. This is great to use with a block of columns. In the following figure. select A1:H1, copy, then select J1 and Alt+E, S, V, Enter to copy all 8 column widths.

	A	B	C	D	E	F	G	H	I	J
1	Jan		Feb		Mar		Q1			Apr
2	Sales	%	Sales	%	Sales	%	Sales	%		Sales
3	7709	20%	5406	12%	9193	15%	22308	15%		8094

31. Alt+E, S, D, V to Paste Special Add

Alt+E, S, D, V does a Paste Special Add, but does not screw up the formatting.

32. Alt+E, S, E to Turn Data Sideways, I

Alt+E, S, E does a Transpose. To see all the possibilities, press Alt+E, S and then look for the underlined letters.

33. Alt+T, M, S to Change Macro Security.

This shortut is really useful now that the settings are buried deep in Excel options. Thanks to Ron de Bruin.

34. Alt+T, I to Activate Add-ins

Alt+T, I is faster than File, Options, Add-Ins, Manage Excel Add-ins, Go.

35. Ctrl+Shift+L to Enable the Filter Dropdowns

Toggle the filters on or off with Ctrl+Shift+L. In Excel 2013 and earlier, pressing Ctrl+Shift+L would scroll your screen to the end of the data set. Press Ctrl+Backspace to bring the active cell back in to view. Or, press and release Alt, A, T. Thanks to David Hager and Andrew Walker.

36. Hold Down Alt to Snap to Grid

If you are drawing any shape, Alt will cause that shape to exactly line up with the borders of cells. Thanks to Rickard Wärnelid.

37. Ctrl+W to Close a Workbook but Leave Excel Open

If you have one workbook open and you click the "X" in the top-right corner, you close Excel. Ctrl+W closes that workbook but leaves Excel open. Thanks to Dave Marriott.

38. F5 to Sneak into a Hidden Cell

You've hidden column D, but you need to see what is in D2. Press Ctrl+G or F5 to open the Go To dialog. Type D2 and press Enter. The cell pointer moves to the hidden cell D2, and you can see the value in the formula bar. You can now use the Down Arrow key to move within the hidden column D, and you can always see the value in the formula bar.

39. Alt+D, E, F to Convert Numbers Stored as Text to Numbers

Select a whole column and press Alt+D, E, F. The text numbers are converted to numbers. You are actually doing a default Text to Columns with this shortcut.

40. Alt+O, C, A to AutoFit a Column

Select some cells and press Alt+O, C, A to make the column wide enough for the longest value in the selection.

5

41. Ctrl+' to Copy the Exact Formula Down (aka Ditto)

You have to sum in D10 and average in D11. Create the AutoSum in D10. When you press Enter, you are in D11. Press Ctrl+' to bring the exact formula down without changing the cell reference. If D10 is =SUM(D2:D9), the formula in D11 will also be =SUM(D2:D9).

From there, you can press F2, Home, Right, AVERAGE, Delete, Delete, Delete, Enter. It sounds crazy, but the engineers at General Electric in Cleveland swear by it.

42. Ctrl+Shift+" to Copy the Cell Value from Above

Use Ctrl+Shift+" to bring the value from above into the current cell, eliminating any formula.

43. Hold down Alt while launching Excel to force it into a second instance

You might want each Excel workbook to have separate Undo stacks. This is one way.

44. Press F2 to toggle EDIT or ENTER while editing a formula in any dialog

Say you are typing =VLOCKUP(in the conditional formatting dialog. You press the left arrow key to go back to fix the typo, but Excel inserts a cell reference. Press F2 to change the lower left corner of the status bar from ENTER to EDIT and you can use the arrow keys to move through the formula.

45. Alt+W, F, F to Freeze Panes

There are hundreds more shortcuts like the ones above which you can easily learn. Press and release Alt in Excel to see key tips for each tab in the Ribbon (plus numbered key tips for the Quick Access Toolbar. Press the letter corresponding to a Ribbon tab to see the key tips for all of the commands on that tab. In this particular case, clicking Alt, W, F reveals a third level of key tips, and Alt, W, F, F completes the command. Thanks to Bradford Myers.

46. Ctrl+C to Copy

47. Ctrl+V to Paste

48. Ctrl+X to Cut

49. Ctrl+B for Bold

50. Ctrl+I for Italics

51. Ctrl+U for Underline

52. Ctrl+N for New Workbook

53. Ctrl+P to Print

54. Ctrl+T (or Ctrl+L) to Format as Table

55. Never Forget to Right-click

Many timesavers that are linked to the right mouse button that are often forgotten. Thanks to Colin Foster. Hey! This is not a keyboard shortcut! But wait…it is. You can open that right-click menu by using the Application key on the bottom-right side of your keyboard or Shift+F10. For more on the Application key, see "For Those Who Prefer Using Keyboard Shortcuts" on page 122. Release the Application key and then press any underlined letter to invoke the command.

#115 Ctrl+Click to Unselect Cells

You've always had the ability to select multiple selections in Excel by Ctrl+Dragging to select cells. In the images below, you might click in B2 and drag to C6. Then Ctrl+Click in C8 and drag to C11. Then Ctrl+Click on F2:and drag to B8. Then Ctrl+Click in F11.

You realize that you did not want to include F3 or F11 in the selection. In the past, there was no way to unselect one cell. You had to start all over with selecting B2:C6 and so on.

If you still have a copy of Excel 2013, try unselecting cells by Ctrl+Clicking them. An odd bug causes the cell to become progressively darker with each Ctrl+Click.

However - that bug was erased and new functionality added to Excel once a posting on Excel.UserVoice.com garnered 327 votes on Excel.UserVoice.com. This is a new feature released in 2018 to Microsoft 365 subscribers. You can now Ctrl+Click on a cell that is in the selection and remove the cell from the selection:

#116 Collapse the Search Box

It takes up way to much space. If you never use it, go to File, Options, General, Collapse the Microsoft Search Box by default. It will collapse to a magnifying glass and move to the top right of the screen.

#117 More Excel Tips

More than 200 ideas were sent in for this book. While the following ideas did not get much press here, they are self-explanatory in a 140-character tweet.

- To make Excel open full-screen, right-click the Excel icon and change the Run setting to Maximized. -David Ringstrom, CPA

- Use a thin light border line to create useful scrollbar maximums when your worksheet contains charts that the scroll bars don't recognize. -Chris Mack

- Highlight duplicate records with Conditional Formatting, Highlight Cells, Duplicate Records. -@Leaf_xl

- Color every other row with this conditional formatting formula: =MOD(ROW(),2)=0. -Pedro Millers

- Have a photo appear after a dropdown list in Excel http://t.co/TjbAtSkJ3t -Michael A. Rempel

- Use pictographs for charts (column and pie): Copy picture: select series, paste. -Olga Kryuchkova

- For a pie chart with too many slices: move small slices to second pie using Pie of Pie chart. -Olga Kryuchkova

- Use X/Y charts for drawing artwork. -Joerg Decker

- INDEX can return an entire row/column by using 0 for column/row. -Sumit Bansal

- Put an apostrophe in front of an Excel formula to stop it from being evaluated. -@DiffEngineX

- DATEDIF(A2,B2,"Y")&" yrs, "&DATEDIF(A2,B2,"YM")&" mos, "&DATEDIF(A2,B2,"MD")&" days." -Paul Wright

- Insert rows without breaking formulas. Cell above is OFFSET(*thisCell*,-1,0) - Jon Wittwer, Vertex42.com

- Subtract 1 from NPV function to get the Net Present Value of the investment. -Olen L. Greer

- Use EDATE to move the date out one month or year. -Justin Fishman

- Find mystery links in the Name Manager. Ta-da! -Lisa Burkett

- Formulas created in Notepad, saved as CSV, & opened in Excel work. Example: mike,=proper(A1) will give Mike. -@mdhExcel

- Double-click a formula. Excel color codes the cells referenced in the formula. -Cat Parkinson

- Turn off Edit Directly in Cell. Then double-click a formula to show cells used in that formula, even if in external workbook. -Sean Blessitt and David Ringstrom

- Go To Special, Constants helps spot constants within a block of formulas where a formula is overwritten with a number. -@HowToExcel

- Select a random 5% of data using =RAND()<.05. -Olga Kryuchkova

- Mark formulas with Conditional Formatting formula =HASFORMULA(A1). -Justin Fishman

- Double-click a number in a pivot to get the detail behind that number. -@Sheet1

- Array formula to count without COUNT: =SUM(IF(ISNUMBER(MyRange),1,0)). -Meni Porat

- In VBA, use Range("A1").CurrentRegion instead of RANGE(). It is like pressing Ctrl+*. -Arnout Brandt

- You can use hyperlinks to launch VBA macros. Smaller than buttons. -Cecelia Rieb

- Use a macro to color the heading cells that have filters applied. -Peter Edwards

- Use Environ("UserName") in VBA code for restricting workbook access. -Angelina Teneva

- Use a UDF in a hyperlink to change cells mrx.cl/udfhyperlink -Jordan Goldmeier

- There are a variety of games written in Excel (2048, MissileCommand, pleuroku, TowerDefense, Pac-Man, Rubic's Cube, Yahtzee, Tetris). -Olga Kryuchkova

- POINT mode in Excel lets you build a formula using arrow keys to point to cells or ranges. If this stops working, see if you inadvertently pressed ScrLk key. You will see SCROLL LOCK near left side of Status Bar. (ScrLk is near PrtScrn and Break keys). -Vijay Krishnan

#118 Excel Stories

Live – On Stage – In Person: The Power Excel Seminars

That poster from Hatch Show Print on my website sort of started out as a joke. I was flying through Nashville and saw a display of old country music letterpress posters on the wall. The little sign by the posters said they were produced on a 100-year-old hand-cranked press and that the company was still operating in Nashville. I called them and hired them to produce a "concert" poster for my live Excel seminars. They had to think I was a little nuts. The print shop manager, Jim Sherraden, often did an informative presentation about the history of Hatch, and he cited my poster as the first to list a website URL.

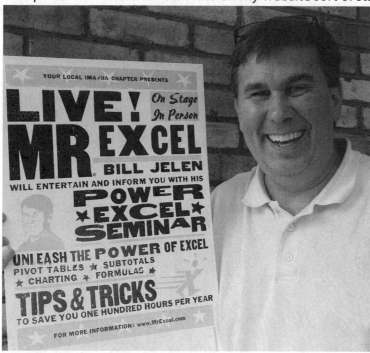

I do my half-day or 1-day seminar for accounting groups across the country. Every large city has a local chapter of the Institute of Managerial Accountants or the Institute of Internal Auditors. The people who belong to these groups usually need 20-30 hours of continuing education (CPE) each year. If you join the organization and go to 12 lunch meetings, half of your CPE is done. The organizations will often sponsor a 1- or 2-day event with speakers so their members can earn the remaining CPE at one time. I often am invited to speak at these events. The poster on the door lets people know that they are not in for the usual tax update. (I don't mean to offend the wonderful people going through the new tax laws…someone's got to do that.)

Excel is used on 750 million devices. I've met a lady in Appalachia who used Excel to design original quilt patterns. I've met people who have designed workbooks in Excel that train people how to fly 737 jets. From quilts to jets, Excel is used everywhere.

When you hand the world's most flexible software to 750 million people, everyone finds interesting things to do or interesting ways to use Excel. I love traveling to do the in-person Excel seminars because I get to meet these people. At every seminar, someone has an interesting story of how they are using Excel. At every seminar, I always learn a few new Excel tricks from the people in the seminar. I joke that my job is collecting the cool and obscure tricks in Excel from people along the road and passing them on to people further on up the road. Many of the amazing tricks in this book came from people in my live Excel seminars.

This is truly a win-win. I have fun doing the seminars. The audience get to take home a cool Excel book. Among the 75 tricks that I show in a day, hopefully everyone will find a few that they can take back to work to start becoming more efficient the next day. Plus, people earn the CPE hours without hearing about any tax updates. Even at the Association for Computers and Taxation, where their annual meeting is all about tax updates, they bring me in to do a 2-hour session to offer a little levity between the tax updates!

The Excel Guru Mission Patch

Do you own a the highly-coveted Excel Guru mission patch?

When I do my live Power Excel seminars, I always encourage the audience to "show me up." Someone in that room is going to have a better way to do something in Excel. I used to offer a small prize to the first person to teach me something during the seminar. I would also predict that the first person to show me up that day walked into the room and sat in row 2.

I have no idea why they often sit in row 2. But I noticed early on that the best Exceller often chooses a seat in row 2. They want to be close. But not front-row close. Almost every time, the first cool idea from the audience comes to row 2. (On the times when the first tip comes from another row, I quip, "Did you arrive late, and row 2 was already full?")

Over the years, the prize varied from a laminated tip card to an Excel Master enamel pin. The current prize is an embroidered Excel Guru patch designed by the same guy who designs mission patches for Cape Canaveral rocket launches.

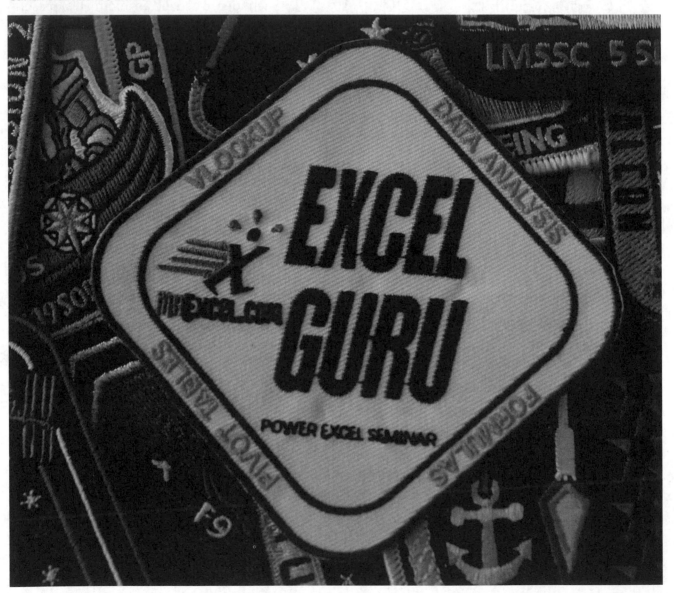

As Seen in the Wall Street Journal: the Excel Function Clock

It was a Friday afternoon at work and time was dragging. I would look at the clock, do some VLOOKUPs, then look back at the clock and barely a minute had passed.

it struck me that it would be funny if someone made a clock where the 3 was replaced with the Excel function =PI(). This simple function with no arguments returns 3.14. So, =PI() wouldn't be exactly at 3. It would have to be just a bit beyond the 3. The solution would be to use the INT function to return just the integer portion of PI(). =INT(PI()) returns just 3. Perfect! I am sure I pitched both of these ideas to Kevin Adkins, who probably didn't think it was a funny as I did. That never deters me, though.

After writing all 12 functions, I actually found the graphic designer who designed the clocks for the old Signals mail order catalog. The Excel function clock was on Call For Help a few times. Once, Leo Laporte attached it to a lanyard and wore the clock as if he were rapper Flavor Flav. It was funny stuff.

The clock became famous, though, in 2017 when it was featured in a Wall Street Journal article about the CFO of PF Changs saying he was going to dump Excel. People were furious and the WSJ ran a follow-up article with a quote by me and also a picture of my clock. I sold a lot of clocks that week!

Here are the 12 formulas:

1. =MIN(1,10). Min returns the minimum number. Since 1<10, the function returns 1.

2. =MONTH(23790). That is the serial number for my birthday, February 17, 1965. That is month number 2.

3. =INT(PI()). =PI() would've been 1/7 of the way past 3, so =INT returns the integer 3.

4. =LEN("FOUR"). I used LEN daily. =MID(A2,LEN(A2)-7,2) gets the last 2 characters. How long is FOUR? 4.

5. =SQRT(25). The square root of 25 is 5.

6. =FACT(3). Factorials are used to calculate lottery probability. The Factorial of 3 is 3x2x1 or 6.

7. =GCD(77,49). Middle school match is simpler with Excel. The greatest common divisor of 77 and 49 is 7

8. =2^3. The ^ raises 2 to the 3 power. =2*2*2 is 8.

9. =PMT(9%,9,-53.96). If you borrowed $53.96 from the bank to buy some MrExcel books and had to pay it back over 9 years with a 9% interest rate, each yearly payment would be $9.

10. =LCM(2,5). Another one for the 7th graders. The Lowest Common Multiple of 2 and 5 is 10.

11. =ROMAN(2). Hmm. My fascination with =ROMAN() began before my 40th book. The =ROMAN(2) is II, which looks sort of like 11. Just like XL sounds sort of like Excel.

12. =COLUMN(L1). tells you the column number of a cell. L is column number 12.

If you are thinking you need to get one of these for yourself, head over to mrx.cl/excelclock.

The MrExcel Message Board Community Answered 1 Million Excel Questions

When I launched MrExcel.com in November 1998, I would get up every morning and answers yesterday's e-mailed questions before heading in to work. Initially, it was a question or two each weekday. But, by May 1999, I was getting more questions than I could answer in an hour. I was answering questions from 5 AM to 6 AM and then heading in to work. I either had to start getting up at 4 AM or find another way.

I downloaded WWWBoard from Matt's Script Archive. I asked people to post their question at the message board. And I asked that, after posting, they look at the last few questions to see if they could help someone else out. It was like the take-a-penny, leave-a-penny tray at a cash register. If you need help, post a question. If you can help someone else out, help them out. It worked. People started posting and answering questions.

In the early days, I noticed a few people would stop by almost every day and answer a question or two. Ivan F. Moala. Cecilia. The late Dave Hawley.

One day, at work. I was stumped. I went out to my own message board, and described my problem. An hour later, Ivan F. Moala from New Zealand had posted an amazing answer. I knew I had something.

The board transformed over the years, morphing into bigger platforms. I was on a $10-a-month hosting plan at Pair Networks in Pittsburgh. One day, I get a call from them wondering what I was doing. "You are on a $10-a-month plan, but you are using as much traffic as our $1,000-a-month plan!" Apparently, the MrExcel Message Board had taken on a life of its own.

Today, the amazing people at the MrExcel Message Board have answered 1 million questions about Excel. We've attempted to keep every question live on the site. There are some massive competitors (I won't name them, but their anagram is "is Comfort" or "of Mr Stoic") who have competing forums, but they have no problem wiping out their history. I run into people all the time who say they use my forum. I ask what their UserID is. "Oh – I've never had to post – I just search. Every answer is already there."

The MrExcel community is staffed by volunteers. Over the years, various experts have worked tirelessly as moderators and administrators. My sincere thanks to Andrew Poulsom, barry houdini, Colo, fairwinds, Ivan F Moala, Joe4, Jon von der Heyden, Juan Pablo Gonzalez, NateO, PaddyD, Peter_SSs, Richard Schollar, RoryA, Scott Huish, Smitty, Starl, SydneyGeek, VoG, Von Pookie, zenou, and Zack Barresse. Suat Ozgur and Scott Pierson handled the tech issues with the board.

As far as the people answering questions, 45 people have answered more than 10,000 questions at the board. This is a staggering contribution to the Excel community. Thanks to Aladin Akyurek with 85,000 posts. Norie and Andrew Poulsom have over 70,000 posts each. VoG has over 63,000 posts. Others with over 10K posts: Joe4, Jonmo1, Peter SSs, Rick Rothstein, RoryA, Fluff, Smitty, Richard Schollar, mikerickson, shg, barry houdini, Scott Huish, pgc01, Domenic, erik.van.geit, Michael M, hiker95, jindon, JoeMo, T. Valko, xenou, Marcelo Branco, AlphaFrog, My Aswer Is This, MickG, PaddyD, Ienze, Von Pookie, SydneyGeek, Juan Pablo Gonzalez, Mark W., Yogi Anand, MARK858, Tom Urtis, JLGWhiz, GlennUK, tusharm, oldbrewer, Zack Barresse, Jon von der Heyden, just jon, and Greg Truby, and Mole999. Many of the experts at MrExcel.com are awarded the MVP Award in Excel from Microsoft.

If you ask Google any Excel question, the odds are pretty good that one of the top answers will be from MrExcel. If you can't find your answer on Google, it is free to post a new question. Make sure to give the post a title that describes what you are trying to do. Even in the middle of the night, someone will likely have an answer.

In late 2019, the message board was migrated to a modern Xenforo platform, complete with the ability to post screenshots of your Excel problem.

How to Post Your Question to the MrExcel Forum

Here are a few tips to getting an answer quickly at the MrExcel forum.

1. Before posting, do a <u>Search</u>. With a million threads, it is likely someone has had this problem before. You do not have to register to search.

2. In order to post, you have to <u>Register</u>. Give yourself a clever name such as XLGoddess or VLOOKUPKing. We ask for your e-mail address for password resets. I am not doing this to spam you. I won't spam you (because I can't figure out how to spam this many people without getting thrown off the Internet). We used to allow "Anonymous" to post to the board, but when five different "Anonymous" started posting in the same thread, it became impossible to follow the conversation. After registering, click the link in the confirmation e-mail that we send.

3. Start in the <u>Excel Questions</u> forum (there are other forums for Access, Power BI, and so on).

4. Click the Post Thread button in the top right.

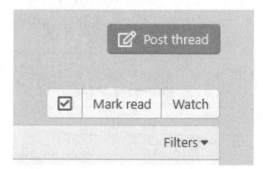

5. Include a meaningful title that is specific to your question. Here is an example of a good title: "Excel VBA Type Mismatch Error". Your goal with the title is to get an expert to be interested in your question. Titles such as "Excel Help" or "Help" are not useful.

6. State your question clearly, including your entire need at the start.

7. Add some representative sample data - actual data is much better than an image. There are free tools to help you post your data to the board. See "How to Show Your Worksheet in a Post" below.

8. Tell us what formula/code you have currently, and why your results are not what you want.

9. Include which version of Excel and Operating System you are using.

10. If you are looking for help with an error received, what is the actual error message and where exactly does it occur?

11. Before posting, read your question back to yourself to check it will make sense to somebody unfamiliar with your worksheet.

12. If the answer you receive is inadequate for some reason, post a reply stating why the answer does not work and/or with more information (if needed) in the same thread.

If one or more posts were particularly helpful, click the Like button on that post. Getting Likes increases a person's reputation.

How to Show Your Worksheet in a Post

There are two ways to show your worksheet when posting to the MrExcel Message Board. First, you can use any screen clipping tool, copy a portion of the screen to your clipboard, then paste it into a post at the board. While pasting a picture can allow someone to see what is going on, in many cases, the volunteer who is going to answer your question will want to test some formulas in Excel, and a picture forces them to re-create your worksheet. Instead, our awesome web developer, Suat Ozgur has produced a free Excel add-in called XL2BB which allows you to post your worksheet to the board and allows the volunteer to then copy this data to Excel.

1. Download XL2BB and install following the instructions at http://mrx.cl/XL2BB.

2. You will see a new xl2BB tab in the Ribbon.

3. Select the portion of the worksheet you would like to share and click Mini Sheet.

4. Switch back to the MrExcel forum and Ctrl+V to paste the code into your question. Initially, it will be a scary-looking bunch of codes, like this:

6. Click the Preview button

7. And you will see a version of your worksheet:

Preview
Can you help with this worksheet?

xl2bb.xlam				
f(x) Click formula cells to copy formulas.				

	A	B	C	D	E
1		Jan	Feb	Mar	Apr
2	Andy	4	6	8	10
3	Barb	6	9	12	15
4	Chris	8	12	16	20
5	Diane	10	15	20	25
6	Ed	12	18	24	30
7	Flo	14	21	28	35

Sheet1   XL2BB

Cell Formulas

Range(s)	Formula	
B2:E7	**B2**	=ROW()*COLUMN()

Here is why going to these extra steps will get you a better answer. When you post your worksheet to the board, the volunteer Excel experts love this view of the data for several reasons:

1. They can hover over any value in a cell with a yellow triangle to see the formula in that cell.

2. If they click the value, the formula is displayed in the formula bar and automatically copied to the clipboard so the volunteer expert can paste it into their copy of Excel.

3. If they click the "Select All" icon above and to the left of cell A1, the code for the worksheet is copied to the clipboard. They can then paste this code to a blank workbook and test their formula ideas.

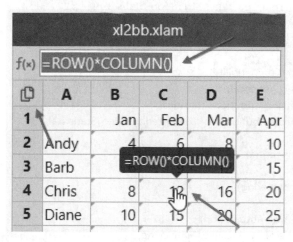

#119 Excel Function Quick Reference

This is an alphabetical listing of Excel's functions as of February 2021.

ABS - Returns the absolute value of a number (Math & trig)

ACCRINT - Returns the accrued interest for a security that pays periodic interest (Financial)

ACCRINTM - Returns the accrued interest for a security that pays interest at maturity (Financial)

ACOS - Returns the arccosine of a number (Math & trig)

ACOSH - Returns the inverse hyperbolic cosine of a number (Math & trig)

ACOT - Returns the arccotangent of a number (Math & trig)

ACOTH - Returns the hyperbolic arccotangent of a number (Math & trig)

AGGREGATE - Returns an aggregate in a list or database (Math & trig)

ADDRESS - Returns a reference as text to a single cell in a worksheet (Lookup & reference)

AMORDEGRC - Returns the depreciation for each accounting period by using a depreciation coefficient (Financial)

AMORLINC - Returns the depreciation for each accounting period (Financial)

AND - Returns TRUE if all of its arguments are TRUE (Logical)

ARABIC - Converts a Roman number to Arabic, as a number (Math & trig)

AREAS - Returns the number of areas in a reference (Lookup & reference)

ARRAYTOTEXT - Returns an array of text values from any specified range (Text)

ASC - Changes full-width (double-byte) English letters or katakana within a character string to half-width (single-byte) characters (Text)

ASIN - Returns the arcsine of a number (Math & trig)

ASINH - Returns the inverse hyperbolic sine of a number (Math & trig)

ATAN - Returns the arctangent of a number (Math & trig)

ATAN2 - Returns the arctangent from x- and y-coordinates (Math & trig)

ATANH - Returns the inverse hyperbolic tangent of a number (Math & trig)

AVEDEV - Returns the average of the absolute deviations of data points from their mean (Statistical)

AVERAGE - Returns the average of its arguments (Statistical)

AVERAGEA - Returns the average of its arguments, including numbers, text, and logical values (Statistical)

AVERAGEIF - Returns the average (arithmetic mean) of all the cells in a range that meet a given criteria (Statistical)

AVERAGEIFS - Returns the average (arithmetic mean) of all cells that meet multiple criteria. (Statistical)

BAHTTEXT - Converts a number to text, using the ß (baht) currency format (Text)

BASE - Converts a number into a text representation with the given radix (base) (Math & trig)

BESSELI - Returns the modified Bessel function In(x) (Engineering)

BESSELJ - Returns the Bessel function Jn(x) (Engineering)

BESSELK - Returns the modified Bessel function Kn(x) (Engineering)

BESSELY - Returns the Bessel function Yn(x) (Engineering)

BETADIST - Returns the beta cumulative distribution function (Compatibility)

BETA.DIST - Returns the beta cumulative distribution function (Statistical)

BETAINV - Returns the inverse of the cumulative distribution function for a specified beta distribution (Compatibility)

BETA.INV - Returns the inverse of the cumulative distribution function for a specified beta distribution (Statistical)

BIN2DEC - Converts a binary number to decimal (Engineering)

BIN2HEX - Converts a binary number to hexadecimal (Engineering)

BIN2OCT - Converts a binary number to octal (Engineering)

BINOMDIST - Returns the individual term binomial distribution probability (Compatibility)

BINOM.DIST - Returns the individual term binomial distribution probability (Statistical)

BINOM.DIST.RANGE - Returns the probability of a trial result using a binomial distribution (Statistical)

BINOM.INV - Returns the smallest value for which the cumulative binomial distribution is <= to a criterion value (Statistical)

BITAND - Returns a 'Bitwise And' of two numbers (Engineering)

BITLSHIFT - Returns a value number shifted left by shift_amount bits (Engineering)

BITOR - Returns a bitwise OR of 2 numbers (Engineering)

BITRSHIFT - Returns a value number shifted right by shift_amount bits (Engineering)

BITXOR - Returns a bitwise 'Exclusive Or' of two numbers (Engineering)

CALL - Calls a procedure in a dynamic link library or code resource (Add-in and Automation)

CEILING - Rounds a number to the nearest integer or to the nearest multiple of significance (Math & trig)

CEILING.MATH - Rounds a number up, to the nearest integer or to the nearest multiple of significance (Math & trig)

CEILING.PRECISE - Rounds a number the nearest integer or to the nearest multiple of significance. Regardless of the sign of the number, the number is rounded up. (Math & trig)

CELL - Returns information about the formatting, location, or contents of a cell (Information)

CHAR - Returns the character specified by the code number (Text)

CHIDIST - Returns the one-tailed probability of the chi-squared distribution (Compatibility)

CHIINV - Returns the inverse of the one-tailed probability of the chi-squared distribution (Compatibility)

CHITEST - Returns the test for independence (Compatibility)

CHISQ.DIST - Returns the cumulative beta probability density function (Statistical)

CHISQ.DIST.RT - Returns the one-tailed probability of the chi-squared distribution (Statistical)

CHISQ.INV - Returns the cumulative beta probability density function (Statistical)

CHISQ.INV.RT - Returns the inverse of the one-tailed probability of the chi-squared distribution (Statistical)

CHISQ.TEST - Returns the test for independence (Statistical)

CHOOSE - Chooses a value from a list of values (Lookup & reference)

CLEAN - Removes all nonprintable characters from text (Text)

CODE - Returns a numeric code for the first character in a text string (Text)

COLUMN - Returns the column number of a reference (Lookup & reference)

COLUMNS - Returns the number of columns in a reference (Lookup & reference)

COMBIN - Returns the number of combinations for a given number of objects (Math & trig)

COMBINA - Returns the number of combinations with repetitions for a given number of items (Math & trig)

COMPLEX - Converts real and imaginary coefficients into a complex number (Engineering)

CONCAT - Combines the text from multiple ranges and/or strings, without the delimiter or IgnoreEmpty arguments. (Text)

CONCATENATE - Joins several text items into one text item (Text)

CONFIDENCE - Returns the confidence interval for a population mean (Compatibility)

CONFIDENCE.NORM - Returns the confidence interval for a population mean (Statistical)

CONFIDENCE.T - Returns the confidence interval for a population mean, using a Student's t distribution (Statistical)

CONVERT - Converts a number from one measurement system to another (Engineering)

CORREL - Returns the correlation coefficient between two data sets (Statistical)

COS - Returns the cosine of a number (Math & trig)

COSH - Returns the hyperbolic cosine of a number (Math & trig)

COT - Returns the hyperbolic cosine of a number (Math & trig)

COTH - Returns the cotangent of an angle (Math & trig)

COUNT - Counts how many numbers are in the list of arguments (Statistical)

COUNTA - Counts how many values are in the list of arguments (Statistical)

COUNTBLANK - Counts the number of blank cells within a range (Statistical)

COUNTIF - Counts the number of cells within a range that meet the given criteria (Statistical)

COUNTIFS - Counts the number of cells within a range that meet multiple criteria (Statistical)

COUPDAYBS - Returns the number of days from the beginning of the coupon period to the settlement date (Financial)

COUPDAYS - Returns the number of days in the coupon period that contains the settlement date (Financial)

COUPDAYSNC - Returns the number of days from the settlement date to the next coupon date (Financial)

COUPNCD - Returns the next coupon date after the settlement date (Financial)

COUPNUM - Returns the number of coupons payable between the settlement date and maturity date (Financial)

COUPPCD - Returns the previous coupon date before the settlement date (Financial)

COVAR - Returns covariance, the average of the products of paired deviations (Compatibility)

COVARIANCE.P - Returns covariance, the average of the products of paired deviations (Statistical)

COVARIANCE.S - Returns a sample covariance, the average of the products deviations for each data point pair in 2 data sets (Stats)

CRITBINOM - Returns the smallest value for which the cumulative binomial distribution is <= to a criterion value (Compatibility)

CSC - Returns the cosecant of an angle (Math & trig)

CSCH - Returns the hyperbolic cosecant of an angle (Math & trig)

CUBEKPIMEMBER - Returns a key performance indicator (KPI) name, property, and measure, and displays the name and property in the cell. A KPI is a quantifiable measurement, such as monthly gross profit or quarterly employee turnover, used to monitor an organization's performance. (Cube)

CUBEMEMBER - Returns a member or tuple in a cube hierarchy. Use to validate that the member or tuple exists in the cube. (Cube)

CUBEMEMBERPROPERTY - Returns the value of a member property in the cube. Use to validate that a member name exists within the cube and to return the specified property for this member. (Cube)

CUBERANKEDMEMBER - Returns the nth, or ranked, member in a set. Use to return one or more elements in a set, such as the top sales performer or top 10 students. (Cube)

CUBESET - Defines a calculated set of members or tuples by sending a set expression to the cube on the server, which creates the set, and then returns that set to Microsoft Office Excel. (Cube)

CUBESETCOUNT - Returns the number of items in a set. (Cube)

CUBEVALUE - Returns an aggregated value from a cube. (Cube)

CUMIPMT - Returns the cumulative interest paid between two periods (Financial)

CUMPRINC - Returns the cumulative principal paid on a loan between two periods (Financial)

DATE - Returns the serial number of a particular date (Date & time)

DATEDIF - Calculates the number of days, months, or years between two dates. This function is useful in formulas where you need to calculate an age. (Date & time)

DATEVALUE - Converts a date in the form of text to a serial number (Date & time)

DAVERAGE - Returns the average of selected database entries (Database)

DAY - Converts a serial number to a day of the month (Date & time)

DAYS - Returns the number of days between two dates (Date & time)

DAYS360 - Calculates the number of days between two dates based on a 360-day year (Date & time)

DB - Returns the depreciation of an asset for a specified period by using the fixed-declining balance method (Financial)

DBCS - Changes half-width (single-byte) English letters or katakana within a character string to double-byte characters (Text)

DCOUNT - Counts the cells that contain numbers in a database (Database)

DCOUNTA - Counts nonblank cells in a database (Database)

DDB - Returns the depreciation of an asset for a specified period by using the double-declining balance method or some other method that you specify (Financial)

DEC2BIN - Converts a decimal number to binary (Engineering)

DEC2HEX - Converts a decimal number to hexadecimal (Engineering)

DEC2OCT - Converts a decimal number to octal (Engineering)

DECIMAL - Converts a text representation of a number in a given base into a decimal number (Math & trig)

DEGREES - Converts radians to degrees (Math & trig)

DELTA - Tests whether two values are equal (Engineering)

DEVSQ - Returns the sum of squares of deviations (Statistical)

DGET - Extracts from a database a single record that matches the specified criteria (Database)

DISC - Returns the discount rate for a security (Financial)

DMAX - Returns the maximum value from selected database entries (Database)

DMIN - Returns the minimum value from selected database entries (Database)

DOLLAR - Converts a number to text, using the $ (dollar) currency format (Text)

DOLLARDE - Converts a dollar price, expressed as a fraction, into a dollar price, expressed as a decimal number (Financial)

DOLLARFR - Converts a dollar price, expressed as a decimal number, into a dollar price, expressed as a fraction (Financial)

DPRODUCT - Multiplies the values in a particular field of records that match the criteria in a database (Database)

DSTDEV - Estimates the standard deviation based on a sample of selected database entries (Database)

DSTDEVP - Calculates the standard deviation based on the entire population of selected database entries (Database)

DSUM - Adds the numbers in the field column of records in the database that match the criteria (Database)

DURATION - Returns the annual duration of a security with periodic interest payments (Financial)

DVAR - Estimates variance based on a sample from selected database entries (Database)

DVARP - Calculates variance based on the entire population of selected database entries (Database)

EDATE - Returns the serial number of the date that is the indicated number of months before or after the start date (Date & time)

EFFECT - Returns the effective annual interest rate (Financial)

ENCODEURL - Returns a URL-encoded string (Web)

EOMONTH - Returns the serial number of the last day of the month before or after a specified number of months (Date & time)

ERF - Returns the error function (Engineering)

ERF.PRECISE - Returns the error function (Engineering)

ERFC - Returns the complementary error function (Engineering)

ERFC.PRECISE - Returns the complementary ERF function integrated between x and infinity (Engineering)

ERROR.TYPE - Returns a number corresponding to an error type (Information)

EUROCONVERT - Converts a number to euros, converts a number from euros to a euro member currency, or converts a number from one euro member currency to another by using the euro as an intermediary (triangulation). (Add-in and Automation)

EVEN - Rounds a number up to the nearest even integer (Math & trig)

EXACT - Checks to see if two text values are identical (Text)

EXP - Returns e raised to the power of a given number (Math & trig)

EXPON.DIST - Returns the exponential distribution (Statistical)

EXPONDIST - Returns the exponential distribution (Compatibility)

FACT - Returns the factorial of a number (Math & trig)

FACTDOUBLE - Returns the double factorial of a number (Math & trig)

FALSE - Returns the logical value FALSE (Logical)

F.DIST - Returns the F probability distribution (Statistical)

FDIST - Returns the F probability distribution (Compatibility)

F.DIST.RT - Returns the F probability distribution (Statistical)

FILTER - Filters a range of data based on criteria you define (Lookup & reference)

FILTERXML - Returns specific data from the XML content by using the specified XPath (Web)

FIND, FINDBs - Finds one text value within another (case-sensitive) (Text)

F.INV - Returns the inverse of the F probability distribution (Statistical)

F.INV.RT - Returns the inverse of the F probability distribution (Statistical)

FINV - Returns the inverse of the F probability distribution (Statistical)

FISHER - Returns the Fisher transformation (Statistical)

FISHERINV - Returns the inverse of the Fisher transformation (Statistical)

FIXED - Formats a number as text with a fixed number of decimals (Text)

FLOOR - Rounds a number down, toward zero (Compatibility)

FLOOR.MATH - Rounds a number down, to the nearest integer or to the nearest multiple of significance (Math & trig)

FLOOR.PRECISE - Rounds a number the nearest integer or to the nearest multiple of significance. Regardless of the sign of the number, the number is rounded up. (Math & trig)

FORECAST - Returns a value along a linear trend (Statistical)

FORECAST.ETS - Returns a future value based on existing (historical) values by using the AAA version of the Exponential Smoothing (ETS) algorithm (Statistical)

FORECAST.ETS.CONFINT - Returns a confidence interval for the forecast value at the specified target date (Statistical)

FORECAST.ETS.SEASONALITY - Returns the length of the repetitive pattern Excel detects for the specified time series (Statistical)

FORECAST.ETS.STAT - Returns a statistical value as a result of time series forecasting (Statistical)

FORECAST.LINEAR - Returns a future value based on existing values (Statistical)

FORMULATEXT - Returns the formula at the given reference as text (Lookup & reference)

FREQUENCY - Returns a frequency distribution as a vertical array (Statistical)

F.TEST - Returns the result of an F-test (Statistical)

FTEST - Returns the result of an F-test (Compatibility)

FV - Returns the future value of an investment (Financial)

FVSCHEDULE - Returns the future value of an initial principal after applying a series of compound interest rates (Financial)

GAMMA - Returns the Gamma function value (Statistical)

GAMMA.DIST - Returns the gamma distribution (Statistical)

GAMMADIST - Returns the gamma distribution (Compatibility)

GAMMA.INV - Returns the inverse of the gamma cumulative distribution (Statistical)

GAMMAINV - Returns the inverse of the gamma cumulative distribution (Compatibility)

GAMMALN - Returns the natural logarithm of the gamma function, $\Gamma(x)$ (Statistical)

GAMMALN.PRECISE - Returns the natural logarithm of the gamma function, $\Gamma(x)$ (Statistical)

GAUSS - Returns 0.5 less than the standard normal cumulative distribution (Statistical)

GCD - Returns the greatest common divisor (Math & trig)

GEOMEAN - Returns the geometric mean (Statistical)

GESTEP - Tests whether a number is greater than a threshold value (Engineering)

GETPIVOTDATA - Returns data stored in a PivotTable report (Lookup & reference)

GROWTH - Returns values along an exponential trend (Statistical)

HARMEAN - Returns the harmonic mean (Statistical)

HEX2BIN - Converts a hexadecimal number to binary (Engineering)

HEX2DEC - Converts a hexadecimal number to decimal (Engineering)

HEX2OCT - Converts a hexadecimal number to octal (Engineering)

HLOOKUP - Looks in the top row of an array and returns the value of the indicated cell (Lookup & reference)

HOUR - Converts a serial number to an hour (Date & time)

HYPERLINK - Creates a shortcut that opens a document stored on a network, an intranet, or the Internet (Lookup & reference)

HYPGEOM.DIST - Returns the hypergeometric distribution (Statistical)

HYPGEOMDIST - Returns the hypergeometric distribution (Compatibility)

IF - Specifies a logical test to perform (Logical)

IFERROR - Returns a value you specify if a formula evaluates to an error; otherwise, returns the result of the formula (Logical)

IFNA - Returns the value you specify if the expression resolves to #N/A, otherwise returns the result of the expression (Logical)

IFS - Checks whether one or more conditions are met and returns a value that corresponds to the first TRUE condition. (Logical)

IMABS - Returns the absolute value (modulus) of a complex number (Engineering)

IMAGINARY - Returns the imaginary coefficient of a complex number (Engineering)

IMARGUMENT - Returns the argument theta, an angle expressed in radians (Engineering)

IMCONJUGATE - Returns the complex conjugate of a complex number (Engineering)

IMCOS - Returns the cosine of a complex number (Engineering)

IMCOSH - Returns the hyperbolic cosine of a complex number (Engineering)

IMCOT - Returns the cotangent of a complex number (Engineering)

IMCSC - Returns the cosecant of a complex number (Engineering)

IMCSCH - Returns the hyperbolic cosecant of a complex number (Engineering)

IMDIV - Returns the quotient of two complex numbers (Engineering)

IMEXP - Returns the exponential of a complex number (Engineering)

IMLN - Returns the natural logarithm of a complex number (Engineering)

IMLOG10 - Returns the base-10 logarithm of a complex number (Engineering)

IMLOG2 - Returns the base-2 logarithm of a complex number (Engineering)

IMPOWER - Returns a complex number raised to an integer power (Engineering)

IMPRODUCT - Returns the product of complex numbers (Engineering)

IMREAL - Returns the real coefficient of a complex number (Engineering)

IMSEC - Returns the secant of a complex number (Engineering)

IMSECH - Returns the hyperbolic secant of a complex number (Engineering)

IMSIN - Returns the sine of a complex number (Engineering)

IMSINH - Returns the hyperbolic sine of a complex number (Engineering)

IMSQRT - Returns the square root of a complex number (Engineering)

IMSUB - Returns the difference between two complex numbers (Engineering)

IMSUM - Returns the sum of complex numbers (Engineering)

IMTAN - Returns the tangent of a complex number (Engineering)

INDEX - Uses an index to choose a value from a reference or array (Lookup & reference)

INDIRECT - Returns a reference indicated by a text value (Lookup & reference)

INFO - Returns information about the current operating environment (Information)

INT - Rounds a number down to the nearest integer (Math & trig)

INTERCEPT - Returns the intercept of the linear regression line (Statistical)

INTRATE - Returns the interest rate for a fully invested security (Financial)

IPMT - Returns the interest payment for an investment for a given period (Financial)

IRR - Returns the internal rate of return for a series of cash flows (Financial)

ISBLANK - Returns TRUE if the value is blank (Information)

ISERR - Returns TRUE if the value is any error value except #N/A (Information)

ISERROR - Returns TRUE if the value is any error value (Information)

ISEVEN - Returns TRUE if the number is even (Information)

ISFORMULA - Returns TRUE if there is a reference to a cell that contains a formula (Information)

ISLOGICAL - Returns TRUE if the value is a logical value (Information)

ISNA - Returns TRUE if the value is the #N/A error value (Information)

ISNONTEXT - Returns TRUE if the value is not text (Information)

ISNUMBER - Returns TRUE if the value is a number (Information)

ISODD - Returns TRUE if the number is odd (Information)

ISREF - Returns TRUE if the value is a reference (Information)

ISTEXT - Returns TRUE if the value is text (Information)

ISO.CEILING - Returns a number that is rounded up to the nearest integer or to the nearest multiple of significance (Math & trig)

ISOWEEKNUM - Returns the number of the ISO week number of the year for a given date (Date & time)

ISPMT - Calculates the interest paid during a specific period of an investment (Financial)

JIS - Changes half-width (single-byte) characters within a string to full-width (double-byte) characters (Text)

KURT - Returns the kurtosis of a data set (Statistical)

LARGE - Returns the k-th largest value in a data set (Statistical)

LCM - Returns the least common multiple (Math & trig)

LEFT, LEFTBs - Returns the leftmost characters from a text value (Text)

LEN, LENBs - Returns the number of characters in a text string (Text)

LET - Assigns names to intermediate calculations, values, or defining names inside a formula (Math & trig)

LINEST - Returns the parameters of a linear trend (Statistical)

LN - Returns the natural logarithm of a number (Math & trig)

LOG - Returns the logarithm of a number to a specified base (Math & trig)

LOG10 - Returns the base-10 logarithm of a number (Math & trig)

LOGEST - Returns the parameters of an exponential trend (Statistical)

LOGINV - Returns the inverse of the lognormal cumulative distribution (Compatibility)

LOGNORM.DIST - Returns the cumulative lognormal distribution (Statistical)

LOGNORMDIST - Returns the cumulative lognormal distribution (Compatibility)

LOGNORM.INV - Returns the inverse of the lognormal cumulative distribution (Statistical)

LOOKUP - Looks up values in a vector or array (Lookup & reference)

LOWER - Converts text to lowercase (Text)

MATCH - Looks up values in a reference or array (Lookup & reference)

MAX - Returns the maximum value in a list of arguments (Statistical)

MAXA - Returns the maximum value in a list of arguments, including numbers, text, and logical values (Statistical)

MAXIFS - Returns the maximum value among cells specified by a given set of conditions or criteria (Statistical)

MDETERM - Returns the matrix determinant of an array (Math & trig)

MDURATION - Returns the Macauley modified duration for a security with an assumed par value of $100 (Financial)

MEDIAN - Returns the median of the given numbers (Statistical)

MID, MIDBs - Returns a specific number of characters from a text string starting at the position you specify (Text)

MIN - Returns the minimum value in a list of arguments (Statistical)

MINIFS - Returns the minimum value among cells specified by a given set of conditions or criteria. (Statistical)

MINA - Returns the smallest value in a list of arguments, including numbers, text, and logical values (Statistical)

MINUTE - Converts a serial number to a minute (Date & time)

MINVERSE - Returns the matrix inverse of an array (Math & trig)

MIRR - Returns the internal rate of return where positive and negative cash flows are financed at different rates (Financial)

MMULT - Returns the matrix product of two arrays (Math & trig)

MOD - Returns the remainder from division (Math & trig)

MODE - Returns the most common value in a data set (Compatibility)

MODE.MULT - Returns a vertical array of the most frequently occurring, or repetitive values in an array or range of data (Statistical)

MODE.SNGL - Returns the most common value in a data set (Statistical)

MONTH - Converts a serial number to a month (Date & time)

MROUND - Returns a number rounded to the desired multiple (Math & trig)

MULTINOMIAL - Returns the multinomial of a set of numbers (Math & trig)

MUNIT - Returns the unit matrix or the specified dimension (Math & trig)

N - Returns a value converted to a number (Information)

NA - Returns the error value #N/A (Information)

NEGBINOM.DIST - Returns the negative binomial distribution (Statistical)

NEGBINOMDIST - Returns the negative binomial distribution (Compatibility)

NETWORKDAYS - Returns the number of whole workdays between two dates (Date & time)

NETWORKDAYS.INTL - Returns the number of whole workdays between two dates using parameters to indicate which and how many days are weekend days (Date & time)

NOMINAL - Returns the annual nominal interest rate (Financial)

NORM.DIST - Returns the normal cumulative distribution (Statistical)

NORMDIST - Returns the normal cumulative distribution (Compatibility)

NORMINV - Returns the inverse of the normal cumulative distribution (Statistical)

NORM.INV - Returns the inverse of the normal cumulative distribution (Compatibility)

NORM.S.DIST - Returns the standard normal cumulative distribution (Statistical)

NORMSDIST - Returns the standard normal cumulative distribution (Compatibility)

NORM.S.INV - Returns the inverse of the standard normal cumulative distribution (Statistical)

NORMSINV - Returns the inverse of the standard normal cumulative distribution (Compatibility)

NOT - Reverses the logic of its argument (Logical)

NOW - Returns the serial number of the current Date & time (Date & time)

NPER - Returns the number of periods for an investment (Financial)

NPV - Returns the net present value of an investment based on a series of periodic cash flows and a discount rate (Financial)

NUMBERVALUE - Converts text to number in a locale-independent manner (Text)

OCT2BIN - Converts an octal number to binary (Engineering)

OCT2DEC - Converts an octal number to decimal (Engineering)

OCT2HEX - Converts an octal number to hexadecimal (Engineering)

ODD - Rounds a number up to the nearest odd integer (Math & trig)

ODDFPRICE - Returns the price per $100 face value of a security with an odd first period (Financial)

ODDFYIELD - Returns the yield of a security with an odd first period (Financial)

ODDLPRICE - Returns the price per $100 face value of a security with an odd last period (Financial)

ODDLYIELD - Returns the yield of a security with an odd last period (Financial)

OFFSET - Returns a reference offset from a given reference (Lookup & reference)

OR - Returns TRUE if any argument is TRUE (Logical)

PDURATION - Returns the number of periods required by an investment to reach a specified value (Financial)

PEARSON - Returns the Pearson product moment correlation coefficient (Statistical)

PERCENTILE.EXC - Returns the k-th percentile of values in a range, where k is in the range 0..1, exclusive (Statistical)

PERCENTILE.INC - Returns the k-th percentile of values in a range (Statistical)

PERCENTILE - Returns the k-th percentile of values in a range (Compatibility)

PERCENTRANK.EXC - Returns the rank of a value in a data set as a percentage (0..1, exclusive) of the data set (Statistical)

PERCENTRANK.INC - Returns the percentage rank of a value in a data set (Statistical)

PERCENTRANK - Returns the percentage rank of a value in a data set (Compatibility)

PERMUT - Returns the number of permutations for a given number of objects (Statistical)

PERMUTATIONA - Returns the number of permutations for a given number of objects (with repetitions) that can be selected from the total objects (Statistical)

PHI - Returns the value of the density function for a standard normal distribution (Statistical)

PHONETIC - Extracts the phonetic (furigana) characters from a text string (Text)

PI - Returns the value of pi (Math & trig)

PMT - Returns the periodic payment for an annuity (Financial)

POISSON.DIST - Returns the Poisson distribution (Statistical)

POISSON - Returns the Poisson distribution (Compatibility)

POWER - Returns the result of a number raised to a power (Math & trig)

PPMT - Returns the payment on the principal for an investment for a given period (Financial)

PRICE - Returns the price per $100 face value of a security that pays periodic interest (Financial)

PRICEDISC - Returns the price per $100 face value of a discounted security (Financial)

PRICEMAT - Returns the price per $100 face value of a security that pays interest at maturity (Financial)

PROB - Returns the probability that values in a range are between two limits (Statistical)

PRODUCT - Multiplies its arguments (Math & trig)

PROPER - Capitalizes the first letter in each word of a text value (Text)

PV - Returns the present value of an investment (Financial)

QUARTILE - Returns the quartile of a data set (Compatibility)

QUARTILE.EXC - Returns the quartile of the data set, based on percentile values from 0..1, exclusive (Statistical)

QUARTILE.INC - Returns the quartile of a data set (Statistical)

QUOTIENT - Returns the integer portion of a division (Math & trig)

RADIANS - Converts degrees to radians (Math & trig)

RAND - Returns a random number between 0 and 1 (Math & trig)

RANDARRAY - Returns an array of random numbers between 0 and 1. However, you can specify the number of rows and columns to fill, minimum and maximum values, and whether to return whole numbers or decimal values. (Math & trig)

RANDBETWEEN - Returns a random number between the numbers you specify (Math & trig)

RANK.AVG - Returns the rank of a number in a list of numbers (Statistical)

RANK.EQ - Returns the rank of a number in a list of numbers (Statistical)

RANK - Returns the rank of a number in a list of numbers (Compatibility)

RATE - Returns the interest rate per period of an annuity (Financial)

RECEIVED - Returns the amount received at maturity for a fully invested security (Financial)

REGISTER.ID - Returns the register ID of the specified dynamic link library (DLL) or code resource that has been previously registered (Add-in and Automation)

REPLACE, REPLACEBs - Replaces characters within text (Text)

REPT - Repeats text a given number of times (Text)

RIGHT, RIGHTBs - Returns the rightmost characters from a text value (Text)

ROMAN - Converts an arabic numeral to roman, as text (Math & trig)

ROUND - Rounds a number to a specified number of digits (Math & trig)

ROUNDDOWN - Rounds a number down, toward zero (Math & trig)

ROUNDUP - Rounds a number up, away from zero (Math & trig)

ROW - Returns the row number of a reference (Lookup & reference)

ROWS - Returns the number of rows in a reference (Lookup & reference)

RRI - Returns an equivalent interest rate for the growth of an investment (Financial)

RSQ - Returns the square of the Pearson product moment correlation coefficient (Statistical)

RTD - Retrieves real-time data from a program that supports COM automation (Lookup & reference)

SEARCH, SEARCHBs - Finds one text value within another (not case-sensitive) (Text)

SEC - Returns the secant of an angle (Math & trig)

SECH - Returns the hyperbolic secant of an angle (Math & trig)

SECOND - Converts a serial number to a second (Date & time)

SEQUENCE - Generates a list of sequential numbers in an array, such as 1, 2, 3, 4 (Math & trig)

SERIESSUM - Returns the sum of a power series based on the formula (Math & trig)

SHEET - Returns the sheet number of the referenced sheet (Information)

SHEETS - Returns the number of sheets in a reference (Information)

SIGN - Returns the sign of a number (Math & trig)

SIN - Returns the sine of the given angle (Math & trig)

SINH - Returns the hyperbolic sine of a number (Math & trig)

SKEW - Returns the skewness of a distribution (Statistical)

SKEW.P - Returns the skewness of a distribution based on a population: a characterization of the degree of asymmetry of a distribution around its mean (Statistical)

SLN - Returns the straight-line depreciation of an asset for one period (Financial)

SLOPE - Returns the slope of the linear regression line (Statistical)

SMALL - Returns the k-th smallest value in a data set (Statistical)

SORT - Sorts the contents of a range or array (Lookup & reference)

SORTBY - Sorts the contents of a range or array based on the values in a corresponding range or array (Lookup & reference)

SQRT - Returns a positive square root (Math & trig)

SQRTPI - Returns the square root of (number * pi) (Math & trig)

STANDARDIZE - Returns a normalized value (Statistical)

STDEV - Estimates standard deviation based on a sample (Compatibility)

STDEV.P - Calculates standard deviation based on the entire population (Statistical)

STDEV.S - Estimates standard deviation based on a sample (Statistical)

STDEVA - Estimates standard deviation based on a sample, including numbers, text, and logical values (Statistical)

STDEVP - Calculates standard deviation based on the entire population (Compatibility)

STDEVPA - Calculates standard deviation based on the entire population, including numbers, text, and logical values (Statistical)

STEYX - Returns the standard error of the predicted y-value for each x in the regression (Statistical)

SUBSTITUTE - Substitutes new text for old text in a text string (Text)

SUBTOTAL - Returns a subtotal in a list or database (Math & trig)

SUM - Adds its arguments (Math & trig)

SUMIF - Adds the cells specified by a given criteria (Math & trig)

SUMIFS - Adds the cells in a range that meet multiple criteria (Math & trig)

SUMPRODUCT - Returns the sum of the products of corresponding array components (Math & trig)

SUMSQ - Returns the sum of the squares of the arguments (Math & trig)

SUMX2MY2 - Returns the sum of the difference of squares of corresponding values in two arrays (Math & trig)

SUMX2PY2 - Returns the sum of the sum of squares of corresponding values in two arrays (Math & trig)

SUMXMY2 - Returns the sum of squares of differences of corresponding values in two arrays (Math & trig)

SWITCH - Evaluates an expression against a list of values and returns the result corresponding to the first matching value. If there is no match, an optional default value may be returned. (Logical)

SYD - Returns the sum-of-years' digits depreciation of an asset for a specified period (Financial)

T - Converts its arguments to text (Text)

TAN - Returns the tangent of a number (Math & trig)

TANH - Returns the hyperbolic tangent of a number (Math & trig)

TBILLEQ - Returns the bond-equivalent yield for a Treasury bill (Financial)

TBILLPRICE - Returns the price per $100 face value for a Treasury bill (Financial)

TBILLYIELD - Returns the yield for a Treasury bill (Financial)

T.DIST - Returns the Percentage Points (probability) for the Student t-distribution (Statistical)

T.DIST.2T - Returns the Percentage Points (probability) for the Student t-distribution (Statistical)

T.DIST.RT - Returns the Student's t-distribution (Statistical)

TDIST - Returns the Student's t-distribution (Compatibility)

TEXT - Formats a number and converts it to text (Text)

TEXTJOIN - Combines the text from multiple ranges and/or strings, and includes a delimiter you specify between each text value that will be combined. If the delimiter is an empty text string, this function will effectively concatenate the ranges. (Text)

TIME - Returns the serial number of a particular time (Date & time)

TIMEVALUE - Converts a time in the form of text to a serial number (Date & time)

T.INV - Returns the t-value of the Student's t-distribution as a function of the probability and the degrees of freedom (Statistical)

T.INV.2T - Returns the inverse of the Student's t-distribution (Statistical)

TINV - Returns the inverse of the Student's t-distribution (Compatibility)

TODAY - Returns the serial number of today's date (Date & time)

TRANSPOSE - Returns the transpose of an array (Lookup & reference)

TREND - Returns values along a linear trend (Statistical)

TRIM - Removes spaces from text (Text)

TRIMMEAN - Returns the mean of the interior of a data set (Statistical)

TRUE - Returns the logical value TRUE (Logical)

TRUNC - Truncates a number to an integer (Math & trig)

T.TEST - Returns the probability associated with a Student's t-test (Statistical)

TTEST - Returns the probability associated with a Student's t-test (Compatibility)

TYPE - Returns a number indicating the data type of a value (Information)

UNICHAR - Returns the Unicode character that is references by the given numeric value (Text)

UNICODE - Returns the number (code point) that corresponds to the first character of the text (Text)

UNIQUE - Returns a list of unique values in a list or range (Lookup & reference)

UPPER - Converts text to uppercase (Text)

VALUE - Converts a text argument to a number (Text)

VALUETOTEXT - Returns text from any specified value (Text)

VAR - Estimates variance based on a sample (Compatibility)

VAR.P - Calculates variance based on the entire population (Statistical)

VAR.S - Estimates variance based on a sample (Statistical)

VARA - Estimates variance based on a sample, including numbers, text, and logical values (Statistical)

VARP - Calculates variance based on the entire population (Compatibility)

VARPA - Calculates variance based on the entire population, including numbers, text, and logical values (Statistical)

VDB - Returns the depreciation of an asset for a specified or partial period by using a declining balance method (Financial)

VLOOKUP - Looks in the first column of an array and moves across the row to return the value of a cell (Lookup & reference)

WEBSERVICE - Returns data from a web service. (Web)

WEEKDAY - Converts a serial number to a day of the week (Date & time)

WEEKNUM - Converts a serial number to a number representing where the week falls numerically with a year (Date & time)

WEIBULL - Calculates variance based on the entire population, including numbers, text, and logical values (Compatibility)

WEIBULL.DIST - Returns the Weibull distribution (Statistical)

WORKDAY - Returns the serial number of the date before or after a specified number of workdays (Date & time)

WORKDAY.INTL - Returns the serial number of the date before or after a specified number of workdays using parameters to indicate which and how many days are weekend days (Date & time)

XIRR - Returns the internal rate of return for a schedule of cash flows that is not necessarily periodic (Financial)

XLOOKUP - Searches a range or an array, and returns an item corresponding to the first match it finds. If a match doesn't exist, then XLOOKUP can return the closest (approximate) match. (Lookup & reference)

XMATCH - Returns the relative position of an item in an array or range of cells. (Lookup & reference)

XNPV - Returns the net present value for a schedule of cash flows that is not necessarily periodic (Financial)

XOR - Returns a logical exclusive OR of all arguments (Logical)

YEAR - Converts a serial number to a year (Date & time)

YEARFRAC - Returns the year fraction representing the number of whole days between start_date and end_date (Date & time)

YIELD - Returns the yield on a security that pays periodic interest (Financial)

YIELDDISC - Returns the annual yield for a discounted security; for example, a Treasury bill (Financial)

YIELDMAT - Returns the annual yield of a security that pays interest at maturity (Financial)

Z.TEST - Returns the one-tailed probability-value of a z-test (Statistical)

ZTEST - Returns the one-tailed probability-value of a z-test (Compatibility)

Tip: The sample workbook for this chapter contains a refreshable Power Query script to update this list.

#120 Index

Connect with Bill Jelen on Twitter, LinkedIn and YouTube

Follow @MrExcel on Twitter for Excel Tips in 280 characters plus retweets of cool Excel tips from my friends.

Search for Bill Jelen on LinkedIn and click Connect. Optionally, mention "I was in your seminar" or "I read your book". However - I accept all connection requests on LinkedIn.

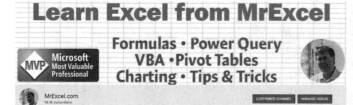

Search for MrExcel.com on YouTube for a collection of 2200 Excel videos. Click Subscribe and ring the bell to hear when there is a feature newer than this book.

What is New in this 2021 Edition

Updates to "#1 Ask Excel's A.I. a Question About Your Data" on page 1
Faster "#4 Convert Text Numbers to Numbers Quickly" on page 8
"#7 Save Filter & Sorting in Sheet View" on page 13
Resolve comments in "#13 New Threaded Comments Allow Conversations" on page 35
Look-ahead validation video link mentioned on page 37
"#24 Use People to Add Interest to Your Worksheet" on page 54
"Bonus Tip: Add Text to the Sign Held by a Person" on page 56
"Bonus Tip: Use a Formula to Toggle Pictures" on page 57
"#25 Make an Image Semi-Transparent" on page 59
"#26 Save Any Object as an Image" on page 60
"#27 Set Up Your Data for Data Analysis" on page 60
"Bonus Tip: Use Accounting Underline to Avoid Tiny Blank Columns" on page 60
"Bonus Tip: Rearrange Fields Pane" on page 78
"#65 Get Historical Stock History from STOCKHISTORY" on page 163
"#66 More Data Types from Wolfram Alpha" on page 164
"#67 Getting Historical Weather For a City" on page 165
"#68 Create Your Own Data Types Using Power Query" on page 168
"#69 IF Based on Installed Language in a Bilingual Worksheet" on page 173
"#82 Performance Improvements in 2020 for Microsoft 365" on page 187
"#83 Unhide Multiple Worksheets" on page 188
"#84 Write Your Data with the Action Pen" on page 188
"#85 Many Task Panes Now Collapse into a Tab Strip" on page 189
"#87 Date Tricks in Excel" on page 190
"#88 Use the LET Function to Re-Use Variables in a Formula" on page 190
"#89 Store Complex Formula Logic in LAMBDA function" on page 192
"Bonus Tip: Use TypeScript to Write Macros for Excel Online" on page 213
"Bonus Tip: Tame the Sequence of Refresh All" on page 217
"#119 Excel Function Quick Reference" on page 266

What was introduced in the MrExcel 2020 - Seeing Excel Clearly edition:
XLOOKUP on page 145.
Power Query's Data Profiling tools on page 217.
How Geography Data Types decide which Madison on page 159.
A SEQUENCE example for descending 52 weeks on page 181.
Exchange Rates support in Stock Data Types on page 161.
How to collapse the Search box on page 257.
How to leave effective feedback for Microsoft on page 190 .
How to post your worksheet to the MrExcel Board on page 263.